MAJORITY WORLD THEOLOGY SERIES

SERIES EDITORS

Gene L. Green, Stephen T. Pardue, and K. K. Yeo

The Majority World Theology series exists because of the seismic shifts in the makeup of world Christianity. At this moment in history, more Christians live in the Majority World than in Europe and North America. However, most theological literature does not reflect the rising tide of Christian reflection coming from these regions. The Majority World authors in this series seek to produce, collaboratively, biblical and theological textbooks that are about, from, and to the Majority World. By assembling scholars from around the globe who share a concern to do theology in light of Christian Scripture and in dialogue with Christian tradition coming from the Western church, this series offers readers the chance to listen in on insightful, productive, and unprecedented in-person conversations. Each volume pursues a specific theological topic and is designed to be accessible to students and scholars alike.

Jesus without Borders

Christology in the Majority World

Edited by

Gene L. Green, Stephen T. Pardue, and K. K. Yeo

WILLIAM B. EERDMANS PUBLISHING COMPANY
GRAND RAPIDS, MICHIGAN / CAMBRIDGE, U.K.

Published 2014 by
Wm. B. Eerdmans Publishing Co.
2140 Oak Industrial Drive N.E., Grand Rapids, Michigan 49505 /
P.O. Box 163, Cambridge CB3 9PU U.K.

Printed in the United States of America

20 19 18 17 16 15 14   7 6 5 4 3 2 1

Library of Congress Cataloging-in-Publication Data

ISBN 978-0-8028-7082-7

www.eerdmans.com

To our brothers and sisters in the Majority World
who offer us renewed visions of the Faith

Contents

Introduction: An Invitation to Discuss Christology
with the Global Church   1
Stephen T. Pardue

PART I: THEOLOGICAL ENGAGEMENTS

1. Christology in the West: Conversations
   in Europe and North America   11
   Kevin J. Vanhoozer

2. Jesus as God's Communicative and Hermeneutical Act:
   African Christians on the Person and Significance
   of Jesus Christ   37
   Victor I. Ezigbo

3. Christologies in Asia: Trends and Reflections   59
   Timoteo D. Gener

4. ¿Quién Vive? ¡Cristo! Christology
   in Latin American Perspectives   80
   Jules A. Martínez-Olivieri

Contents

PART II: BIBLICAL EXPLORATIONS

5. Reading the Gospel of John through Palestinian Eyes   103
   Yohanna Katanacho

6. From Artemis to Mary: Misplaced Veneration versus
   True Worship of Jesus in the Latino/a Context   123
   Aída Besançon Spencer

7. Christology and *Cultus* in 1 Peter:
   An African (Kenyan) Appraisal   141
   Andrew M. Mbuvi

8. Biblical Christologies of the Global Church:
   Beyond Chalcedon? Toward a Fully Christian
   and Fully Cultural Theology   162
   K. K. Yeo

   Contributors   180

   Index of Authors   183

   Index of Subjects   188

   Index of Scripture References   190

An Invitation to Discuss Christology with the Global Church

STEPHEN T. PARDUE

World Christianity: So What?

You may have heard about the tectonic shift in global Christianity that is happening before our eyes. A teacher or a friend may have noted that 80 percent of Christians lived in North America and Europe at the turn of the twentieth century but currently almost 70 percent live in the Majority World. If you are like many Christians around the world today, you understand that these changes are not just about numbers, but also about real people. If you have not experienced church life in a rapidly growing part of the world firsthand, you likely know someone who has, and that means you are connected to the people that this statistical story is all about. The increasing interconnectedness of the world and our awareness of people once invisible to us – a phenomenon often called globalization – ensure that we cannot remain disconnected from what is happening elsewhere.

This massive shift has received significant attention in recent years from missiologists, sociologists, and historians. All of them agree that the trends in global Christianity (decline in Europe and North America and swift growth on every other continent and Oceania) will continue more or less unabated for the foreseeable future. Many have pointed out an important reality: the kind of Christianity growing in the Majority World has a number of characteristics that differentiate it from the kind that has historically thrived in the North Atlantic region. Indeed, while the core tenets of the faith may not change from Berlin to Nairobi, its texture and trajectories differ from place to place. What

1

Stephen T. Pardue

it means, in thought, word, and deed, to make Jesus Lord in Bangkok
is quite different from what it means to do the same in Chicago (although there are many commonalities, of course). What's more, in
learning what it means for Jesus to be Lord in other places, we often
grasp the gospel more fully for ourselves and are more able to see
the blind spots of our own locally embodied versions of Christianity.
Learning from the church throughout the world, as well as through
history, is an essential activity for Christians since we are a catholic, or
universal, church.

The Majority World Theology series exists because it is increasingly evident that Christianity in its current state requires theological
resources quite different from those that have been available thus far.
The great shift in Christianity's makeup cannot be merely observed
as a fascinating phenomenon. If we take the Spirit's work around the
world seriously, we are obligated as thoughtful Christians to consider
how these shifts should enliven, inform, and challenge the church in its
proclamation of and reflection on the gospel of Jesus Christ. The changing world and God's providential use of it for our benefit is what makes
the theological task new in every generation and distinct in every place,
and so it will not do simply to make the same old theological arguments
we always have, as good as they might be. The gospel must be understood in relation to the multiplex cultures where the church proclaims
and celebrates Christ's good news. As the church has sought to hear the
gospel afresh and anew throughout Christian history, so now the Majority World church is doing the same as it seeks to relevantly apply and
faithfully proclaim the gospel where its members live.

But just as it would be a mistake to ignore the best thinking and
practice emerging from the Majority World, where the church is currently thriving, it would be equally problematic to do theology only
in light of the here and now, ignoring the best aspects of Christian
tradition. Theology at its best not only considers the proposals of those
present and living, but also facilitates the "democracy of the dead,"
letting our spiritual forebears help us as we sort out our present challenges. The complexity of this interplay of past and present interests
should not be underestimated, especially because much of church tradition emerges in the shadow of Western thought, and Christians today are primarily living outside the West.

So we need the strongest theological resources available, from both
past and present, both West and East, to do theology in our current

2

context. But theology at its best ultimately takes its cues from somewhere beyond these two streams: God's self-revelation in Scripture. As a theological resource, Scripture does not simply stand alongside traditional and contemporary reflection. Rather, it stands above these two, orienting and judging the theological task from start to finish.

This series aims to bring all of these resources together, with an eye especially toward discerning how Christians attentive to the global shape of the faith should be interacting with Scripture and tradition. That is, we want to move beyond *mere observation* of world Christianity and into the realm of actually *reading the Bible* and *thinking Christianly* together in light of these realities. In doing so, we want to invite you, the reader, into a lively and rich exchange that is possible today in a way that it never was before. In this conversation, you will meet scholars and pastors from around the globe, and you will see them sort out how Scripture, tradition, and culture fit together to guide the church's theological reflection today. We think you will find this a useful and transforming experience, and we hope that it will inspire further conversation in your community, whether you are in Los Angeles, Madrid, Beijing, Buenos Aires, or Bethlehem.

Why Christology?

This book is the first in the Majority World Theology series, and it deals with the person and work of Jesus of Nazareth. We chose this topic to inaugurate the series because it is both easy and hard. It is easy because one of the first things revealed by even a superficial examination of Christianity around the world is that every culture observes Jesus differently, with various culturally relevant nuances. This is perhaps most notable in Christian art: whatever continent you are on, at least some depictions of Jesus are likely to make him look like the people there.[1] At its worst, there can be a kind of self-idolatry in these depictions − a legitimation of oneself or one's culture by self-projection onto the God-man. But often, something more profound is happening: artists are signifying the contextual nature of the Christian faith and

---

1. There are, of course, plenty of exceptions, such as images of Jesus that have been exported around the world, in which he is often depicted as a white European or American.

3

communicating the profound truth that God in Jesus has sympathized with *all* humanity, in all of its bewildering and awe-inspiring diversity.

Jesus is revealed as a person for all people, a singular figure with universal and cross-cultural significance. And so when the Gospels are translated into various languages, different things stand out to different people groups, and these diverse emphases lead Christians to latch onto various aspects of Jesus' identity. So, for example, while many Europeans in the nineteenth and twentieth centuries found the image of adoption as sons and daughters to be a guiding metaphor in the New Testament, and so highlighted Jesus as brother, they often ignored another image that has been more noticed in other times and places: Jesus as King.[2] These different emphases shape everything from theology to prayer to worship, which is part of what gives Christianity in different places and cultures distinct "flavor." And so in the study of Jesus, it is easy to see how people from different times, places, and cultures come to different conclusions about the same biblical data.

But as promising as Christology may be as a starting point for renovating theology in light of global Christianity, it also presents some particular challenges. Students of early church history will recall that Christians spent hundreds of years discussing appropriate and problematic ways of talking about Jesus and his relationship to God. Over the years, the legacy of these debates grew and grew, with the result that creedal treatment of Christology is longer and more specific than creedal treatment of any other doctrine.

And all of this discussion and creed-writing occurred in a particular historical and cultural context. That context, generally speaking, has more historical continuity with Western ways of thinking about the world than with the conceptual frameworks that are familiar in the places where Christianity is currently growing. Many languages spoken in the Majority World, for example, lack vocabulary equivalents for common creedal words like "essence" or "hypostasis," and this is sometimes (though not always) indicative of a lack of concern for the questions being answered with such terms. In the face of this reality, significant debate has emerged regarding how heavily to favor

---

2. Scot McKnight and N. T. Wright have recently emphasized the shortsightedness of this approach. See Scot McKnight, *The King Jesus Gospel: The Original Good News Revisited* (Grand Rapids: Zondervan, 2011); N. T. Wright, *Jesus and the Victory of God* (Minneapolis: Fortress, 1997).

each of the three sources we mentioned earlier: Scripture, tradition, and culture. And so while Christology is, in some ways, an easy place to begin a renovation of theology in light of contemporary realities, it is not without significant challenges. Yet even in these challenges there lies the potential for tremendous theological profit, as we are forced to stare head-on at the tangle of ancient and contemporary realities that hold together in Jesus Christ.

The Plan of the Book

This book, and the series of which it is a part, takes a collaborative approach to the challenge of developing a theological approach to Jesus that makes the most of Christians' best resources, both ancient and contemporary. In concrete terms, we asked eight leading scholars from around the world to discuss what Christology looks like in their region, and what they hope it might look like in the future. To help bring focus to the analysis of tradition's contribution to the discussion, we asked each author to investigate the relationship between the Christology of the Chalcedonian Definition and their own contextual Christological observations and proposals.[3] This approach to the issue is indebted to Andrew Walls, a scholar who has spent his career calling for recognition of the similarities between what is happening in the Majority World church today and what happened in the first few centuries of Christianity.[4]

Because theological dialogue is best done in person, we helped to bring all the authors together for a few crisp fall days in 2012, during the annual meetings of the Evangelical Theological Society and the

3. The Council of Chalcedon was the fourth ecumenical (worldwide) council convened by the early church, and it was focused especially on how Christians should think about Jesus' divinity and humanity. The substance of the Chalcedonian definition is that Jesus is one person with two natures — divine and human — and that these two natures are neither mixed nor separated. This definition, while rejected by a minority of Christians at the time (and today), has set the tone for much Christological debate for more than a millennium. For an accessible introduction to Chalcedon, including primary sources, see Richard A. Norris Jr., trans. and ed., *The Christological Controversy* (Minneapolis: Fortress, 1980).

4. See Walls's excellent essay, "The Rise of Global Theologies," in *Global Theology in Evangelical Perspective*, ed. Jeffrey P. Greenman and Gene L. Green (Downers Grove: InterVarsity, 2012), pp. 19-34.

Institute for Biblical Research, as part of a consultation called "Scripture and Theology in Global Context." During this time, the authors discussed their papers with each other, as well as with other scholars present at the meetings, and then revised their essays for this book. This approach was designed to foster genuine dialogue between people who would otherwise not get to see one another, and we are confident that the book is much better because of it.

The eight essays in the book can be divided into two halves. The first half is written by theologians, reflecting on Christology as an enterprise that unites philosophy, history, and cultural anthropology with reflection on Scripture; the second half is written by biblical scholars, reflecting on Christology through deeper interaction with specific biblical texts freighted with Christological significance.

In the opening essay, Kevin J. Vanhoozer reflects on Christological developments in the West over the centuries, and considers what kind of continuity is important for contemporary Christians seeking to talk about and worship Jesus in the same way that early Christians did. Next, Victor I. Ezigbo discusses the history of Christology in Africa, considers and critiques contemporary proposals, and then offers his own suggestions for a biblical Christology relevant for Africans. After that, Timoteo D. Gener assesses the available proposals on offer regarding what it means to see Jesus through Asian eyes, and suggests that as members of a minority faith, Christians in Asia are best served by thinking about Christology through a missiological lens. Finally, Jules A. Martínez-Olivieri wraps up the first half of essays by examining Christological trends in Latin America, and arguing that the region is an ideal place to bridge the gap between Jesus' heavenly and earthly identities.

At the beginning of the second half of the book, Yohanna Katanacho reads the Gospel of John as a Palestinian, with a particular interest in its relevance for the Palestinian-Israeli conflict. He argues forcefully that John depicts Jesus as establishing a new world order that precludes approaches to Christology that exclude either Palestinians or Jews. Next, Aída Besançon Spencer takes a closer look at New Testament passages relating to Mary, and then considers and critiques the approach to Mariology and Christology in Latino communities. Andrew M. Mbuvi considers the sacrificial system and its usage in 1 Peter in relation to Christ, offering a close examination of the book from the perspective of an Akamba reader. And finally, K. K. Yeo concludes this collection with an essay that sheds light on the challenge of unity and diversity in New Testament Christologies, and also proposes a Christology that reflects on the image of God from a Chinese perspective.

Given the limited time at the conference and limited space in this book, we cannot claim to represent fully the Christologies emerging from the Majority World. We are aware also that many equally significant voices from other parts of the world are not represented here. We wish to express our thanks to the many individuals and organizations that made this collaborative work possible. We are thankful to the Evangelical Theological Society and the Institute for Biblical Research, each of which graciously hosted our group for its in-person discussions. We are thankful, as well, to the Combs Foundation and First Presbyterian Church of Evanston that helped make the consultation and this book possible. We owe a debt of gratitude to Jessica Hawthorne for her timely help with the indices, and to Michael Thomson and Jenny Hoffman at Eerdmans for their support for and assistance with the book. Finally, it is with joy that we dedicate this book to our brothers and sisters in the Majority World who are offering us renewed visions of the faith. This collection of essays is from them, for them, and about them.

All three of us who edited this volume are thrilled with the outcome of this collaborative experiment in the renovation of theology. While it should be clear that there are ongoing disagreements regarding what it means to do contextual Christology well, each essay you are about to read is rich with insight that has been gleaned from Christianity around the world and strengthened by interaction with Scripture and tradition. We hope you enjoy the book.

PART I

THEOLOGICAL ENGAGEMENTS

CHAPTER 1

Christology in the West: Conversations in Europe and North America

KEVIN J. VANHOOZER

Introduction

If theology is the doctrine of "living to God," as the seventeenth-century English Puritan William Ames held, then we may define Christology as the doctrine of "living to follow Jesus Christ."[1] This means following his story in the fullest sense of the term "following": understanding who he is, the significance of what he has done, and how to live to God as Christ's disciples in our present contexts. Christology is faith seeking understanding of its prime confession: "I believe in the Lord Jesus Christ." It is the joyful response of heart, mind, soul, and strength to our Lord's own self-communication. To be a disciple — to perform Christology — means knowing (1) who Jesus Christ is for us "yesterday and today and forever" (Heb. 13:8) and (2) how to follow this *same* Jesus today, in *different* contexts. Christology is thus about discerning the same (Christ) in the midst of the different (context).

The Marriage of Theology and Missiology: Homage to Andrew Walls

The history of Christian mission is that of successive translations of the gospel into the languages, thought forms, and practices of other cultures. As Andrew Walls rightly notes, the church, in transmitting

1. William Ames, *The Marrow of Theology* (Durham, N.C.: Labyrinth, 1983), 1.1.

the gospel, is simply imitating God's own missionary movement (so to speak), the sending of Son and Spirit: "Christian faith rests on a divine act of translation: 'the Word became flesh, and dwelt among us' (John 1:14)."[2] Theology too is the attempt to "translate" what we read on the sacred page into sacred doctrine, to restate teaching from God about God in concepts and categories that speak coherently and compellingly to people today. Theology and missiology share a common passion and vocation: to translate the way, truth, and life of Jesus Christ.

The geographic progress of the gospel recorded in the book of Acts ("so the word of the Lord continued to increase," 6:7; 12:24; 19:20) continued after the closing of the canon. This missionary movement and the development of doctrine went hand in hand: "In order to explain in the Greek world who Christ is and what he did and does, a new conceptual vocabulary had to be constructed."[3] Yes, there was conflict and confusion, but in the providence of God, as Walls notes, "the process was hugely enriching; it proved to be a discovery of the Christ. . . . It is as though Christ himself actually grows through the work of mission,"[4] and, we might add, theology.

The study of Christianity in the non-Western world affords a glimpse into the future of Christian theology, as well as into the present and perennial fact that all Christian theology is to a greater or lesser extent *contextual.* This is as true of the ecumenical Councils of Nicaea and Chalcedon as it is of North American theology today. The Spirit guides the church into the unity of truth precisely by guiding it into greater diversity: "It is a delightful paradox that the more Christ is translated into the various thought forms and life systems which form our various national identities, the richer all of us will be in our common Christian identity."[5]

Walls divides Christian history into six phases. Watch out for that first post-apostolic step; it's a doozy. The gospel's entry into Hellenistic culture has "left its mark on all later Christianity,"[6] for better or for worse. Indeed, many today believe that this first step was a serious

2. Andrew Walls, *The Missionary Movement in Christian History: Studies in the Transmission of Faith* (Maryknoll: Orbis, 1996), p. 26.
3. Walls, *Missionary Movement*, p. xvii.
4. Walls, *Missionary Movement*, p. xvii.
5. Walls, *Missionary Movement*, p. 54.
6. Walls, *Missionary Movement*, p. 18.

misstep, not a spring forward but a "Fall back into Hellenistic philosophy."[7] A remnant nevertheless remains who insists that the conciliar formulations of the early church fathers is best seen, by way of contrast, as the evangelization of Hellenism.[8] Whether Western Christology is simply a series of footnotes to this "Fall" into Hellenistic philosophy rather than a deepening of the church's understanding of Jesus Christ is the urgent question before us.

Premodern Roots: The Deep-Seated Shape of Western Christology

Christology: The Question and the Project

A newcomer to Western theology might be forgiven for thinking that Western theologians misheard Jesus' question; it is as if he had asked, "*What* do you say that I am?" On the other hand, Dietrich Bonhoeffer thinks that's what Jesus may have been asking in the first place:

> The christological question is fundamentally an ontological question. Its aim is to work out the ontological structure of the "Who?", without plunging on the Scylla of the "How?" or the Charybdis of the question of the "truth" of the revelation. The early Church foundered on the former; modern theology since the Enlightenment and Schleiermacher, on the latter. The New Testament, Paul and Luther sailed through the middle.[9]

Bonhoeffer goes on to distinguish Christology from soteriology, and discusses whether one's work interprets the person or the person the work.[10] Luther believed that if the person is good then his work will be good, even if it does not appear to be so. Still, one cannot conclude that the person is good just because the work is: a work can

7. For a description, and rebuttal, of the "theory of theology's Fall into Hellenistic philosophy," see Paul Gavrilyuk, *The Suffering of the Impassible God: The Dialectics of Patristic Thought* (New York: Oxford University Press, 2004), chapter 1.

8. Robert Wilken speaks of a "Christianization of Hellenism" in *The Spirit of Early Christian Thought* (New Haven, Conn.: Yale University Press, 2003), p. xvi.

9. Dietrich Bonhoeffer, *Christ the Center* (New York: Harper & Row, 1978), pp. 32-33.

10. Bonhoeffer, *Christ the Center*, p. 37.

appear good, but it can still be the work of the devil in the guise of an angel of light. Who a person *is* thus takes precedence over what a person *does*. Christology for Bonhoeffer is first and foremost a matter of "who he is" (the person) rather than "what he does" (the work). Western theology has, with some prominent exceptions, focused on the project that Bonhoeffer describes.[11]

Background: The Council of Chalcedon

We will not understand Western theology without appreciating its deep roots in the Council of Chalcedon. Philip Jenkins, no stranger to the discussion of global theology, alludes to these roots in the subtitle of his book, *Jesus Wars: How Four Patriarchs, Three Queens, and Two Emperors Decided What Christians Would Believe for the Next 1,500 Years*,[12] though he overstates the role political powers played. It is one thing to explain where a belief came from, or why people came to adopt it, but quite another to assess its truth. His claim that the church's core beliefs "gained the status they did as a result of what appears to be . . . the workings of raw chance"[13] is unconvincing. Readers should read with a critical eye. Fair to say some of the historical sources he relies on are dubious. He quotes Edward Gibbon's *Decline and Fall of the Roman Empire* and its account of the aftermath of Chalcedon, saying, "in the pursuit of a metaphysical quarrel, many thousands were slain."[14]

This so-called metaphysical quarrel was nothing less than an attempt to articulate the central Christian conviction "that God was incarnate in Jesus, that Jesus is God and Man."[15] The early Christological councils were attempts to explain the underlying logic and ontology

11. The three most important methodological questions in contemporary Western Christology are: (1) should one start "from above" by presupposing the Son's heavenly preexistence or "from below" with the humanity of the historical Jesus?; (2) which takes priority as to subject matter, Jesus' person or work?; (3) what kind of explanation takes priority, ontological or functional (i.e., is Jesus the "Christ" because of what he *is* or what he *does*)? See Myk Habets, *The Anointed Son: A Trinitarian Spirit Christology*, Princeton Theological Monograph 129 (Eugene, Ore.: Pickwick, 2010), p. 11.

12. (New York: HarperCollins, 2010).

13. Jenkins, *Jesus Wars* (New York: HarperOne, 2011), p. xiv.

14. Cited in Jenkins, *Jesus Wars*, p. xii.

15. D. M. Baillie, *God Was in Christ: An Essay on Incarnation and Atonement* (London: Faber & Faber, 1961), p. 83.

of the biblical teaching and narrative of Jesus Christ with the conceptual tools at hand. This required the deliberations of 6 councils over a span of 350 years.[16] The most important of these councils for our purposes is Chalcedon (451), and its formulation of the so-called hypostatic union: "two natures in one person . . . without confusion, without change, without division, without separation."

Is this an imposition of Greek metaphysics on the gospel? Must Christians subscribe to a particular theory about "natures" and "persons," to the conceptual scheme of a particular culture? Jacques Derrida deflates whatever totalitarian ambitions metaphysics might have by calling it "a white mythology which assembles and reflects Western culture: the white man takes his own mythology . . . his *logos* — that is, the *mythos* of his idiom, for the universal form of that which it is still his inescapable desire to call Reason."[17] Chalcedon employs the notion of *phusis,* or "nature," to refer to those essential characteristics that make an entity one thing rather than another. To say that Jesus Christ is "one person in two natures" is to think of him as having both human-making and God-making properties that coexist alongside one another with no admixture.[18] Does this make Christology a white mythology? Not necessarily. It is possible to read Chalcedon's two-natures-in-one-person formula not as a metaphysical proposition but as a grammatical rule for correct speech about Jesus Christ, a rule that stipulates the kind of thing we *can* say and what we must *not* say. On this reading, Chalcedon exhibits metaphysical restraint: the formula gives us guidance for talking about persons and natures but does not tell us in what each consists.

---

16. The relevant councils are: Nicaea (325), which proclaimed Jesus *homoousios* with God as opposed to Arius's suggestion that Jesus was a splendid creature; Constantinople I (381), which affirmed the Logos's assumption of a true human soul, contra Apollinaris; Ephesus (431), which upheld the unity of Jesus' person (contra Nestorius) and proclaimed Mary *Theotokos*; Chalcedon (451); Constantinople II (553), which recognized the divine Son as the person that is the subject of both natures *(enhypostasis);* Constantinople III (681), which further clarified Chalcedon, specifying that Jesus had two wills, divine and human.

17. Jacques Derrida, "White Mythology: Metaphor in the Text of Philosophy," *New Literary History* 6 (1974): 11.

18. See John McIntyre, *The Shape of Christology: Studies in the Doctrine of the Person of Christ,* 2nd ed. (Edinburgh: T&T Clark, 1998), chapter 4, "The Two-Nature Model," esp. pp. 104-5.

Modern Reactions to Two-Nature Christology: From Metaphysics to Morals, History, and Myth (and Back Again)

Western theologians have been busy preserving, modifying, or reject-ing two-nature Christology. With the advent of modernity, theologians began to react against it, as they did all things metaphysical, largely because of Kant's delimitation of knowledge to things that we can ex-perience in space and time. The two alternatives to the heavenly, meta-physical Christ in the eighteenth century were the Jesus of history and the Jesus of moral value: "The central Christological problem of the present day is not the ontological problem which dominated the pa-tristic period, but the question of the relationship between revelation and history."[19] We begin our survey of modern Western Christology by examining two nineteenth- and three twentieth-century responses to Chalcedon.

From Metaphysics to Religious-Moral Function

Enlightenment thinkers such as Kant wanted to be rational and to de-termine the limits of reason. Kant believed that metaphysics — the attempt to know ultimate reality, things like God, which transcend space and time — is a futile, speculative ambition that modern think-ers ought to abandon. Theologians can continue talking about God, however, if they are willing to do so in terms not of divine nature but of divine function. "Functional" Christologies focus not on Christ's on-tological constitution but on what he does, and on the effects of what he does on others.[20]

Friedrich Schleiermacher (1768-1834) espoused a Christology that was very much a product of its non-metaphysical times. Jesus says "the kingdom is within you" (Luke 17:21 KJV) because the kingdom — the rule of God in the human will — was first and foremost in him (i.e., his subjectivity). He was uniquely receptive to the divine causality every-

---

19. Alister McGrath, *The Making of Modern German Christology* (Oxford: Basil Black-well, 1986), p. 2. On the other hand, McIntyre thinks that the influence of Chalcedon is far from over, not least because even reactions against Chalcedon, like process theology, "remained deeply under its spell" (*Shape of Christology*, p. ix).

20. See Donald Macleod, *The Person of Christ* (Downers Grove: InterVarsity, 1998), pp. 245-48.

where and always at work in the world. God-consciousness, the feeling of being absolutely dependent on God, "was a real being of God in him."[21] It is precisely as archetype of humanity (the second Adam) that Jesus functions as Redeemer, the ideal example and historical source of God-consciousness, which is to say, divinity itself. Jesus is unlike all other men because of "the constant power of his consciousness of God, which was a genuine being of God in him."[22] For Schleiermacher, the historical Jesus is the Christ of faith because he is the agent of redemption: he is the catalyst who communicates his God-consciousness to the apostles, hence mediating between humanity and God. The apostles in turn communicated this God-consciousness to the church, and it is through participation in the community that Jesus founded that men and women find redemption, the purging and strengthening of their religious subjectivity.

Albert Ritschl (1822-89) too began his Christology "from within" the this-worldly historical nexus with Jesus' subjectivity or moral consciousness. Ritschl focuses on Jesus' earthly ministry, in particular his proclamation of the kingdom of God — "the organization of humanity through action inspired by love."[23] Jesus serves as a catalyst for what amounts to an ethical commonwealth, a society that does God's will on earth as it is in heaven. Jesus' "divinity" is a function of his will being perfectly aligned with God's will. When Jesus says, "I and the Father are one" (John 10:30), Ritschl hears "one in moral purpose." Jesus' divinity is a function of what he does that is Godlike, namely, giving himself in love for the sake of greater community. In this, Ritschl anticipates twentieth-century Christologies that similarly locate Jesus' significance in terms of what he does to bring about justice, liberation, equality, or anything else that advances the kingdom of God: "Ritschl represented Jesus' continuing influence on the world as that of a powerful moral image that continually energizes the community of the kingdom of God."[24]

---

21. Friedrich Schleiermacher, *The Christian Faith* (Edinburgh: T&T Clark, 1999), p. 385.

22. Cited in John P. Galvin, "Modern Western Christology," in *The Blackwell Companion to Jesus,* ed. Delbert Burkett (Oxford: Wiley-Blackwell, 2010), p. 359.

23. Ritschl, *Justification and Reconciliation*, vol. 3 (Edinburgh: T&T Clark, 1900), p. 12.

24. Stanley J. Grenz, *Twentieth-Century Theology: God and the World in a Transitional Age* (Downers Grove: InterVarsity, 1992), p. 58.

Kenosis

So-called kenotic Christology (from *kenosis,* or "self-emptying," Phil. 2:7) attempts to both preserve Chalcedon's two-nature framework and do justice to the realities of Jesus' human psychological development. How can we reconcile Jesus' divinity with his limited human knowledge and fully human psychology? Instead of saying the eternal Logos assumed or *took on* something (i.e., humanity), the Lutheran theologian Gottfried Thomasius (1802-73) proposed that the second person of the Trinity temporarily *divested* (i.e., emptied) himself of divine attributes incompatible with the normal functioning of the finite human mind. Properties like omnipotence, omniscience, and omnipresence define God in his relation to the world, but they are not *essential* divine attributes like truth, holiness, and love. In Thomasius's words: "He [Jesus] exercised no other lordship at all than the ethical one of truth and love."[25]

Subsequent kenotic theologians vacillated between saying that the Son put aside the divine nature and saying that he merely chose not to exercise divine functions like omniscience while in his incarnate state. What remained constant — the kenotic *cantus firmus* — was the idea that the Son emptied himself of everything not compatible with a genuinely human experience. According to kenotic Christology, Jesus is a divine consciousness within a human nature. According to P. T. Forsyth, "We could not have in the same person both knowledge and ignorance of the same thing."[26] While the overarching framework of kenotic Christology is Chalcedonian, its content is distinctly modern.[27]

The Jesus of History

Twentieth-century European theologians who pursued Christology "from below" did justice to Jesus' humanity another way, proposing

25. From Thomasius, *Christ's Person and Work,* cited in Claude Welch, ed., *God and Incarnation in Mid-nineteenth-century German Thought* (Oxford: Oxford University Press, 1965), p. 70.

26. P. T. Forsyth, *The Person and Place of Jesus Christ,* 2nd ed. (London: Hodder and Stoughton, 1910), p. 319.

27. For a recent examination of the viability of the notion of kenosis vis-à-vis Chalcedon, see C. Stephen Evans, ed., *Exploring Kenotic Christology: The Self-Emptying of God* (Oxford: Oxford University Press, 2006).

to examine the historical evidence for signs that Jesus was (humanly) conscious of his divine identity.[28] Unlike their kenotic counterparts, however, they were unwilling to presuppose a Chalcedonian framework. The Belgian Roman Catholic Edward Schillebeeckx (1914-2009) is representative of this approach.[29] Schillebeeckx discovered a Jesus who proclaimed a liberating message (concerning the radical hospitality of God and the liberation of the oppressed from suffering) and practiced what he preached (i.e., by having table-fellowship with sinners and healing the sick). Jesus was an eschatological prophet who proclaimed and practiced his powerful "Abba" experience of intimacy with God. Schillebeeckx uses this historical conclusion as a norm for judging all other theological statements about Jesus' identity, including that of Chalcedon. On his view, Jesus' other titles — Lord, Son of God, Christ — reflect the various ways the apostles sought to describe their experience of the significance of the eschatological prophet's work: "This means that all the later titles must be interpreted functionally, not ontologically."[30]

The Christ of Myth

The so-called myth of God incarnate theologians represent the most extreme Western rejection of Chalcedon, and of metaphysics more generally. Their "non-incarnational Christology"[31] denies both the pre- and post-existence of Jesus Christ. John Hick, the organizer of the symposium that later became *The Myth of God Incarnate*,[32] argued that Chalcedon was not only inexplicable — how could a mere mortal be God? — but "pernicious" and unjust inasmuch as it limits salvation to the Judeo-Christian tradition alone. It is precisely the exclusivism associated with Chalcedonian Christology — the uniqueness of the

28. Representative theologians include Wolfhart Pannenberg, Walter Kasper, and Hans Küng.

29. See his *Jesus: An Experiment in Christology* (New York: Seabury, 1979), and *Christ: The Christian Experience in the Modern World* (New York: Seabury, 1980).

30. Edward T. Oakes, *Infinity Dwindled to Infancy: A Catholic and Evangelical Christology* (Grand Rapids: Eerdmans, 2011), p. 406.

31. So Brian Hebblethwaite, *The Incarnation: Collected Essays in Christology* (Cambridge: Cambridge University Press, 1987), p. 2.

32. Hick, ed., *Myth of God Incarnate* (London: SCM, 1977).

God-man — that renders it objectionable to these thinkers. According to Hick, Jesus was "a man approved by God" for a special role, and the incarnation is simply a poetic way or metaphor that the church used to express his significance for us.[33] For a religious pluralist like Hick, viewing Jesus as *one* way rather than *the* way to God "can only be regarded as a gain."[34] However, in the words of one contemporary: "A Savior not quite God is a bridge broken at the farther end."[35]

Revisionist Ontologies and Metaphysics

Several twentieth-century Christologies revised the tradition in light of newer philosophies. Paul Tillich (1886-1965) was alert to the wide-spread problem of anxiety and used categories drawn from existentialist philosophy to explain how Christ is the answer to questions implied in human existence. In Tillich's hands, Christology is the answer to the question of how to cope with the anxiety that human existence is not simply finite but threatened by meaninglessness, a form of "non-being." According to Tillich, the story of Jesus' cross and resurrection is a symbolic representation of the power of "new being" to overcome existential estrangement (this is ontology in a new existentialist key). The way Jesus dies shows that it is possible to have victory over anxiety through trust in God — Being itself, the source or ground of one's particular being — whatever the negativities of one's life.[36]

One of the most surprising developments in twentieth-century Christology was the return to metaphysics, though one that employed categories not of being and substance but of becoming and process. Process thinkers follow Alfred North Whitehead in thinking that a focus on events rather than essences allows them to construct a theory of reality that does justice to Einstein's physics. According to process theology, God is not "over" the world, sovereignly decreeing what-

---

33. Hick, *Myth of God Incarnate*, p. ix.

34. Maurice Wiles, "Christianity without Incarnation?" in *Myth of God Incarnate*, ed. Hick, p. 9.

35. Handley Moule, preface to Robert Anderson, *The Lord from Heaven: Chapters on the Deity of Christ* (London: James Nisbet, 1910).

36. For an evaluation of Tillich's Christology as overly beholden to his mid-twentieth-century context, see Colin J. D. Greene, *Christology in Cultural Perspective: Marking Out the Horizons* (Grand Rapids: Eerdmans, 2003), pp. 128-32.

ever comes to pass, but rather the "soul" of the world who loves and lures the world to actualize its own good. Process theology privileges divine immanence, not transcendence; God acts not on but within the world's natural processes. Hence Christ's incarnation was "not by intrusion from outside but by emergence from within" the world.[37] There is no place for the virgin birth in process theology. Jesus is a man who makes a great leap forward for humanity by perfectly following God's desire for the human creature, the divine lure ("My food is to do the will of the one who sent me," John 4:34). In so doing, Jesus acts as catalyst in the becoming of a new kind of human community: the church, a way of being together that transcends the usual divisions of race, gender, and class.[38] Jesus is not the God-man but the human who becomes fully open to the divine influence, the person in whom we best see the divine process of creative transformation.

Back to (or Beyond) Chalcedon? Conversations in Contemporary Western Christology

We turn now to survey contemporary trends in European and North American Christology. There is a vast amount of material, but little consensus on how to order it. Textbooks disagree about the organizing categories: some treat Jürgen Moltmann (b. 1926) under "The Cruci-fied God," others under "Eschatological Christology," and still others under "Postmodern Christology." The following classification stems in part from an interest in seeing how various approaches (1) attend to the biblical narrative, (2) remain faithful to Chalcedon's ontology, and (3) genuinely contextualize the gospel rather than merely reflect (or impose) the concerns of cultural contexts.

The Humanity of Jesus Christ

Though Chalcedon affirms that Jesus Christ is "truly human," contem-porary Christological discussions make the humanity of Jesus the focal

---

37. Norman Pittenger, *The Word Incarnate* (New York: Harper & Row, 1959), p. 192.

38. A significant problem with process Christology is that, in principle, other in-dividuals could respond to God's lure too, thus calling Jesus' uniqueness into question.

point and assess its significance in new ways. Don Schweitzer concludes his survey of contemporary Christologies with this observation: "The genuine humanity of Jesus is a basic assumption of contemporary Christologies."[39] Whereas Chalcedon asks, "How did God become man?" contemporary theologians ask, "In what does Jesus' humanity really consist, and how can a particular individual who lived in one context be universally relevant, significant to people in every context?"

Faith. Some suggest that Jesus is never more human than when he puts his faith in God. On this view, Jesus is a representative of perfect humanity precisely because, as one who accepts and obeys the word of God (cf. Heb. 11:6), he is the paradigm of covenant faithfulness. T. F. Torrance encourages us to "think of Jesus Christ as believing, trusting, and having faith in God the Father on our behalf and in our place."[40]

Fellow feeling. Many contemporary approaches in the West are sensitive to social context, focusing on "how Jesus empowers those who believe in him to love others, accept themselves, and remain faithful" and viewing Jesus as "the bearer of a universal principle of justice that is not limited by creed or race."[41] Their goal is to apply and expand the patristic axiom, "that which is unassumed is unhealed," so as to include all kinds of human beings. Jesus is the embodiment of the compassion of God, and "the principal evil that Jesus saves people from is a misapprehension of God and a lack of concern for the victims of society."[42]

The awareness of social context has led some to put the accent in Bonhoeffer's question on the person asking it: "Who is Jesus Christ *for us* today?" The "us" in question might be Latinos, African Americans, Asian Americans, or any other marginalized group excluded from the power and influence of the mainstream. Women are a case in point. Elizabeth Johnson observes that the creedal formulation of the incarnation *(homo factus est)* should be translated "was made human," not "was made man."[43] Feminist Christology emphasizes Jesus' full hu-

39. Don Schweitzer, *Contemporary Christologies* (Minneapolis: Fortress, 2010), p. 128.

40. T. F. Torrance, *The Mediation of Christ*, rev. ed. (Colorado Springs: Helmers & Howard, 1992), pp. 92-93. See further R. Michael Allen, *The Christ's Faith: A Dogmatic Account* (London: T&T Clark, 2009).

41. Schweitzer, *Contemporary Christologies*, p. 130.

42. Schweitzer, *Contemporary Christologies*, p. 34.

43. *She Who Is: The Mystery of God in Feminist Theological Discourse* (New York: Crossroad, 1992), p. 165.

manity, in particular his loving acceptance and compassion for the outcast, as well as his willingness to subvert unjust social structures, including patriarchy. It is not his sex but his spirit — his identification with and liberating preference for the poor — that qualifies him as God's representative.

Fallenness. Another conversation that falls under this general rubric is whether Jesus assumed a *fallen* humanity. Those who say yes do so in order to underscore Jesus' identification with sinners. Those who disagree do so to avoid denying Jesus' sinlessness, on the grounds that if Jesus were a sinner he could not be our Savior. This dispute is a good example of how debates about the person of Jesus are inextricably tied to discussions about his saving work.[44]

The (Narrative) Identity of Jesus Christ

As we have seen, Western theologians typically tended to respond to Jesus' question ("Who do you say that I am?") in one of two ways: (1) by saying *what* he is or (2) by saying what he *does* for us. The 1980s ushered in a new approach that responds by (3) narrating his *identity*, thereby focusing on the *who* question in a new way. The philosopher Paul Ricoeur argues that narrative is not simply a way of packaging information, but a cognitive instrument in its own right, capable of providing explanations that elude the grasp of metaphysics. The "turn to narrative" in Christology, often associated with Karl Barth (1886-1968), is thus a highpoint in twentieth-century Western Christology's attempt to explain how Jesus is the Christ.

Hans Frei (1922-88) castigated both conservatives and liberals for "eclipsing" biblical narrative. The former read the Gospels as histories, mining them for nuggets of factual information; the latter read the Gospels as myth, demythologizing them in search of existential truth. Neither read the Gospels as history-like narratives whose unique purpose is to render personal identity. It is one thing to describe a person by listing that person's objective characteristics, or "properties" (e.g.,

44. See further Kelly M. Kapic, "The Son's Assumption of a Human Nature: A Call for Clarity," *International Journal of Systematic Theology* 3 (2011): 154-66, and Oliver Crisp, *Divinity and Humanity* (Cambridge: Cambridge University Press, 2007), chapter 4, "Did Christ Have a *Fallen* Human Nature?" pp. 90-117.

six feet tall, brown hair, good sense of humor, hardworking, etc.). It is quite another to read the Gospels on their own terms, as "realistic" narratives, that identify Jesus as "the one-who-cannot-be-thought-of-except-as-now-living." In Frei's words: "To know who he is in connection with what took place is to know that he is. This is the climax of the story and its claims. What the accounts are saying, in effect, is that the being and identity of Jesus in the resurrection are such that his non-resurrection becomes inconceivable."[45]

The New Testament scholar Richard Bauckham (b. 1946) argues that the unified narrative of Old and New Testaments includes the man Jesus in the unique identity of the God of Israel. "Identity" responds to the *who* question. As God identifies himself to Israel as the one who redeems Israel, rules all things, and alone is deserving of worship, so the New Testament identifies Jesus as one who saves the world, receives worship, and rules all things ("even the wind and the sea obey him," Mark 4:41). Because Jesus does things that only God can do, like forgive sins, and because God is one (Deut. 6:4), Bauckham argues that the biblical narrative drives readers to the inescapable conclusion that Jesus Christ participates in the divine identity.[46] As to *homoousios* ("of the same substance"), far from being a piece of abstract ontological speculation, it instead "functions to ensure that this divine identity is truly the identity of the one and only God."[47]

Focal Points in the Narrative of Jesus Christ

It is difficult to keep the whole of Jesus' story in mind simultaneously. Many theologians who have made the "turn to narrative" therefore tend to emphasize one moment in Jesus' story and use it as the lens for viewing everything else. Four particular moments stand out as being of particular importance to Western Christology.[48]

Incarnation. For T. F. Torrance, the event that overshadows all oth-

45. *The Identity of Jesus Christ: The Hermeneutical Bases of Dogmatic Theology* (Philadelphia: Fortress, 1975), p. 145.

46. *God Crucified: Monotheism and Christology in the New Testament* (Grand Rapids: Eerdmans, 1998), p. 71.

47. Bauckham, *God Crucified*, pp. 78-79.

48. Other focal points (e.g., the transfiguration; the descent into hell) figure less frequently.

ers in importance is when God assumed humanity and "became flesh" (John 1:14). The incarnation is God's loving "Yes" to every human being. The Son of God enters into a "carnal union" with all humanity. All are objectively "in Christ" and thus (ontologically) related to God, whether they realize it (subjectively) or not. The work of Christ is here identical with his person: Jesus atones for humanity by becoming human and living out a human life (a life that includes death). In Kathryn Tanner's words: "Incarnation becomes the primary mechanism of atonement."[49] Jesus is the one in whom God and humanity coexist in a harmonious relationship. *Homoousios* implies reconciliation.[50]

Crucifixion. No other event better characterizes the story of Jesus than his suffering and death on a cross, which is why Martin Kähler can describe the Gospel of Mark as "a passion narrative with an extended introduction."[51] According to Moltmann, Jesus' crucifixion reminds us that hope is always for something other than what is present in the world. The cross reveals God's willingness to take on the suffering of the world in order to make all things new. Indeed, Moltmann wrote *The Crucified God*[52] in order to criticize the idea that God sovereignly supports the oppressive status quo: "For me the cross of Christ became the 'foundation and critique of Christian theology.'"[53] Interestingly, nowhere in his book *The Way of Jesus Christ*[54] does Moltmann even mention Chalcedon. He is less interested in speculating on how the cross affects the two natures than in understanding how the death of the Son enables the Father to absorb, and so overcome, all the forces of death and destruction that threaten the world.

Resurrection. Wolfhart Pannenberg (b. 1928) pins his whole Christology on the historical event of Jesus' resurrection. With an eye to

49. Kathryn Tanner, *Christ the Key* (Cambridge: Cambridge University Press, 2010), p. 252.

50. Though I have emphasized the incarnation as a "moment," both Torrance and Tanner intend what they say about it to extend to the whole of Jesus' life, and not his birth only. For a critique of Tanner's notion that incarnation is atoning, see Oliver Crisp, *Revisioning Christology: Theology in the Reformed Tradition* (Farnham: Ashgate, 2011), pp. 111-31.

51. *The So-Called Historical Jesus and the Historic, Biblical Christ* (Philadelphia: Fortress, 1964), p. 80.

52. (London: SCM, 1974).

53. Moltmann, *How I Have Changed: Reflections on Thirty Years of Theology* (London: SCM, 1997), p. 18.

54. (Minneapolis: Fortress, 1993).

biblical (and late Jewish) apocalyptic and eschatology, Pannenberg argues that the meaning of any event of history can only be determined in light of the end of history, for only then will the revelation of God be complete. Pannenberg's signal contribution is to insist that the end of history has broken into the middle of history in the resurrection of Jesus Christ, a harbinger of the general resurrection of the dead that God will bring about at the consummation.[55] Only on the basis of this historical event can we say that Jesus' preaching of the coming kingdom is true. We can also confess that "Jesus is God" (i.e., the future of God's rule and the meaning of universal history), but only *after, and because of,* the resurrection.

Ascension. Some theologians have made the very last incident of Jesus' story – his ascension into heaven (Luke 24:51; cf. Acts 1:9-11) – rather than the resurrection the climax of Jesus' story, a crucial lens for understanding not only Christology but also the church.[56] The ascension reminds us that the incarnation (i.e., the Son's assumption of human nature-flesh) continues, that Jesus now lives, and that he will return to earth. In ascending, Jesus went up to heaven in our flesh: "I go and prepare a place for you" (John 14:2). The ascension reminds us that what is now true of the Son of God – that he has not simply a spiritualized existence but an exalted human, and bodily, existence – will eventually be true for the saints. The ascended Jesus Christ is the hope of the saints' glorification.

Analytic Christology

The relationship of faith and rationality has long been a concern of Western thinkers. Recently, however, a group of theologians has enlisted tools typically used in analytic philosophy and applied them to the project of faith seeking understanding. Analytic theologians prioritize precision, clarity, and logical coherence and seek to clarify basic concepts that play important roles in Christian doctrine.[57] In particu-

---

55. Pannenberg, *Jesus: God and Man* (Philadelphia: Westminster, 1977).

56. Gerrit Dawson, *Jesus Ascended: The Meaning of Christ's Continuing Incarnation* (London: T&T Clark, 2004); Douglas Farrow, *Ascension Theology* (London: T&T Clark, 2011).

57. See Oliver D. Crisp and Michael C. Rea, eds., *Analytic Theology: New Essays in the Philosophy of Theology* (Oxford: Oxford University Press, 2009), esp. the introduction and chapter 1.

lar, analytic theologians strive to give as clear a picture as possible of the ultimate constituents of reality, including (as far as is possible) the mystery of the Triune God. It follows that analytic theologians are concerned to read the biblical narrative with a view to making (conceptually and ontologically) explicit what is (metaphorically and narratively) implicit.

Chalcedonian Christology, with its central postulate "two natures in one person," is an apt candidate for analysis, not least because many Westerners charge it with being not only mysterious but also incoherent. Analytic theologians therefore devote considerable energy to refining definitions and clarifying distinctions (e.g., What is "human nature"? Does the God-man have one mind or two?). Thomas V. Morris's *The Logic of God Incarnate*[58] is a good example of analytic Christology. Morris draws a number of helpful distinctions (e.g., Chalcedon's "fully human" does not mean "merely human") in an effort to demonstrate the coherence of the concept of the hypostatic union.

Christology as Lens for Viewing Other Doctrines and Domains

We turn now from approaches that think *about* Christology to those that think *with* and *through* it. It was Karl Barth who made the famous "turn to Christology," insisting that the history of Jesus Christ — a unified series of personal and agential events — is the sole basis for everything we know about God, true humanity, and their relationship. Barth preserves Chalcedon in a new conceptual key by radically "actualizing" his understanding of both persons and natures, however, insisting that we do not know what "divinity" and "humanity" truly mean apart from Jesus' concrete history.[59] God *is* what he *does* in Jesus Christ: "He acts as God when He acts as a human being, and as a human being when He acts as God."[60] Largely because of Barth's influence, Christology has become not simply one theological locus among others but the key to unlocking every other doctrine — and not only doctrine! Three examples will have to suffice.

58. (Ithaca, N.Y.: Cornell University Press, 1986).
59. For a fuller description of Barth's radically actualized Christology, see Paul Dafydd Jones, *The Humanity of Christ: Christology in Karl Barth's Church Dogmatics* (London: T&T Clark, 2008).
60. Karl Barth, *Church Dogmatics* IV/2 (Edinburgh: T&T Clark, 1958), p. 115.

Election. Barth reworks every other doctrine – creation, the divine attributes, anthropology – on the basis of his Christology, thus prompting some to wonder whether Christian theology has perhaps become *too* Christological. The doctrine of election is the most stunning example. On Barth's view, God does not choose particular human beings to elect, but rather elects *all* human beings in Christ. There is no electing decree "behind Christ's back." Further, election pertains to God's self-determination not to be God *apart* from his union with humanity in Christ. Election "in Christ" therefore determines both the being of humanity and of God. Hence a "christologically conditioned" doctrine of election is the sum of the gospel: that God essentially is the one who is with us and for us is the totality of the good news.

Metaphysics. Robert Jenson radicalizes Barth's insight, offering a Christologically conditioned understanding of God's very being. Specifically, Jenson corrects Greek metaphysics with what he calls a "metaphysics of the gospel" that identifies God's being with the events of Jesus' life. Consistently to follow Barth's "turn to the subject of Jesus Christ" is to substitute Jesus' concrete history for what Western metaphysics traditionally referred to as the Ground of Being. Jesus' *individuality* is constitutive of God's *infinity:* "God is what happens between Jesus and his Father in their Spirit."[61] This is the necessary consequence of turning Christology into first theology, the norm for all speaking and thinking about God.

Ethics. Christology is the attempt to formulate *what is* in Jesus Christ. In Christ there is "the fullness of God" (Col. 1:19) and the covenant fellowship (union) between God and humanity. In Christ, as the apostle Paul says, there is "a new creation" (2 Cor. 5:17). Christian ethics may be described as the attempt to show how *is* implies *ought* "in Christ." Jesus is not merely a moral example to emulate in our respective contexts; rather, disciples participate in who he is. Jesus Christ is the truth and life of the new creation: he is what God is doing by the Spirit's power to make all things new (Rev. 21:5). Viewed through the lens of Christology, ethics is the human response to what Jesus is *now doing* and *now is.*[62] Regardless of their particular context, then,

---

61. Robert Jenson, *Systematic Theology,* vol. 1, *The Triune God* (Oxford: Oxford University Press, 1997), p. 221. McIntyre wonders whether some theologians ask Christology to perform tasks for which the doctrine was not originally designed.

62. So Christopher R. J. Holmes, *Ethics in the Presence of Christ* (London: T&T Clark, 2012).

disciples participate in reality rightly only if and when they know who Jesus is and what he is now doing to renew all things. Christology, on this view, is indeed all-encompassing: it directs us how best to become the kind of people that correspond to Jesus' person and work, a person and work that reveals and establishes the really real. Christology says *what is* and *what therefore ought to be.*

Concluding Ontological-Contextual Postscript: On the Development of Any Future Global Christology

The question now before us is *how to go on globally* without either letting Western Christology dominate the discussion or dismissing it altogether. If Christology today is "lived in the tension between continuity with the church's doctrinal tradition on the one hand and, on the other, openness to new experiences and understandings of Christ arising out of the particular contexts of suffering and hope,"[63] we cannot shirk the question: whither Chalcedon?

Church history is the story of contextualization as the gospel encountered new frontiers (i.e., a new space) and ethnic groups (i.e., a new people). There are still a few people groups left that have not heard of Jesus Christ; yet global theology poses a distinctly new contextual challenge. It is no longer simply a matter of the gospel entering new contexts, but rather of the *intersection of contexts,* including some that have already received the gospel.

We stand at the threshold of an exciting new stage of church history: "The full-grown humanity of Christ requires all the Christian generations, just as it embodies all the cultural variety that six continents can bring."[64] Andrews Walls acknowledges that all Christians affirm "the ultimate significance" of Jesus of Nazareth, but is reluctant to state the coherence of historical Christianity in creedal or propositional form since such formulation "is itself a necessary product of a particular Christian culture."[65] I believe the global church can still and ought to confess that Chalcedon, while not the *whole* truth, is never-

---

63. Daniel L. Migliore, "Christology in Context: The Doctrinal and Contextual Tasks of Christology Today," *Interpretation* 49 (1995): 242.

64. Walls, *Missionary Movement,* p. xvii.

65. Walls, *Missionary Movement,* p. 23.

theless "the truth and nothing but the truth," stated in the conceptual terms of the Greco-Roman context.

Is there a global future for Christology without ontology? Must we apologize when using concepts like *homoousios* for the unbearable *whiteness* of "being"? The ecumenical councils, in invoking ontological terms, showed themselves to be Western, but not necessarily provincial, or metaphysical. Bruce McCormack's verdict is worth pondering: "If Barth has taught us anything, it is that . . . theological ontology can be constructed on the basis of the narrated history of Jesus of Nazareth without the help of metaphysics."[66] I want to make three suggestions about the development of any future global Christology, especially as it concerns the vexed question of Nicaea and Chalcedon's ontology and its normative status. I argue that these creedal statements are essential for thinking rightly about the biblical narratives as stories and histories about Jesus, for maintaining the unity of the church, and for assisting the church to faithfully to improvise new cultural scenes of discipleship in context. In the final analysis, however, we will see that it takes a global village – churches from West, East, and South – fully to say who Jesus Christ is for us today.

1. *What is normative in Chalcedon is not a particular metaphysical scheme but the underlying biblical ontology, not the particular concepts but the underlying judgments that they express.*

Let me explain. To claim that Nicaea and Chalcedon preserve necessary evangelical *judgments* is not to insist that subsequent doctrinal formulations must use Greek, or that Christian cultural practices must be Hellenistic. Everything hinges on the distinction between language and concepts on the one hand and judgments and wisdom – the ability to draw proper distinctions and make fundamental connections – on the other.[67] Judgments "are intellectual (and therefore moral and spiritual) acts in which we struggle to order our thinking and speaking in response to reality, and so to think and speak truthfully."[68] To un-

---

66. Bruce McCormack, "The Person of Christ," in *Mapping Modern Theology: A Thematic and Historical Introduction,* ed. Kelly M. Kapic and Bruce L. McCormack (Grand Rapids: Baker Academic, 2012), pp. 171-72.

67. Humans typically think, and achieve understanding, by making appropriate connections and distinctions. The mind, most basically, identifies, relates, and distinguishes. Hence the typical form of judgments: "this is an x"; "this is not an x"; "all x's are y's"; "no x's are y's," etc.

68. John Webster, *Word and Church: Essays in Christian Dogmatics* (Edinburgh: T&T Clark, 2001), p. 4.

derstand the biblical witness theologians must make many kinds of judgments — moral, logical, historical, and yes, ontological: "The Bible conceives life as a drama in which human and divine actions create the dramatic whole. There are ontological presuppositions for this drama, but they are not spelled out."[69] Making "theodramatic" judgments — about the identity of the divine agents in the drama of redemption, about what the drama is about, about what we should do fittingly to participate — is perhaps the quintessential theological skill.

I owe the concept-judgment distinction to David Yeago, who in a seminal essay developed it in connection to Nicaea. He thinks Paul's language in Philippians 2:6, about the Son's *isos theos* ("equality with God"), is saying the same thing as Nicaea's very different concept *homoousios* ("of the same substance"). It is essential "to distinguish between judgments and the conceptual terms in which those judgments are rendered" so that "the same judgment can be rendered in a variety of conceptual terms."[70] The technical concept *homoousios* expresses a non-identical equivalence with Paul's "equality with God." Chalcedon's "two natures in one person" language is similarly faithful to biblical discourse, not because it repeats the same biblical words or concepts (it does not), but because it renders in *different* terms the *same* underlying (ontological) judgments. *It is not the propositional content alone but the biblical judgments of which they are ingredients — that the man Jesus is God; that humanity is not divinity — that are theologically binding.*

This account may be open to what appears to be a serious objection: why should the rest of the world care about the West's grand ontological obsession? My answer: because the Christian faith necessarily involves certain ontological presuppositions, namely, "the question of being, of what is real and how it is real."[71] Consider, for example, the "ontological difference" between Being and beings. We may not want to use the same expression, but global Christians need to express the same judgment in some way in order rightly to respond to the prime theological imperative (also known as the First Commandment): "You

69. Reinhold Niebuhr, "Biblical Thought and Ontological Speculation in Tillich's Theology," in *The Theology of Paul Tillich,* ed. Charles W. Kegley and Robert W. Bretall (New York: Macmillan, 1952), p. 216.

70. David Yeago, "The New Testament and the Nicene Dogma: A Contribution to the Recovery of Theological Exegesis," in *The Theological Interpretation of Scripture: Classic and Contemporary Readings,* ed. Stephen Fowl (Oxford: Blackwell, 1997), p. 93.

71. McCormack, "Person of Christ," p. 150.

shall have no other gods before me" (Exod. 20:3). We can only keep ourselves from idols if we get into the habit of thinking of God in some kind of absolute distinction to all other creatures (i.e., what Western theologians call the "ontological difference").

The church's use of concepts like "nature" and "person" should not be viewed as a betrayal of the faith to philosophical tradition but rather as an attempt, by particular people of faith, to gain a greater understanding of the biblical drama of redemption (i.e., by identifying its protagonist). This is a crucial point. Chalcedon does not define for all time what a person is or what is in a nature; instead, it *provides direction, and a concrete example, for the kinds of things all Christians ought to say about Jesus Christ.* We can speak of Jesus without (cultural) borders but not without some (conceptual) boundaries. For example: "We might say that a 'person' is what there are three of in the Trinity and one in Christ, and 'nature' is what there is one of in the Trinity and two in Christ."[72] What is normative about Chalcedon is the underlying ontological judgment that it preserves, in Greek conceptual form, from Scripture: whatever it means to be human, and whatever it means to be God, Chalcedon stipulates that we must say that the one person Jesus Christ is fully both.

2. *While the Bible alone has magisterial authority, the early catholic consensus has ministerial authority insofar as it displays biblical judgments. It thus provides pedagogical direction and an important opportunity for global theology to display catholic sensibility, which is to say a concern for doing theology in communion with the saints.*

Jesus Christ is "the same yesterday and today and forever" (Heb. 13:8). The same cannot be said for Christology. Whereas the previous point dealt with apostolicity (preserving authoritative biblical judgments), the focus here is on the oneness and catholicity of the church and its doctrine. Clearly, the West has not exhausted the riches of the knowledge of Jesus Christ. There is more, much more, to be said on the basis of God's word. However, we should no more despise or relativize the hypostatic union simply because it is culturally situated than we should relativize Newton's Second Law of Motion — $F = ma$ (force = mass × acceleration) — just because he was a seventeenth-century Englishman.

---

72. Bernard Lonergan, "The Origins of Christian Realism," in *A Second Collection: Papers* (London: Darton, Longman, & Todd, 1974), p. 259.

How do we know if Chalcedon, or our local church, is saying the same thing about Jesus Christ as the apostles? Kevin Hector offers a "postmetaphysical" account of the way one's doctrinal concepts can be judged to be the same. Everything depends on *using* concepts in ways that others recognize as attempts to carry on the normative trajectory implicit in a chain of precedent performances recognized as authoritative or, in our case, apostolic.[73] Hector's account relies heavily on our ability to recognize other Christians as "one of us." In the New Testament, this happened dramatically when various groups of people received the Holy Spirit. The illumination of the word-ministering Spirit enables the church eventually to distinguish whether or not a judgment counts as "going on in the same way" as Jesus Christ.

Can we merge Hector's account of the transmission of the faith with that of Walls? In each case it is important to carry on, in the power of the Spirit, the normative trajectory implicit in the church's confession of Jesus as the Christ. Both Hector and Walls acknowledge that the trajectory looks a bit different each time a new use is recognized as "going on in the same way." We must not overlook the significance of this point. *The non-Western church can "go on in the same way" as Nicaea and Chalcedon without having to do so in a slavish, repetitive manner.* Nicaea and Chalcedon are nevertheless important developments that help anchor the trajectory by embodying biblically sound judgments in terms of their respective cultural situations. Subsequent Christologies would do well to continue "going on in the same way."

Non-Western Christianity does not need to become Western. Yet non-Western Christianity should strive to stay authentically Christian, and one way to do that is to remain in communion with catholic theological tradition. The way forward for global theology is so to know both Scripture and tradition well enough to make judgments about whether the church's speech and action today participates rightly in the "same doing" — *homodrao,* one might say — as the biblically attested story of the Christ.

3. *Western Christology is ultimately a matter of regional, perhaps even masterpiece theater that, while not providing an exhaustive description, nevertheless affords precious insight into the identity of the main protagonist of the drama of redemption.*

---

73. Kevin Hector, *Theology Without Metaphysics: God, Language, and the Spirit of Recognition* (Cambridge: Cambridge University Press, 2011), p. 48.

No single way of embodying the gospel or identifying Jesus Christ is exhaustive of his way, truth, and life. However, occasional performances — and all attempts to act out theological understanding are "occasional" — can produce permanent gains. I believe the formulas of Nicaea and Chalcedon to be "great performances" — responses to their own historical contexts that contain lessons for the rest of the church as well.[74]

Like it or not, Western theology is part of the catholic heritage of the church, and hence an intrinsic part of global theology. Whatever the locale, the church's performance of the gospel should be informed by the magisterially authoritative canonical performance of the apostles as well as the ministerially authoritative catholic performance of their successors, Western and non-Western. The goal of global theology is not simply to maintain Chalcedon, of course, but rather to promote what we might call *theodramatic understanding*: a grasp of what God is doing in Christ through the Spirit to renew all things, and a sense of how the church in its particular place and time can participate in the action.

If Newton's Second Law holds good for people in twenty-first-century Guatemala and Tibet, how much more ought the global church attend to the Chalcedonian formula, if it correctly identifies Jesus' ontological constitution. To the extent that it makes the ontology presupposed by the biblical drama explicit, doctrinal formulations are true for everyone, everywhere, and at all times. The global church will of course find new things to say about what Jesus Christ means for us today, but I respectfully submit that these new things must "go on in the same way" — or at least not go *against* — the way indicated by Chalcedon.[75]

---

74. See further my "'One Rule to Rule Them All?' Theological Method in an Era of World Christianity," in *Doing Theology in a Globalized World*, ed. Craig Ott and Harold Netland (Grand Rapids: Baker, 2006), pp. 85-126.

75. Cf. the Brazilian composer Heitor Villa-Lobos's comment about the influence of Western counterpoint, paradigmatically expressed in the person and work of Johann Sebastian Bach on his *Bachianas Brasileiras:* "This is a special kind of musical composition, based on an intimate knowledge of the great works of Bach. . . . The composer considered Bach a universal and rich folklore source, deeply rooted in the folk music of every country in the world. Thus Bach is a mediator among all races." I submit that Bach is to Villa-Lobos what Chalcedon is to non-Western Christology.

What we are after is creative understanding: the ability to "go on in the same way," only differently. How can we think this sameness and difference together? I submit that what stays the same is the drama of redemption. The church needs to remain faithful to the apostolic testimony (the inspired transcript), for there is no other gospel, no other drama of redemption. What is different, however, is the scene the local church is now being asked to play. Put differently: the theological judgments about the essential nature of the theodrama must remain the same, but the particular way we perform it — the way we go on — in our present context may differ from previous performances. The task of systematic theology is to form actors with good improvisatory judgment, disciples who know how to go on in the same way as their Lord in terms of their different cultural contexts. Global theology is a "Pentecostal" plurality of languages and concepts ruled by biblical judgments, especially as these have come to be expressed in the classic formulations of Nicaea and Chalcedon. Creedal Christianity is a precious guide to the global church's confession of Christ, ensuring that it is "according to the Scriptures," grammatically correct no matter what the language or conceptuality.

The task of Christology, says T. F. Torrance, "is to yield the obedience of our mind to what is given, which is God's self-revelation in its objective reality, Jesus Christ."[76] It is only through sustained apprenticeship to Scripture that the church learns how to make judgments about *what is* in Christ and about what it must do to follow Christ today in our myriad present contexts.

Christology requires a plurality of tongues — languages, vocabularies, and concepts. Yet whatever language or conceptual scheme Christians speak and think, let them confess in line with the Chalcedonian (ontological) grammar. Let "every tongue confess *that Jesus Christ is Lord*" (Phil. 2:11). That *Jesus is Lord* is the preeminent theological judgment. May the Spirit of Jesus Christ direct the global church, in all its diversity, to "go on in the same way" — for there is no other way, "no other name under heaven . . . by which we must be saved" (Acts 4:12).

76. T. F. Torrance, *Incarnation: The Person and Work of Christ* (Downers Grove: Inter-Varsity, 2008), p. 1.

35

For Further Reading

Dupuis, Jacques. *Who Do You Say I Am? Introduction to Christology.* Maryknoll: Orbis, 1994.

Greene, Colin J. D. *Christology in Cultural Perspective: Marking Out the Horizons.* Grand Rapids: Eerdmans, 2003.

Macleod, Donald. *The Person of Christ.* Downers Grove: InterVarsity, 1998.

Macquarrie, John. *Jesus Christ in Modern Thought.* London: SCM, 1990.

McCormack, Bruce L. "The Person of Christ." In *Mapping Modern Theology: A Thematic and Historical Introduction,* edited by Kelly M. Kapic and Bruce L. McCormack, pp. 149-74. Grand Rapids: Baker Academic, 2012.

McGrath, Alister. *The Making of Modern German Christology: From the Enlightenment to Pannenberg.* Oxford: Basil Blackwell, 1986.

Migliore, Daniel L. "Christology in Context: The Doctrinal and Contextual Tasks of Christology Today." *Interpretation* 49 (1995): 242-54.

Oakes, Edward T. *Infinity Dwindled to Infancy: A Catholic and Evangelical Christology.* Grand Rapids: Eerdmans, 2011.

O'Collins, Gerald. *Christology: A Biblical, Historical, and Systematic Study of Jesus.* 2nd ed. Oxford: Oxford University Press, 2009.

Schweitzer, Don. *Contemporary Christologies: A Fortress Introduction.* Minneapolis: Fortress, 2010.

CHAPTER 2

Jesus as God's Communicative and Hermeneutical Act: African Christians on the Person and Significance of Jesus Christ

VICTOR I. EZIGBO

Introduction

An African Christian Christology should pass both the test of "African-ness" and the test of "Christian-ness."[1] The Christology should demonstrate simultaneously its Christian identity and its relevance to the Christological questions of African Christians. The Christology should engage the experience, history, cultures, and religious aspirations of Africans. The Christology should also demonstrate its faithfulness to the understandings of Jesus Christ that are present in the Christian Scripture and the Christologies of the earliest ecumenical Christian councils — in particular, the Councils of Nicaea (325), Constantinople (381), and Chalcedon (451). A Christology that fails to pass these two tests ought not to bear the name "African Christian Christology."

The complexity of these two tests is noteworthy. Christian theologians disagree on what constitutes a faithful or an adequate interpretation of the Christological themes in Scripture and the Christological statements of the Councils of Nicaea, Constantinople, and Chalcedon. African Christian theologians disagree in their views of the value of Africans' history, experience, cultures, and religious aspiration in constructing Christologies. They also disagree on what constitutes an "appropriate" relationship between Christianity and African indigenous

---

1. The word "Africa" is used in this essay to describe nations in the sub-Saharan African region. This is because the essay focuses only on sub-Saharan African Christianity.

religions. I attempt to deal with the complexity of the two tests by working with the following broad theological framework: an African Christian Christology (1) should use the Africans' contexts – experience, cultures, indigenous thoughts, language, and social location – as an indispensable source; (2) should learn from Christological statements of the earliest ecumenical councils; and (3) should not be in contradiction with the understandings of Jesus Christ that are expressed in Scripture.

Jesus as the Problem of Christology: Lessons from the Ecumenical Councils

Many Christian theologians, especially systematicians, are preoccupied with the task of assembling Christian beliefs about Jesus Christ into a coherent and tidy formula. These theologians have forgotten rather quickly that all Christologies are *human*, and as such, are incapable of encapsulating the full ramifications of God's action in and through Jesus Christ. Theologians, therefore, need the "vision" of other theologians, particularly those from outside their cultural contexts, church traditions, and religious traditions in order to successfully imagine, understand, and appreciate the breadth, width, and length of the person and significance of Jesus Christ (Eph. 4:12-13). This is because the significance of Jesus Christ will always overflow our theological boundaries. Theologians ought to strive to construct Christologies that identify with the multifarious representations of Jesus Christ in the Bible. Such Christologies also should intentionally engage the religious, cultural, and social issues of the communities for which they are intended.

The earliest Christian communities set the example for this way of doing Christology when the Hebraic Christians expressed Jesus' significance in light of the context of the Jewish notion of God's chosen Messiah. "Everything about Jesus made sense for them in terms of Jewish history and Jewish destiny."[2] Similarly, the Hellenistic Greek-speaking theologians such as Justin Martyr (martyred ca. 165) boldly expressed

2. Andrew F. Walls, "Old Athens and New Jerusalem: Some Signposts for Christian Scholarship in the Early History of Mission Studies," *International Bulletin of Missionary Research* 21 (1997): 146.

Jesus' significance in the Greco-Roman cultures by presenting him as the divine *logos* — a divine agent through whom God creates and maintains order in the universe.[3] An earlier example of this theological move by the Greek-speaking Christians could be found in the apostle Paul, who seized the "Hellenistic idea of *pleroma*, the totality of emanations between the transcendent God and the material universe, and identified it with Christ (Col. 1:19)."[4]

In the fourth and fifth centuries, the Councils of Nicaea, Constantinople, and Chalcedon adopted a highly slippery Greek term *homoousios* ("same substance") to explain the relationship between Jesus Christ and God (the Father). The Christologies of these councils continue to exert an enormous influence on Christian views of God and Jesus Christ. What lessons can twenty-first-century African Christians learn from the Christologies of these councils? I see two main lessons.

First, there is a *lesson of contextualization*. The attendees of the Council of Nicaea borrowed words and ideas (such as *homoousios*, "similar substance") from their Hellenistic world to articulate Jesus' relationship with God (the Father). That *homoousios* is culturally conditioned is evident in its meaninglessness or limited relevance to the twenty-first-century people who are not schooled in *Koine* Greek and Hellenistic thought. No Christian community can successfully and meaningfully answer Jesus' question — "Who do you say that I am" (Mark 8:29) — in foreign thoughts and concepts. Our contexts — social locations, cultures, histories, languages, and experiences — supply the cognitive framework we use to interpret and appropriate our encounters with Jesus Christ.

The error of the theologians who do not think contextually is the presumption that their theological questions are universally relevant and, therefore, are not bound by their contexts. For example, a North American evangelical theologian who thinks in this way may be enthusiastic about posing questions relating to open theism and classical theism in an evangelical seminary in Nigeria. It would be surprising, however, if the immediate reaction of most Nigerian students to such

3. Justin Martyr, *Apologia* 1.5, in *The Early Christian Fathers: A Selection from the Writings of the Fathers from St. Clement of Rome to St. Athanasius*, ed. and trans. Henry Bettenson (New York: Oxford University Press, 1956), pp. 58-64. See Kwame Bediako, *Theology and Identity: The Impact of Culture upon Christian Thought in the Second Century and Modern Africa* (Oxford: Regnum, 1992).

4. Walls, "Old Athens and New Jerusalem," p. 149.

questions was not: "Really? Who cares about such questions?" This is because many Nigerian Christians live in cultures where gods are believed to compete for recognition, and who construe omniscience as an essential attribute of any being worthy of the name God. Many of these Christians take for granted the omniscience of the Christian God, even though they ground their trust on God's ability to heal, provide, and protect them on God's ability to know God's creation exhaustively. Contextualization reminds us that diversity of culture and thought does not inhibit Christology. On the contrary, diversity of culture and thoughts takes our understandings of Jesus into new realms of thought and meaning.[5]

Second, there is a *lesson of the danger of imperial romance.* The early church's preoccupation with the quest to safeguard the purity of faith and beliefs sometimes led to the physical abuse and deaths of many Christians who propounded the Christological positions that lost in the "theological elections" sponsored by the emperors. In the case of the Council of Nicaea (325), Emperor Constantine might not only have influenced the acceptance and insertion of *homoousios* in the creed, he also endorsed and enforced the punishment of the council on those who refused to sign the Nicene Creed. The possibility that Constantine was not interested entirely in the purity of Christian beliefs was demonstrated in his demand for Arius's restoration into the ecclesiastical fellowship and his decision to exile Athanasius, whose theological camp won the debate at the Council of Nicaea. By flirting with the empire, the Council of Nicaea might have unwittingly drawn Jesus Christ into the support of the political agenda of Constantine's empire.[6]

In the sixth century, North African Christianity was tested by the horror of the imperial-ecclesial persecutions when some Copts who opted for the Miaphysite Christology refused to sign the Chalcedonian Definition (451).[7] The persecution of the Copts was so severe that, on hearing the footsteps of the invading Arab Muslims approaching Egypt, they limped for joy and praised God for sending the invaders to rescue them from the hands of the ruthless Melkites or Chalcedonian Christians. In moments such as this, one wonders if some Christians had

5. Walls, "Old Athens and New Jerusalem," p. 146.

6. Joerg Rieger, *Christ and Empire: From Paul to Postcolonial Times* (Minneapolis: Fortress, 2007), p. 69.

7. Alfred Joshua Butler, *The Arab Conquest of Egypt and the Last Thirty Years of the Roman Dominion* (Oxford: Clarendon, 1978), p. 158.

not made Jesus Christ, the embodiment of God's gospel, bad news. Human ambitions, albeit directed toward the preservation of the purity of Christian doctrines, may have denied the gospel its freedom to be God's liberating good news to all people.

African Christology from the 1980s to the Present: Imagining Jesus Christ from the Contexts of Africa

Moving from the sixth century to the sixteenth century through the mid-twentieth century, a careful scholar of African Christianity would notice a similar experience in sub-Saharan Africa. Many Christians who sought to express the Christian message with indigenous religious thoughts were severely hampered by the traditional Western derogatory attitudes toward African peoples and cultures. The majority of the missionaries who worked in sub-Saharan Africa from the 1400s considered Africans to be irreligious and incapable of conceiving Christian theology adequately without the guiding hands of the West.[8]

In the mid-twentieth century, new opportunities appeared as several Africans, of their own volition, crossed the Atlantic Ocean to study theology and world religions in Europe and North America. Broadly, two kinds of theology emerged: the theologies that presented the Christian message as the defeater of indigenous religions of Africa, and the theologies that construed the indigenous religions of Africa as *preparatio evangelica*. Some theologians returned to Africa as the protégés of the missionaries who gave them connections to the European and North American funding agencies. Like the missionaries, they aimed to rid Africa of its idolatrous way of life and idolatrous religions.[9] The irony was that the missionaries themselves presented Africans with an idolatrous form of Christianity when they introduced an imperialist and a colonialist Christ whose aim was to civilize the uncivil Africans and to send them on their way to "whiteness."[10] Some theologians,

8. For example, see the Annual Report of CMS Committee (May 3, 1921), *Proceedings of the Church Missionary Society for Africa in the East, 1920-1921*.

9. E. Bolaji Idowu, "The Predicament of the Church in Africa," in *Christianity in Tropical Africa: Studies Presented and Discussed at the Seventh International African Seminar, University of Ghana, April 1965*, ed. C. G. Baeta (Oxford: Oxford University Press, 1968), p. 426.

10. Kari Miettinen, *On the Way to Whiteness: Christianization, Conflict and Change in Colonial Ovamboland, 1910-1965* (Helsinki: Suomalasen Kirjallisuuden Seura, 2005).

however, began to question the usefulness of foreign theologies for African Christianity. They aimed to construct theologies that took into account the indigenous beliefs and customs of Africa and also to lay theological foundations for the gospel message of Christianity to interact meaningfully with African indigenous religions.[11]

The state of Christological discourses in sub-Saharan African Christianity has changed significantly since the 1960s and 1970s. During these periods, because of the pressing theological needs at the time, African theologians focused on broader theological issues of the relationship between African indigenous religions and Christianity. While discussions on the person and significance of Jesus were not entirely absent in the works of theologians, there were no substantive works on Christology. The lack of substantive Christological discussions was partly responsible for John Mbiti's comments in 1972 that "African concepts of Christology do not exist."[12] Earlier commentators on the condition of Christological discussions in sub-Saharan African Christianity such as John Taylor and Bolaji Idowu were highly critical of the ineffectiveness of the "imperialist" Christologies Western missionaries imposed on African Christian communities. In *Primal Vision: Christian Presence amid African Religion,* Taylor wrote: "Christ has been presented as the answer to the questions a white man would ask, the solution to the needs that Western man would feel . . . if Christ were to appear as the answer to the questions that Africans are asking, what would he look like?"[13] In 1969, Bolaji Idowu beckoned African theologians to seek to discover ways "the Christian faith could best be presented, interpreted, and inculcated in Africa so that Africans will hear God in Jesus Christ addressing Himself immediately to them in their own native situation and particular circumstances."[14] Taylor's and Idowu's concerns ignited a new zeal in many African theologians for constructing context-oriented Christologies.

Beginning in the 1980s, some theologians began to do construc-

11. Idowu, "Predicament of the Church in Africa," p. 433.

12. John S. Mbiti, "Some African Concepts of Christology," in *Christ and the Younger Churches: Theological Contributions from Asia, Africa, and Latin America* (London: SPCK, 1972), p. 51.

13. John V. Taylor, *The Primal Vision: Christian Presence amid African Religion* (London: SCM, 1963), p. 23.

14. E. Bolaji Idowu, "Introduction," in *Biblical Revelation and African Beliefs,* ed. Kwesi A. Dickson and Paul Ellingworth (London: Lutterworth, 1969), pp. 9-16.

tive reflections on the person and significance of Jesus.[15] A chronicle of all the Christologies that have appeared in the works of African theologians from the 1980s to the present is beyond the scope of this essay. Instead, I will discuss three Christological models that represent the major presuppositions underlying Christological discourses in sub-Saharan African Christianity: Neo-missionary Christologies, Ancestor Christologies, and Revealer Christology.

Neo-Missionary Christologies

Description and Context What I call "Neo-missionary Christologies" are the Christologies that retain some Western missionaries' derogatory views of the cultures and indigenous religions of Africa but also seek to contextualize the Christian message in their communities.[16]

These views developed as a result of concerns about the danger universalism posed to African Christianity and simultaneous explorations of the relationship between Jesus Christ and African indigenous religions.

Method and Presupposition Neo-missionary Christologies use a Bible-oriented theological approach that is grounded in a "destructionist presupposition."[17] This presupposition argues that Christianity and Jesus Christ must destroy the core beliefs and practices of the indigenous religions of Africa in order to create true Christian converts. The destructionist presupposition also upholds the position of discontinuity between Christianity and African indigenous religions.[18] These Christologies warn that the assumption of continuity between Afri-

---

15. Prior to 1980s, the majority of African theologians focused their attention on theology of religions, concentrating on the relationship between Christianity and African indigenous religions. This, of course, does not mean there were no Christological works before the 1980s. For example, the All African Conference of Churches (AACC) in its 1969 official statement insisted that Christology is central to Christian theological discussions.

16. Victor I. Ezigbo, *Re-imagining African Christologies: Conversing with the Interpretations and Appropriations of Jesus in Contemporary African Christianity* (Eugene, Ore.: Pickwick, 2010), pp. 55-64.

17. For extensive discussions on the destructionist presupposition, see Ezigbo, *Re-imagining African Christologies*, pp. 35-42.

18. Ezigbo, *Re-imagining African Christologies*, pp. 35-42.

can indigenous religions and Christianity threatens the uniqueness of Christianity. This assumption is based largely on the belief that African indigenous religions are "human-made" but Christianity is a "divinely instituted" religion.[19]

Assessment Neo-missionary Christologies have been instrumental in the preservation of the uniqueness of Christianity's theological identity and the primacy of Christian Scripture in the midst of other competing religions in Africa. Byang Kato, the Nigerian evangelical theologian, exemplifies the Neo-missionary approach. Although Kato did not write primarily in the field of Christology, Christological ideas permeated his theological reflections. Kato warned against African theologians who were critical of the missionaries for emphasizing the uniqueness of Christianity. For Kato, "Christianity stands to judge every culture, destroying elements that are incompatible models of expression for its advancement, and bringing new life to its adherents, the qualitative life that begins at the moment of conversion and culminates eternally with the imminent return of our Lord Jesus Christ."[20] Kato likened the indigenous religions of Africa to cancerous tumors and contended that the indigenous religions were unhelpful in expressing the Christian message. "For anyone who has been involved in pagan religion," Kato argued, "the suggestion for 'integral Christianity' . . . is like telling an ex-cancer patient that it was a mistake that he received a complete cure. . . . African traditional [or indigenous] religions only locate the problem; the Incarnate risen Christ alone is the answer. Christianity is a radical faith and it must transform sinners radically."[21] Christianity, for Kato, did not merely fulfill the gaps in the indigenous religions (contra the "gap and fulfillment presupposition").[22] On the contrary, Kato argued that Christianity must destroy the religious aspirations

---

19. Byang H. Kato, *Theological Pitfalls in Africa* (Kisumu: Evangel, 1975), p. 114.

20. Byang H. Kato, *Biblical Christianity in Africa* (Achimota: African Christian Press, 1985), p. 29.

21. Kato, *Theological Pitfalls in Africa*, p. 38.

22. The gap and fulfillment presupposition states that Christianity fulfills the spiritual aspirations of Africans that the indigenous religions do not satisfy sufficiently. Rather than destroying the indigenous religions, the proponents of this presupposition argue that Christianity should build on and utilize the path the indigenous religions have created. For an extensive discussion, see Ezigbo, *Re-imagining African Christologies*, pp. 26-35.

embedded in the indigenous religions of Africa. This view of Christianity is more evident in the work of theologians who follow Kato's theological vision. For example, Tokunboh Adeyemo has written: "Some . . . African theologians have asserted that Jesus came to fulfill not only the Old Testament but the African traditional expectations. Besides the fact that this is neither biblical nor traditionally true, it is pertinent to ask why the shadow is still embraced (that is, the Traditional Religion) when the perfect reality (Jesus Christ) has come?"[23]

Neo-missionary Christologies are not only interested in discrediting the claims that the indigenous religions of Africa contain substantive traces of God's revelation and are helpful for expressing the Christian message about God's action in Jesus Christ.[24] These Christologies are also preoccupied with the quest to preserve what Kato called "biblical Christianity" against the threat of universalism. In *Theological Pitfalls in Africa*, Kato attacked theologians he perceived as promoting universalism.[25] For him, the Bible is the inerrant and authoritative word or revelation of God. The Bible, he argued, must be the final authority in judging the truthfulness of any non-Christian religions. And since he judged the indigenous religions of Africa to be inherently idolatrous, Kato contended that seeing the indigenous religions as *preparatio evangelica* posed a serious threat to the uniqueness of the Bible, Christianity, and Jesus Christ.

I summarize three major criticisms against Neo-missionary Christologies. First, Neo-missionary Christologies fail to separate the "Jesus of Christian Scripture" from the "Jesus of Western missionaries." Neo-missionary Christologies are simplistic in their understanding of the complex relations between Jesus and religions, including Christianity. These Christologies, which share some Western missionaries' antagonist attitude toward African indigenous religious beliefs and practices, fail to utilize African indigenous religions as an indispensable source of African Christian Christologies.[26] These theologians have forgotten that many Western missionaries who worked in Africa from the 1400s

23. Tokunboh Adeyemo, *Salvation in African Tradition* (Kisumu: Evangel, 1978), p. 29.
24. E. Bolaji Idowu, *Towards an Indigenous Church* (London: Oxford University Press, 1965).
25. Kato, *Theological Pitfalls in Africa*, pp. 11-16.
26. I show later that the indigenous religions of Africa have continued to influence the beliefs, hopes, and practices of many Christians in sub-Saharan Africa.

Victor I. Ezigbo

to the 1900s asserted themselves as those who embodied the universal ideals of humanity. The missionaries' condemnation of many indigenous cultures and customs of Africa (such as African names) was the product of the dehumanizing views of Africans prevalent in the psychology of Westerners in the eighteenth and nineteenth centuries.[27] Many of the missionaries believed that Africans were savages, intellectually inferior, and morally repugnant people who must be subdued and savaged "by justice, by kindness [and] by [the] talisman of Christian truth."[28]

The missionaries succeeded in creating an impassable chasm between Christianity and the indigenous cultures of Africa, producing Christians who saw the indigenous religious traditions of Africa as anti-Christian, or viewed Christianity as the great defeater of African indigenous cultures. The irony, as many African theologians such as Kwame Bediako and John Mbiti have pointed out, is that most African Christians do not really abandon the indigenous worldviews of Africa in their understanding and practice of Christianity.[29] Many Christians turn to the indigenous religious beliefs and practices when faced with deep religious and spiritual issues.

Neo-missionary Christologies fail to account properly for the dialectics of God's immanence and transcendence in their theologies of religions. For example, polemics preoccupied Byang Kato, a major proponent of Neo-missionary Christology, making him a crusader against African indigenous religions rather than a constructive theologian who ought to allow the person and work of Jesus to critique and transform both Christianity and the indigenous religions of Africa.[30] Neo-missionary Christologies' belief that Christianity is judge over other religions is gravely mistaken. We are not to equate Christianity with Jesus Christ or to equate our Christologies with Jesus Christ. Our Chris-

27. See Robert Bernasconi and Timothy L. Lott, eds., *The Idea of Race* (Indianapolis: Hackett, 2000).

28. See Pringle's mission manifesto of 1820. Quoted in Dorothy Hammond and Atla Jablow, *Myth of Africa* (New York: Library of Social Science, 1977), p. 44.

29. Kwame Bediako, *Jesus and the Gospel in Africa: History and Experience* (Maryknoll: Orbis, 2004), p. 21.

30. Victor I. Ezigbo, "Religion and Divine Presence: Appropriating Christianity from within African Indigenous Religions' Perspective," in *African Traditions in the Study of Religion in Africa*, ed. Afe Adogame, Ezra Chitando, and Bolaji Bateye (Surrey: Ashgate, 2012), p. 196.

tologies cannot be above Jesus' critique. This is because we are prone to distort and misrepresent Jesus, reducing him to *what we want him to be* rather than allowing him to be *who he is* in our Christologies. The apostle Peter was guilty of this Christological error when he imagined that Jesus, as Yahweh's messiah, could not "suffer many things and be rejected by the elders, chief priests and teachers of law, and that he must be killed" (Mark 8:31 NIV). The magnitude of Peter's wrong Christology is revealed in Jesus' stern rebuke: "Get behind me, Satan! You do not have in mind the things of God, but things of men" (Mark 8:33 NIV).

The second criticism against Neo-missionary Christologies is their view of conversion, "substitution," and "replacement." To convert to Christianity, in this sense, is to substitute and replace the core beliefs of African indigenous religion with Christian beliefs and practices, which typically reflect more of Western missionaries' cultures than the teachings of Jesus Christ. This notion of conversion is theologically misleading. This is partly because in the New Testament *conversion* entails "turning toward" or "turning about."[31] A conversion experience implies redirecting and reinterpreting a person's previous way of life and beliefs in light of God's action in Jesus Christ. Conversion is an encounter in which a person willingly allows Jesus' understanding of God and humanity to critique and remold the person's previous understandings of God and humanity. This encounter does not require wiping out the person's previous understandings and filling the void with foreign understandings. Rather, the encounter requires redirecting the previous understandings in the direction of Jesus Christ. As Andrew F. Walls has noted, "To become a convert . . . is to turn, and turning involves not a change of substance but a change of direction. Conversion, in other words, means to turn what is already there in a new direction. It is not a matter of substituting something new for something old – that is proselytizing, a method that the early church could have adopted but deliberately chose to jettison. . . . Rather, Christian conversion involves redirecting what is already there, turning it in the direction of Christ."[32] Jesus Christ, a Jew, does not turn Africans into

---

31. G. Bertram, *"stréphō," "epistréphō,"* and *"epostrophē,"* in *Theological Dictionary of the New Testament,* abridged vol., ed. Geoffrey W. Bromiley (Grand Rapids: Eerdmans, 1985), pp. 1093-96. See Luke 17:4.

32. Walls, "Old Athens and New Jerusalem," p. 148.

"Jews" before he can truly relate to them. African Christians need not give up their cultural thoughts or adopt the Jewish culture before they can meaningfully imagine and appropriate Jesus in their contexts.

The third criticism relates to Neo-missionary Christologies' view of "biblical Christianity," which is grounded in the inerrantist view of the Bible. Theologians that advocate Neo-missionary Christologies need to reconsider the human elements (cultures, aspirations, and limitations) of the Bible. Neo-missionary Christologies' ideas of "biblical Christianity" do not take seriously the "humanness" of the Bible. The authors of the Bible, although under the direction or inspiration of the Holy Spirit (2 Tim. 3:16-17; 2 Pet. 1:20-21), wrote from their contexts — cultures, thoughts, languages, experiences (both personal and communal), and so on. The Holy Spirit's direction of the biblical authors guarantees Scripture's authority in making human beings "wise for salvation through faith in Christ" (2 Tim. 3:15). Also, the Holy Spirit's direction of the biblical authors makes Scripture an authoritative text that provides guidance in redirecting our inadequate understandings of God and humanity, and turning them in the direction of Jesus Christ (2 Tim. 3:16-17). The humanness of the Bible should remind African theologians that (1) African Christians need not use the Jewish and Greco-Roman Christological metaphors in the New Testament in interpreting and expressing their experience of Jesus, and (2) the Christological themes in the Bible neither exhaust nor encapsulate the meaning and significance of Jesus Christ. The problem with Neo-missionary Christologies' concept of "biblical Christianity" is that the forms of Christianity that are expressed in the New Testament are clothed in the thoughts, cultures, religious aspirations, religious experiences, and theological questions of the earliest Christian communities. Like Christians everywhere, African Christians have the theological freedom to use African thoughts, concepts, and metaphors to express their understanding of Jesus Christ. Some critics of Kato's theology, such as Kwame Bediako and Mercy Amba Oduyoye, have constructed Christologies that use the indigenous cultures and religions of Africans as a source of theological and Christological reflections.[33] The Ancestor Christology model is one of the products of such reflections, and it is to that model that I now turn.

---

33. Mercy Amba Oduyoye, *Beads and Strands: Reflections of an African Woman on Christianity in Africa* (Maryknoll: Orbis, 2004); Bediako, *Theology and Identity*, pp. 386-425.

Ancestor Christologies

Description and Context Ancestor Christologies present Jesus Christ as one whose mediatory role between God and humanity fulfills or satisfies the mediatory roles that are ascribed to ancestors in African indigenous religions. Ancestor Christologies seek to bridge the cultural and theological gap between Christianity and the indigenous religions of Africa. Unlike Neo-missionary Christologies, Ancestor Christologies recognize the value of the indigenous religious beliefs and thoughts of Africans in their expression and appropriation of the person and work of Jesus in Africa.

These approaches developed as a result of explorations of the relationship between Jesus Christ and primal cultures of Africa.

Method and Presupposition Ancestor Christologies are grounded in the claim that Jesus' mediatory role is analogous to the mediatory role ascribed to ancestors in some indigenous religions of Africa.[34] Ancestor Christologies use a culture-oriented theological method that operates with either a gap and fulfillment presupposition or a reconstructionist presupposition (or some combination). In the gap and fulfillment presupposition, Jesus Christ and Christianity can successfully satisfy the aspirations, hopes, and theological questions of Africans, which the indigenous religions do not satisfy. For the advocates of the reconstructionist presupposition, Jesus Christ "deconstructs the indigenous religions and reconstructs them in order to create a new religious understanding of the world."[35]

Assessment Ancestors' actual existence and mediatory functions are central to the beliefs in the indigenous understandings of the ancestor cult. Ancestors are believed to mediate between human beings and gods. They participate in the life of human communities by blessing those who keep the indigenous traditions and customs and by punishing evildoers with misfortune, sickness, or death. They are the guardians and custodians of the moral values of their families and

34. See Charles Nyamiti, *Christ as Our Ancestor* (Gweru: Mabo, 1984), and Uchenna A. Ezeh, *Jesus Christ the Ancestor: African Contextual Christology in the Light of the Major Dogmatic Christological Definitions of the Church from the Council of Nicaea (325) to Chalcedon (451)* (Oxford: Peter Lang, 2003).

35. Ezigbo, *Re-imagining African Christologies*, p. 42.

societies.[36] Ancestors are considered "living" because they take spirit or nonphysical forms at death and also because they are alive in the memory of human communities that know and preserve their earthly accomplishments.[37]

Rarely do recent works about African theology or Christology ignore discussions of Ancestor Christology models. This is a testimony to the growing influence and acceptance that these approaches enjoy in sub-Saharan African Christianity.[38] Theologians who construct Ancestor Christologies see continuity between the cult of ancestors in African traditions and the doctrine of the communion of the saints held by some Christian churches. Some of these theologians devote great efforts to defend the authority of Scripture and the universality of Jesus Christ. Kwame Bediako, for example, has argued that an "understanding of Christ in relation to spirit-power in African context is not necessarily less accurate than any other perception of Jesus. The question is whether such an understanding faithfully reflects biblical revelation and is rooted in true Christian experience."[39]

For some advocates of Ancestor Christologies, Jesus is "proto-ancestor," "ancestor par excellence," or the "greatest ancestor."[40] As the proto-ancestor, Jesus is the "Savior, and the remembrance of his passion, death and resurrection must be retold down the generations, for in him is made visible in a transcendent way that future which the ancestors wish to open up to us."[41] Also, Jesus is the ultimate fulfillment of the mediatory works ascribed to ancestors in the indigenous religions. As Bediako has argued, "Our natural ancestors had no barriers to cross to live among us and share our experience. [Jesus'] incarnation implies that he has achieved a far more profound identification with us in our humanity than the mere ethnic solidarity of lineage

36. Edward W. Fasholé-Luke, "Ancestor Veneration and the Communion of the Saints," in *New Testament Christianity for Africa and the World: Essays in Honor of Harry Sawyer,* ed. Mark E. Glaswell and Edward W. Fasholé-Luke (London: SPCK, 1974), p. 213.

37. John S. Mbiti, *African Religions and Philosophy* (Nairobi: Heinemann, 1969), p. 25.

38. For a survey of Ancestor Christologies, see Diane B. Stinton, *Jesus of Africa: Voices of Contemporary African Christology* (Maryknoll: Orbis, 2004), pp. 112-42.

39. Bediako, *Jesus and the Gospel in Africa,* p. 22.

40. Benezet Bujo, *African Theology in Its Social Context,* trans. John O'Donohue (Eugene, Ore.: Wipf and Stock, 2006), p. 82.

41. Bujo, *African Theology in Its Social Context,* p. 83.

ancestors can ever do. Jesus surpasses our natural ancestors also by virtue of who he is in himself."[42]

Criticisms against Ancestor Christology usually focus on some Christians who associate the ancestor cult with idol worship or demonic forces. For many of these Christians, especially Protestants, Africa's ancestor cult promotes necromancy, which they judge to be an anti-Christian act or ritual.[43] Christians who grew up with the doctrine of the communion of the saints (such as Roman Catholics), however, are more open to accepting Ancestor Christologies.[44] Some theologians have also challenged the usefulness of the ancestor Christological model, given the diminishing knowledge of the cult of ancestors in many African communities.[45]

What I consider a more substantial criticism of Ancestor Christologies is the unlikelihood that Jesus Christ would have met the requirements for ancestorship if he were an African. Anyone whom the elders and religious leaders found guilty of gross negligence of the traditions and who was executed for such crimes could not become an ancestor. In African indigenous tradition, the forebearers protected their community "against the forces of disintegration by their careful observance of law and custom."[46] Since Jewish religious leaders charged Jesus with the crimes of blasphemy and a gross negligence of some Jewish cultural and religious traditions, it would be very unlikely that Jesus could have qualified as an ancestor in Africa if he was found guilty of the same crimes.

One way of responding to this criticism is to construe the cult of ancestors as a "myth" and proceed from the religious aspiration it creates, not focusing on whether ancestors actually exist. According to Kwame Bediako, the cult of ancestors is the "myth-making imagination of the community that sacralises" it and confers on ancestors "the sacred authority . . . they exercise through those in the community, like kings who also expect to become ancestors."[47] Bediako concludes, "Once the meaning of the cult of ancestors as a myth is granted and its function is understood within the overall religious life of traditional society, it

42. Bediako, *Jesus and the Gospel in Africa*, p. 22.
43. These Christians usually cite Leviticus 19 as a proof text.
44. Stinton, *Jesus of Africa*, pp. 123-26.
45. Stinton, *Jesus of Africa*, pp. 130-35.
46. Bujo, *African Theology in Its Social Context*, p. 22.
47. Bediako, *Jesus and the Gospel in Africa*, p. 30.

becomes clear how Jesus Christ fulfills our aspirations in relation to ancestral function too."[48] While Bediako's proposal would be of interest to some Christian theologians, many adherents of indigenous religions may find his proposal offensive because it rejects or dismisses the belief in the actual existence and functions of ancestors.[49] Also, Africans who continue to believe in the existence of ancestors and the relevance of the ancestor cult to African communities may find Bediako's mythological interpretation unhelpful.[50] Herbert Macaulay, the grandson of Bishop Ajayi Crowther, for example, argued that the "African should have been left with his ancestor-worship and that Christianity should not have been allowed to supplant it in certain parts of the continent. Ancestor-worship, it will be readily admitted is Aero-worship, nation-worship, in short patriotism."[51] I now turn to a Revealer Christology model I am proposing as an alternative way to imagine the significance of Jesus' identity and work in sub-Saharan African Christianity.

Revealer Christology

Description and Context The word "revealer," as used here, refers to an individual who embodies a true knowledge of God and humanity and who also communicates such knowledge by redirecting inadequate understandings of God and humanity. The Revealer Christology I propose construes Jesus as the revealer of divinity and humanity through whom African Christians can assess and redirect the knowledge of God and humanity they gained from African indigenous religions and Western forms of Christianity.

This approach arises as a result of an exploration of Jesus' "place"

---

48. Bediako, *Jesus and the Gospel in Africa*, p. 30.

49. Bediako writes, "The presumption that ancestors actually function for the benefit of the community can be seen as part of the same myth-making imagination that projects departed human beings into the transcendent realm." Bediako, *Jesus and the Gospel in Africa*, p. 30.

50. The field research Diana Stinton conducted in Kenya, Uganda, and Ghana shows some African Christians believe that ancestors exist and perform some mediatory roles between humans and gods. See Stinton, *Jesus of Africa*, pp. 123-35.

51. H. Macaulay, "Religion and Native Customs," *Lagos Daily News* 18, no. 1 (1992), in *A History of Christianity in Asia, Africa, and Latin America, 1450-1990*, ed. Klaus Koschorke, Frieder Ludwig, and Mariano Delgado (Grand Rapids: Eerdmans, 2007), p. 239.

in the interaction of African indigenous religions and Christianity in the practice of Christian beliefs and ethics in sub-Saharan African Christianity.

Method and Presupposition I use a Christocentric approach I prefer to term "communicative and hermeneutical." This presupposition, which is grounded in the traditional Christian belief in Jesus' full divinity and humanity, sees Jesus as God's communicative and hermeneutical act in which African Christians can encounter a true knowledge of God's expectation from God's creatures, in particular human beings.

Revealer Christology: Jesus as God's Communicative and Hermeneutical Act The ethnographic study I conducted among five different church denominations in Nigeria in 2006 shows that many Nigerian Christians relate to Jesus as only *a* "solution" among many "solutions" to their religious and spiritual needs.[52] To illustrate this Christological mindset, I cite two interviewees' responses to the question: "Do Christians in Nigeria go outside of Jesus to seek solutions to their religious and spiritual needs?" Moses Attah, an evangelical Christian from northern Nigeria, said that many Christians in his community consult native doctors and priests of local deities when they sense Jesus' slowness to solve their problems.

> In the north [northern Nigeria], you may have problems with somebody and if you call on Jesus the problems may not be solved immediately. Some people will do as we normally say: "Let me put off the shirt of Jesus Christ and put on the cultural shirt." Then they will go to the shrine or any other place to look for help forgetting that Jesus will help them. And sometimes during tribal wars or religious wars between Christians and Muslims some Christians go to the herbalists to collect some charm in order to protect themselves, forgetting that Jesus is there to protect them.[53]

Faith Ukaegbu, a member of a Pentecostal church, shares a similar experience.

52. Ezigbo, *Re-imagining African Christologies*, p. 136.
53. Moses Attah, interview by researcher, tape recording, Aba, February 29, 2006, quoted in Ezigbo, *Re-imagining African Christologies*, p. 136.

53

Many people go to native doctors to get solutions. Well, the problem is when we [call them] Christians. When we call them Christians we are getting it wrong, because if you are a Christian you cannot go to native doctors no matter the situation. So I don't believe that if you are a Christian you can go to that extent, except you are a backsliding Christian.[54]

Ukaegbu's distinction between a "Christian" and a "backsliding Christian" is merely a critique of the practice of deserting Jesus for native doctors and priests of local deities and not a denial of the reality that many Christians relate to Jesus as one among many who provide solutions to their religious and spiritual needs. What drives this practice of deserting Jesus, albeit temporarily, to seek immediate solutions from diviners, native doctors, and priests of local deities? I see three interrelated quests at the heart of these practices: (1) the quest to understand the relationship between the spirit and human worlds; (2) the quest to manipulate, appease, or defeat evil agents in order to attain wellbeing; and (3) the quest to identify a reliable agent through whom they can interpret and appropriate their experiences. These quests, which permeate the daily lives of many Christians in Nigeria, are grounded in the indigenous religions' teaching about the symbiotic relationship between the spirit and human worlds. In this view of the spirit and human worlds, God, lesser gods, malevolent beings, and ancestors can commune with human beings and interfere in human affairs. Human beings also can manipulate or appease these spirit beings in order to avert their punishments or win their favor.

Many Christian communities in sub-Saharan Africa, as some works written on African Christianity and African indigenous religions have shown, share the same view of the relationship between the spirit and human world.[55] While we should exercise caution in extending the three quests (which are drawn from the religious experience of Nigerian Christians) to other Christians in sub-Saharan Africa, the quests are most likely connected with the emphases on spiritual warfare, prosperity, and the focus on drawing transcendent power from the Holy

54. Faith Ukaegbu, interview by researcher, tape recording, Aba, May 6, 2006, quoted in Ezigbo, *Re-imagining African Christologies*, p. 137.

55. See Vincent Mulago, "Traditional African Religion and Christianity," in *African Traditional Religion in Contemporary Society*, ed. Jacob K. Olupona (St. Paul, Minn.: Paragon, 1991), pp. 119-34.

Spirit to combat demonic forces in the preaching, songs, and lived theologies of many sub-Sahara African Christian communities.[56]

Merely assigning titles such as the "Chief Diviner-Healer" to Jesus Christ does not deal adequately with the root Christological issues that are inherent in the three quests.[57] The primary Christological issue inherent in the three quests is not the search for a *heuristic* or *pedagogical device* to express a foreign message (about Jesus) to Africans. Rather, the primary Christological issue is the significance of Jesus to the religious and spiritual questions of Africans. What is needed, therefore, is a constructive Christology that allows Jesus to engage these quests by redirecting them to his vision of God's expectations from humanity. The questions the three quests raise for theologians are: How should these quests function as *sources* for interpreting and appropriating Jesus Christ in Africa? And in what ways could Jesus *engage* these quests in order to answer the questions they generate without betraying his vision for humanity or disregarding the experience of African Christians? An extensive answer to these two questions is beyond the scope of this essay. I only summarize how the Revealer Christology I am proposing approaches these questions.

I classify the sources of Christian Christology into two tiers. The Bible belongs to the first tier (in its capacity as the inspired sacred writing) and functions as the final authority in assessing our understandings of Jesus Christ. The Christologies that contradict scriptural teaching about Jesus Christ have failed the primary test of Christian identity. The Christologies of the classical ecumenical councils and the contemporary contexts of local Christian communities belong to the second tier. African Christology should learn from the Christologies of the earliest ecumenical councils. Since the days of the Councils of Nicaea (325), Constantinople (381), and Chalcedon (451), Christian theologians have understood the identity of Jesus in two major parallel ways. We can describe them as the Arian Way and the Nicene-Chalcedonian Way. The *Arian Way* argues that Jesus is God functionally but not ontologically. God created and has continued to sustain the

56. J. Kwabena Assmoah-Gyadu, "'From Prophetism to Pentecostalism': Religious Innovation in Africa and African Religious Scholarship," in *African Traditions in the Study of Religion in Africa*, ed. Afe Adogame, Ezra Chitando, and Bolaji Bateye (Surrey: Ashgate, 2012), pp. 165-72.

57. Joseph Healey and Donald Sybertz, *Towards an African Narrative Theology* (Maryknoll: Orbis, 1996), pp. 85-87.

world through Jesus Christ. But ontologically, Jesus was a special creature of God, and therefore, was not the true God. On the contrary, the
Nicene-Chalcedonian Way argues that Jesus was ontologically divine and
human. He was truly God and truly human. Both Christological ways,
or views, can be explained successfully in Africa because of the indigenous religions' teaching about the mutual relationship and interconnectedness of the spirit world and human world.

The three quests that drive many African Christians' act of consulting native doctors and priests of local deities for solutions to their problems are part of the intellectual and religious contexts of sub-Saharan
African Christianity. Recognizing these three quests as sources for African Christology will provide a theologian with the intellectual and
religious resources needed to express the person and work of Jesus
in a manner that engages concretely with the religious experience of
African Christians. By allowing the quests and other experiences of African Christians to become an indispensable source of Christology, the
theologian will be drawn into actual Christological needs of African
Christians. The theologian is also able to avoid the error of imposing
foreign Christological questions on African Christians.

In light of Jesus' teaching as it is represented in the Gospels, his
followers are called to commit to his redirection of their previous understandings of God's expectations from humanity and also their understandings of the place of human beings in the world. This "redirection" neither occurs in a vacuum nor requires an obliteration of the
cultures, intellectual histories, or religious beliefs of those who desire
to become his followers. Rather, it is a process in which Jesus invites
and enables people, especially his followers, to critique, rethink, and
reimagine their previous knowledge and beliefs in light of his vision
for humanity and teaching about God. Jesus' response to the questions
and religious aspirations of a certain woman of Samaria (John 4:1-26)
exemplifies his identity as a "revealer" of true divinity and humanity. In his conversation with the woman of Samaria, Jesus critiques
the assumptions of two religions: Judaism and a religion of Samaria.
For Jesus, Jews and Samaritans were guilty of "inadequate theology for
perceiving God in ways that strip God of the ability to simultaneously
interact with and distance God's self from human religions."[58] Jesus
invited the woman to rethink her views of God and true worship, not

58. Ezigbo, "Religion and Divine Presence," p. 197.

from the Jews' and Samaritans' views of an appropriate worship location, but from his view of God. "But the hour is coming, and is now here," Jesus taught her, "when the true worshippers will worship the Father in spirit and truth, for the Father is seeking such people to worship him" (John 4:23 ESV). One of Jesus' aims in the conversation was to critique the theologies of both Judaism and the religion of Samaria and also to "inspire a new imagining of God (on the basis of his identity) from within the perspectives of the two religions."[59]

As the revealer of humanity and divinity, a claim that is grounded in the Christian confession of Jesus' divinity and humanity, Jesus Christ is able to resist our attempts to reduce his significance to what we want him to be. He does not merely provide answers to the questions African Christians are asking about the relationship between the spirit and human worlds, or how to manipulate or defeat evil agents in order to attain wellbeing, or how to identify a reliable agent through whom they can interpret and appropriate their experiences. Jesus also critiques and redirects these questions.

The Christian who temporarily deserts Jesus for diviners in search of a solution to her barrenness, for example, needs to rethink indigenous understandings of barrenness in light of Jesus' understanding of the value of humanity as God's creatures (Matt. 6:25-34). In indigenous African cultures, barrenness is associated with incompleteness and divine curse. These beliefs are shaped by the indigenous African notion of the centrality of human beings in the world. Human beings are to be at the center of existence and "everything else is seen in its relation to the central position" they occupy.[60] Some Christians continue to hold these beliefs. The Revealer Christology that is proposed in this essay invites such Christians to rethink these indigenous beliefs in light of Jesus' teaching about God and humanity. In this way, Jesus does not merely satisfy the religious and spiritual aspirations of such Christians, but he also reorients the aspirations in a manner that allows his vision of humanity to shape and transform African Christians' questions and religious aspirations. Christians need to know that being a follower of Jesus requires committing to his vision of humanity in which God, and not human achievements or inabilities, determines human significance and worth. African Christians who search for God's purpose for their lives and the causes of their mis-

59. Ezigbo, "Religion and Divine Presence," p. 198.
60. Adeyemo, *Salvation in African Tradition*, p. 56.

fortunes, and who sometimes visit the shrines of native doctors to hear from the ancestors or to solve their problems, can find hope in Jesus, who embodies the true knowledge of divinity and humanity.

Concluding Remarks

An African "Christian" Christology should show its commitment to the scriptural teaching that God is in Jesus Christ through the power of the Holy Spirit redeeming, reconciling, and remolding humanity. The Christology should also use Africa's contexts as an indispensable source. Doing so would allow Jesus Christ to meaningfully engage the Christological and theological questions that African Christians' contexts generate for Christology. This means that an African theologian should be intentionally contextual when constructing a Christology for an African community. As the Christologies I examined in this essay show, many African theologians see contextualization as one of Christology's universal traits. Our social locations, cultures, histories, and experiences shape and *ought to shape* our understandings of Jesus' identity and significance. Jesus' question "Who do you say I am?" (Mark 8:29) can only be truly meaningful to contemporary African Christians when they engage it from their own contexts. Revealer Christology offers African Christians the opportunity to commit to Jesus' critique and redirection of their views of him, God, and humanity without disregarding their contexts.

For Further Reading

Bediako, Kwame. *Jesus and the Gospel in Africa: History and Experience.* Maryknoll: Orbis, 2004.

Ezigbo, Victor I. *Re-imagining African Christologies: Conversing with the Interpretations and Appropriations of Jesus in Contemporary African Christianity.* Eugene, Ore.: Pickwick, 2010.

Oduyoye, Mercy Amba. "Jesus Christ." In *The Cambridge Companion to Feminist Theology,* edited by Susan Frank Parsons, pp. 151-70. New York: Cambridge University Press, 2002.

Schreiter, Robert J., ed. *Faces of Jesus in Africa.* Maryknoll: Orbis, 1991.

Stinton, Diane B. *Jesus of Africa: Voices of Contemporary African Christology.* Maryknoll: Orbis, 2004.

CHAPTER 3

Christologies in Asia: Trends and Reflections

Timoteo D. Gener

Introduction

What follows is an overview of Christologies in Asia, and my personal reflections as an evangelical theologian based in the Philippines. Nowadays, the world we live in has become "smaller" and globalized. But still genuine conversation and listening seems hard to come by between and among peoples, even in the body of Christ. The title of William Dyrness's recent article says it all, "I'm Not Hearing You: The Struggle to Hear from a Global Church."[1]

Intercultural conversation and hermeneutics remain vital for biblical interpretation, for we are often unaware how cultural blinders limit our interpretations, even of the gospel. Krister Stendahl's seminal article on Paul and the introspective Western conscience alerted us to this half a century ago.[2] Mainstream evangelical leaders and scholars who were responsible for the Willowbank Report on Gospel and Culture (1978) also made us aware of social and cultural noises affecting our attempt at universal, monologic interpretations of the Bible and the gospel.[3] Part of

1. William A. Dyrness, "I'm Not Hearing You: The Struggle to Hear from a Global Church," *Theology, News and Notes* 57, no. 2 (2011): 14-18. See also Stephen B. Bevans and Katalina Tahaafe-Williams, eds., *Contextual Theology for the Twenty-First Century* (Eugene, Ore.: Pickwick, 2011), pp. 11-16, 38-52.

2. Krister Stendahl, "The Apostle Paul and the Introspective Conscience of the West," *Harvard Theological Review* 56, no. 3 (1963): 199-215.

3. Robert T. Coote and John R. W. Stott, *Down to Earth: Studies in Christianity and Culture: The Papers of the Lausanne Consultation on Gospel and Culture* (Grand Rapids: Eerdmans,

the calling of Christ's followers, as reflected in this report, is to discern true contextualization from shallow alternatives. In this vein, what is needed is not just a knowledge of formal (philosophical) hermeneutics, but an applied intercultural hermeneutic in service of Christ and his church.[4] The thrust of the Scriptures tells us that Christ is inseparable from Christian community. The words of Bishop Azariah of India about a hundred years ago summarize this connection well:

> But what is Christianity? It is often said that Christianity is Christ. That is true; but it is also a way of life. "The Way" was the name given to it in the days of the apostles. Christianity is not a doctrine about God; it is not hero-worship of Jesus, it is a scheme of life in a society; it is an organism, a family, a brotherhood − whose centre, radius and circumference is Christ. In fellowship with all others who are attached to the Lord, bound together by outward rules and rites and throbbing with one inward pulse and purpose, men and women of all ages, races, tongues, colours, and nationalities have accepted this scheme of life, and separated from all others are more and more experiencing in this fellowship the impetus and power from the Spirit who is its indweller and life-giver.[5]

As we will see, the vitality of Christian witness relates integrally to Christology since the point of biblical Christology is discipleship in context. The first Christians' path to faith in Jesus as the Christ may actually be called discipleship-in-context Christology,[6] or missiological Christology/ies.[7]

1980). The paper that emerged out of the consultation, known as the Willowbank Report, is also available online: http://www.lausanne.org/en/documents/lops/73-lop-2.html.

4. I still find useful as an introductory orientation for such hermeneutic William A. Dyrness's *Learning About Theology from the Third World* (Grand Rapids: Zondervan, 1990), with its companion reader, *Emerging Voices in Global Christian Theology* (Grand Rapids: Zondervan, 1994); also Stephen Bevans, *Models of Contextual Theology* (Maryknoll: Orbis, 1992, 2002).

5. Quoted in Susan Billington Harper, *In the Shadow of the Mahatma: Bishop V. S. Azariah and the Travails of Christianity in British India* (Grand Rapids: Eerdmans, 2000), p. 248.

6. The phrase "discipleship-in-context Christology" combines James H. Kroeger's (discipleship Christology) and Minho Song's (discipleship in context) terminologies. The actual methodology, however, is indebted to José de Mesa, *Following the Way of the Disciples: A Guidebook for Doing Christology in Cultural Context* (Quezon City: East Asia Pastoral Institute, 1996). See also James H. Kroeger, ed., *Knowing Christ Jesus: A Christological Sourcebook* (Quezon City: Claretian, 1989), p. 13, and Minho Song, "Contextualization and Discipleship: Closing the Gap between Theory and Practice," *Evangelical Review of Theology* 30, no. 3 (2006): 249-63.

7. This direction limits the study from a mere descriptive account (a report) of

What Is the Asian (Church) Setting?

Asia is a vast continent, and home to the major religions of the world.[8] Asia is also a continent where Christians are a minority, the only exception being the Philippines.

The Federation of Asian Bishops' Conference of the Catholic Church (FABC) as well as key Asian theologians such as Aloysius Pieris and José de Mesa consider the triple realities of poverty, religions, and cultures as defining the Asian situation in general.[9] While there are developed countries in Asia such as Japan, China, and Singapore, poverty still characterizes the majority of Asian nations. In these poverty-ridden countries, Christians reread and relate Scripture, and Jesus Christ, to their socioeconomic plight. Likewise, the Scriptures and Jesus Christ are read in the context of the plurality of religions and cultural identities in these communities. The region demonstrates a flourishing of theological ferment that rereads Scripture in ablative terms, by means of Asia and for Asians. These readings characteristically take stock of Asian worldviews, experiences, and concerns.[10]

Asian Christologies to a combination of description and prescription. Peter C. Phan offers a succinct report of Asian Christologies consisting of four Asian theologians in particular: Aloysius Pieris, Jung Young Lee, C. S. Song, and Chung Hyun Kyung. Peter C. Phan, "Jesus the Christ with an Asian Face," *Theological Studies* 57 (1996): 399-430. While I am aware of these theologians and have engaged them myself, my account differs from theirs in that, aside from being confessional (evangelical), I wish to situate christologizing communally, that is, through the local-regional Asian church as a base. I see doing theology as for every Christian, and not just for the experts. See my "Every Filipino Christian, a Theologian: A Way of Advancing Local Theology for the 21st Century," and "Epilogue," in *Doing Theology in the Philippines*, ed. John Suk (Mandaluyong, Philippines: OMF Lit., 2005), pp. 3-23, 219-23.

8. As Phan sums it up well, it is "the birthplace of all the major religions of the world, not only Hinduism, Buddhism, Jainism, Zoroastrianism (southern Asia), Confucianism, Taoism, Shintoism (eastern Asia), but also Judaism, Christianity, and Islam (western Asia)." Phan, "Jesus the Christ with an Asian Face," p. 402.

9. D. D. Gaudencio Rosales and C. G. Arevalo, S.J., eds., *For All the Peoples of Asia: Federation of Asian Bishops' Conferences Documents from 1970-1991* (Quezon City: Claretian, 1997), pp. 13-17; Aloysius Pieris, *An Asian Theology of Liberation* (Quezon City: Claretian, 1988); de Mesa, "Making Salvation Concrete and Jesus Real," pp. 3-8; see also Phan, "Jesus the Christ with an Asian Face," pp. 400-403.

10. See Anri Morimoto, "Asian Theology in the Ablative Case," *Studies in World Christianity* 17, no. 3 (2011): 201-15. For summary reports, see de Mesa, "Making Salvation Concrete and Jesus Real," and Phan, "Jesus the Christ with an Asian Face."

No less than in the rest of the world, globalization is part and parcel of the new reality that Asians now face.[11] The world has become more interconnected and "smaller" because of the pervasive role of digital media. Transcultural flows of people and capital globe-wide have also contributed to this shrinking world.[12] While these global flows and exchanges heighten a sense of interconnectedness, globalization also intensifies cultural identities as well as ethnification.[13] A renewed awareness of one's own reality in Asia goes alongside a sense of global interconnectedness.[14] More than ever these call for a new vision of a world church, which takes seriously the role of local and regional churches in the body of Christ worldwide.[15]

As Christian awareness of the global church increases, it is important to note the unique contributions Asia brings to Christ's body as a whole. A look at the documents of the FABC reveals that there are important contributions in the areas of spirituality, meditative prayer, helpful approaches to world religions, and a strong family orientation.[16] It is *this* Asia, with its giftings, to which the Christian church offers Jesus Christ as the one who can provide a fuller meaning and value to Asian people's lives.

Is Asia part of what Philip Jenkins calls "the next Christendom"?[17] Asia is, indeed, a vast continent and the numbers do show that Christianity is growing remarkably in Asia. But even if this is

11. B. Nicholls, T. Lua and J. Belding, eds., *The Church in a Changing World: An Asian Response* (Quezon City: ATA, 2010); Schreiter, *New Catholicity*.

12. See my "Theology and Cultural Identity in Global Exchange" and "Case Study: Identity Crisis of Philippine Migrant Workers," in *The Church in a Changing World*, pp. 92-108.

13. See Schreiter, *New Catholicity*, p. 27; also Francisco F. Claver, S.J., *The Making of a Local Church* (Quezon City: Claretian, Jesuit Communications, 2009).

14. Emmanuel Gerrit Singgih, "Globalization and Contextualization: Toward a New Awareness of One's Own Reality," *Exchange* 29, no. 4 (October 2000): 361-72.

15. Karl Rahner called attention to this new understanding of a truly world church and local churches in the Roman Catholic Church ("Toward a Fundamental Theological Interpretation of Vatican II," *Theological Studies* 40, no. 4 [1979]: 716-27). Schreiter labels this new ecclesiological vision as "new catholicity." One senses this ecclesiological tension between global and local even in evangelical circles; see Coote and Stott, *Down to Earth*.

16. Here I follow the points listed down by Francis X. Clark, S.J., *An Introduction to the Catholic Church of Asia* (Quezon City: Loyal School of Theology, Ateneo de Manila University, 1987), pp. 26-29.

17. Philip Jenkins, *The Next Christendom* (Oxford: Oxford University Press, 2007).

so, the figures also show that the "Christian Faith in Asia is still a minority in a vast ocean of Hindu, Buddhist, Confucian, Taoist and Islamic religions."[18] Stephen Bevans, summoning figures from the World Christian Database, likewise describes the Asian church as a minority:

> China . . . with 1.2 billion people, has only about one hundred million Christians by a generous count; India's population of one billion contains about fifty-two million Christians, and Indonesia's twenty-seven million Christians make up less than 10 percent of the country's 226 million people – even though these are more Christians than the entire population of Australia.[19]

The close identification of Christianity in Asia with Euro-American colonization and the church's corresponding lack of rootedness in Asian cultures is likely a major factor for the persistence of this minority status.[20] The lack of cultural roots and engagement fuels doubts that merely planting or multiplying churches is the right agenda for the mission in Asian churches today. The Asian theologians Emmanuel Gerrit Singgih and Samuel Jayakumar suggest that the presence of rapid growth and Christian conversions in Asia does not necessarily mean the church is being obedient to God's work of holistic mission.[21] Rather than "expanding 'Christendom'" Singgih suggests focusing on expanding "'Christ' or 'Christianness'" in the region.[22] This means becoming a servant church, involved in prophetic, healing ministry as well as Christians being instruments of Christ's peace and reconciliation among diverse peoples and religions.[23]

---

18. Emmanuel Gerrit Singgih, "Any Room for Christ in Asia? Statistics and the Location of the Next Christendom," *Exchange* 38 (2009): 143.

19. Stephen Bevans, "What Has Contextual Theology to Offer the Church of the Twenty-First Century?" in *Contextual Theology for the Twenty-First Century*, p. 5.

20. As Dionisio Miranda puts it: "a large part of the failure must be traced back to the alienation or lack of authentic appropriation and [cultural] assimilation by the would-be converters themselves, making them appear no more than clones of foreign missionaries" (*Loob: The Filipino Within* [Manila: Divine Word, 1988], p. 6).

21. Samuel Jayakumar, "God's Work as Holistic Mission: An Asian Perspective," *Evangelical Review of Theology* 35, no. 2 (2011): 227-41.

22. Singgih, "Any Room for Christ in Asia?" pp. 144, 143.

23. Singgih, "Any Room for Christ in Asia?" p. 143.

Christology in the Plural?

Christologies in the New Testament

The plural "Christolog*ies*" in this essay's title may suggest a counter-point to the one Jesus. But biblically speaking, it does not and should not do so here. We have four portraits of the one Jesus in the New Testament Gospels. On the one hand, the four Gospels are what they are because they took into account the location of their respective communities; hence, there was a contextualization of the story of Jesus. On the other hand, the reality of four Gospels underscores a "plurality and diversity in our views about Jesus" while at the same time giving parameters to these views.[24]

In fact, the whole of the New Testament embodies the reality of contextualization.[25] Christolog*ies* in particular point us to the reality of contextual theologizing from biblical times to the present. The biblical writings convey God's transforming word as rooted in particular contexts; that is, the biblical authors engaged thought patterns and behaviors of people in particular historical times and places. These authors expressed the biblical faith in the God of Israel and of Jesus through the interpretive models and available vocabularies of their day. Similarly, the dual commitment to being faithful to God's word and meaningfully expressing that word in context can be discerned in the thought of Christians of different generations as they do the task of expressing Christology for their own particular times and places. This is what the witness of the Gospels themselves do. The "Gospels . . . are simultaneously a model of how to modernize Jesus without losing sight of the history of Jesus."[26]

In the history and theology of the Christian churches, diverse typologies of Christology can be encountered. Following Volker Küster, Veli-Matti Kärkkäinen lists five prominent typologies: (1) the incarnational Christology of the early church and Catholicism; (2) the theology of the

---

24. Richard A. Burridge, *Four Gospels, One Jesus?* (Grand Rapids: Eerdmans, 1994), pp. 174-75.

25. Daniel Von Allmen, "The Birth of Theology: Contextualization as the Dynamic Element in the Formation of New Testament Theology," *International Review of Mission* 64 (1975): 37-55.

26. Insightful on this point is Michael F. Bird's "The Peril of Modernizing Jesus and the Crisis of Not Contemporizing Christ," *Evangelical Quarterly* 78, no. 4 (2006): 311.

cross of Protestantism, especially of the Lutheran tradition; (3) liberation Christology, especially from Latin America; (4) the resurrection and ascension Christology of Eastern Orthodoxy; and (5) the empowerment Christology of Pentecostalism and the Charismatic movements.[27]

Approaching Asian Christologies

The way I would describe Christologies in Asia undoubtedly entails some presuppositions, especially regarding theologizing and doing Christology in particular. This admission is not simply a matter of situating this study within the larger canvas of theological scholarship. Stating one's methodological pre-understandings in Christology is essential as Christians around the globe come to terms with and contextually engage the growth of Christological understandings and traditions from New Testament times down to the present. The word engaging the world is integral to the Christological process, even in the Scriptures themselves. To put it another way, the practice of reflection on Christology, as with the practice of theology in general, involves an interaction between biblical faith and our experiences for the sake of Christ's reign, while preserving the normativity of Scripture.[28] Within the Bible itself and the early Christian movement, theological process always demonstrated this interaction between the knowledge of God and the experiences (issues, concerns, needs) of God's people.[29]

On the one hand the work of Christology requires that we probe what the Scriptures reveal about Jesus Christ. The Judeo-Christian

27. Veli-Matti Kärkkäinen, *Christology: A Global Introduction* (Grand Rapids: Baker Academic, 2003), p. 15. For other typologies, see Lesslie Newbigin, *The Finality of Christ* (London: SCM, 1969), pp. 65-69, also *Gospel in a Pluralist Society*, p. 171; also Singgih, "Any Room for Christ in Asia?" p. 137, which summarizes Pieris's categories from *An Asian Theology of Liberation* (New York: Orbis, 1988), p. 33.

28. *Global Dictionary of Theology*, s.v. "Christology" and "Theological Method." See also Donald K. McKim, who defines "doing theology" as "the process of carrying out theological reflection, articulation and action," in *Westminster Dictionary of Theological Terms* (Louisville: Westminster John Knox, 1996), and Neil Darragh, *Doing Theology Ourselves: A Guide to Research and Action* (Auckland: Accent, 1995). See also Gener, "Every Filipino Christian, a Theologian," p. 7.

29. *Global Dictionary of Theology*, s.v. "Theological Method." See also Daniel Von Allmen, "The Birth of Theology: Contextualization as the Dynamic Element in the Formation of New Testament Theology," *International Review of Mission* 64, no. 253 (January 1975): 37-52.

tradition represents one pole in the task of doing Christology. Historical and literary study of who Jesus is in the Bible remains essential. However, these are not ends in themselves. For the Gospels
themselves proffer the claim that to follow Jesus means to be his
disciple in one's own context.[30] The Gospels demonstrate that to
tell the story of Jesus means to follow him "on the road."[31] Here we
affirm the relative, not absolute, value of the quest for the historical
Jesus, or the pursuit of how much can be reliably discovered about
Jesus as a historical figure.[32] For instance, the so-called third quest
for the Jesus of history helped better root him in his original, Jewish context. Indeed, the various quests for the historical Jesus have
alerted us to the differences "between the Christ proclaimed by the
Christian tradition and the Jesus of history."[33] Still the historical
Jesus is not the real Jesus. The historical Jesus is "the picture of Jesus that emerges from the application of historical tools and by the
formation of historical hypotheses."[34] However, for Christian faith
the real Jesus is the resurrected Jesus. He "is not simply a figure
from the past but very much and above all a figure of the present, a
figure, indeed, who defines believers' present by his presence."[35] In
light of the resurrection, the pole of the Judeo-Christian tradition in
theologizing involves a continuing recognition of the living Christ
in history expressed through the agency of God's people, especially
Christ's body, the church. This view of the church entails recognition of the authority of the creeds and the ecumenical councils in
interpreting Scripture and defining the meaning of Christian faith
and life, though such authority expressed through confessions is
still under the higher authority of Scripture.[36]

30. Personal interview with the Philippine theologian José de Mesa, 2012.

31. Michael F. Bird, "The Purpose and Preservation of the Jesus Tradition," *Bulletin for Biblical Research* 15 (2005): 161-85.

32. For a useful introduction, see Luke Timothy Johnson, *The Real Jesus* (San Francisco: HarperCollins, 1996); also N. T. Wright, *The Challenge of Jesus: Rediscovering Who Jesus Was and Is* (Downers Grove: InterVarsity, 1999).

33. Thomas P. Rausch, S.J., *Who is Jesus? An Introduction to Christology* (Quezon City: Claretian, 2005), p. 23.

34. Bird, "Peril of Modernizing Jesus," p. 306.

35. Johnson, *Real Jesus*, p. 142. See also Robert Jenson, *Systematic Theology*, vol. 1 (Oxford: Oxford University Press, 1997), pp. 171-73.

36. Cf. Shirley C. Guthrie, *Always Being Reformed* (Louisville: Westminster John Knox, 1996), pp. 16-30. For a laudable example of how a biblical scholar engages the

The other pole of doing the task of Christology is human experi-ence. Theologizing is a process that speaks to, but also draws from, human experiences and surrounding cultures to transform them. As we've seen, this is evident in the Bible itself and is essential to the very nature of the theological task. If Christology intrinsically dialogues not just with Scripture, but also lived experiences of people(s), then the Asian setting becomes a source for articulating the gospel afresh. Cul-ture is not just a target for evangelization but also a source for express-ing and reappropriating the gospel anew.

To understand the different Christologies in Asia, it is important to examine how Asian Christians reread Scripture in light of their own local realities and issues. To express Christology in Asian contexts, it is essential to employ cultural terms and local idioms to express Jesus Christ in these particular settings. Asian Christians see their task "as bringing the vision of Jesus to the masses of Asia. . . . The crucial hermeneutical question for them is not what the historical Jesus looked like but what he means for Asia today."[37] This contextual approach to Christology is also the concern of evangelicals from the Majority World as evidenced by the work in advancing a *missiological* Christology. Therefore, Christology is not simply about resolving the intellectual puzzle and historical problem of the original Jesus in the Scriptures and in history. Missiological Christology is also very differ-ent from advocacy-driven, Marxist-inspired, liberation Christologies. Rather, it attempts to be both biblical and missiological as it seeks to discover "the meaning and content of Christology for the agenda of mission" in different contexts.[38] It is a biblical Christology "with a missiological thrust, searching for a new model to inspire and mold missionary action."[39]

Evangelical theologians from Latin America highlight four themes in missiological Christology that I find relevant for the Asian context: the identity of Jesus of Nazareth, the marks of Jesus' mission, the meaning of the gospel, and evangelization from the marginalized or

---

creeds in relation to Christ and the Gospels, see N. T. Wright, *How God Became King* (New York: HarperOne, 2012), pp. 10-20.

37. R. S. Sugirtharajah, ed., *Asian Faces of Jesus* (Maryknoll: Orbis, 1993), p. x.

38. Vinay Samuel and Chris Sugden, eds., *Sharing Jesus in the Two-Thirds World* (Grand Rapids: Eerdmans, 1983), p. 277.

39. Samuel Escobar, "Evangelical Theology in Latin America: The Development of a Missiological Christology," *Missiology* 19, no. 3 (1991): 324.

the periphery.[40] In this missiological paradigm, the approach to the "historical Jesus" is in contrast with the view of liberal theology of the nineteenth century. Here, the Gospels are seen as essentially reliable historical records of Jesus that provide an adequate basis for the life of the church in mission.[41]

In the Asian setting, I view missiological Christology as an approach that seeks a translation of the biblical Christ into the language, thought forms, and idioms of Asian cultures. Translatability allows the Christian faith to find its home in the diverse cultures of the world, while remaining true to biblical faith. Thus, a missiological Christology in Asian settings seeks a rendering of Jesus Christ in ways that will impact Asian peoples. Accordingly, doing Christology is a process of enculturation, the process by which the church weaves itself into a given culture in a transformative way.[42] This involves *critical* syntheses (or critical contextualization) with cultures. It also involves careful interaction with local religious systems toward the development of truly local churches and theologies. Even so, the task requires critical alertness to prevent cultural domestications of the gospel (syncretism).[43]

The local churches (as part of a truly world church) doing their own Christological reflections are the articulators and agents (embodiments) of missiological Christologies in their unique settings. José de Mesa offers a useful approach toward developing missiological Christologies in different cultural contexts. He combines sociological description in identifying views of Christ (the reality of projection) with a biblical-theological act of regauging or evaluating these images of Christ toward making the gospel translatable in a new context, in an act of reappropriation of the biblical tradition.[44] Thus the religious

40. Escobar, "Evangelical Theology in Latin America," pp. 322-28.

41. Escobar, "Evangelical Theology in Latin America," p. 323.

42. Timoteo D. Gener, "Re-imaging Conversion in Lowland Philippine Setting: The Perspective of Gospel Re-rooting," *Journal of Asian Mission* 3, no. 1 (2001): 43-77.

43. I have elaborated my views on syncretism in "Engaging Chung Hyun Kyung's Concept of Syncretism: An Inter-cultural Dialogue on Mission" (forthcoming in *Kenosis*, Journal of the Kenosis Conference, Korean Church in Singapore).

44. José de Mesa, "Pastoral Agents and 'Doing Christology,'" *East Asian Pastoral Review* 29 (1992): 111-22. This methodology grounds itself in the "way of the disciples," where the pattern of the disciples' identification of Jesus is taken as a norm for doing Christology. De Mesa's article is expanded into a book, *Following the Way of the Disciples: A Guidebook for Doing Christology in Cultural Context* (Quezon City: East Asia Pastoral Institute, 1996). On the connection between the translatability of the gospel and the

experiences and habits of various peoples reveal aspects of their theologies, their understanding of God or Christ, which then need to be
assessed biblically and theologically for reappropriation by local Christians.[45]

Toward Missiological Christologies in Asia

If we proceed with the above framework, acknowledging that doing
Christology is a process of translation and enculturation of the Word
(Jesus Christ) now into Asian settings, what then are some of the Chris-
tologies in Asia that offer promising missiological engagement?

Jesus Fully Human

In many Asian religions God is often featured as inaccessible and dis-
tant. As such, a fully human Jesus, or Jesus as God in human form, is
good news in Asia. Influenced by the supernaturalist mindset of Asia,
there is a tendency among Asian Christians to see Jesus as an angel
rather than a full-blooded human being.[46] Alternately, he may just be
viewed as one among the many gods that populate the heavenlies.[47]
The theologians Lode Wostyn and José de Mesa ask probingly: "Does
not Jesus' divinity obscure his power to do so on the grounds that he
did not fully share our human condition? It is already a struggle to follow the example of a saint. At most, we can only dream of imitating an
angel. Is it not simply preposterous for us to dare follow a God-man?"[48]

Asian churches and theologians respond to a misguided, docetic
view of Jesus Christ by recovering the Jesus of the Gospels. One Asian
theologian calls this "A Third Look at Jesus."[49] The first look is the way

---

incarnation, see Timothy C. Tennent, *Invitation to World Missions* (Grand Rapids: Kregel,
2010), pp. 323-53.

45. De Mesa, "Pastoral Agents."

46. José de Mesa and Lode Wostyn, *Doing Christology: The Re-appropriation of a Tradition* (Quezon City: Claretian, 2005), p. 2.

47. This domestication of the gospel was something that Lesslie Newbigin rallied
against. See *The Gospel in a Pluralist Society* (Grand Rapids: Eerdmans, 1989), p. 3.

48. De Mesa and Wostyn, *Doing Christology*, p. 2.

49. Carlos H. Abesamis, *A Third Look at Jesus* (Quezon City: Claretian, 1988).

Jesus and first-generation Christians perceived his life and work. The second look at Jesus was the way the Greco-Roman and Western eyes came to understand Jesus. It is this second view that Asians along with the rest of the Majority World churches have received for the past two thousand years. This is the theology expressed in their textbooks, catechisms, and church homilies. The stress has been on the deity of Christ and salvation understood primarily in terms of Christ's atonement for our sins. The third look is a look at the original Jesus by and through the eyes of the poor. For Carlos H. Abesamis, the poor are not any kind of poor. Rather these poor are the "awakened, struggling and selfless poor, who want to create a just, humane, and sustainable world. Jesus and the poor stand on the same ground and view life from a similar vantage point."[50] This third look illuminates two essential insights. First, Jesus as a human being was in vibrant communion with God the Father and was filled with divine power; and second, Jesus was totally poured out in the mission of God's reign, which was about total salvation, human and cosmic.[51] Christian life and service informed by this third look would be characterized by personal holiness and social commitment.

Evangelical theologians in Asia resonate with the need to recover the Jesus of the Gospels for contextual ministry. Vinay Samuel and Chris Sugden have noted that past historical-theological Christologies usually neglect Jesus' humanity and servanthood to the poor and the marginalized (including his inclusion of women).[52] This unfortunate neglect has produced a truncated gospel. Recovering Jesus' identification with the poor and proclamation of their restoration would provide a major resource to recapture the holism of the gospel Jesus proclaimed. Citing the messianic manifesto in Luke 4, Samuel and Sugden insist,

> For Jesus there was no such thing as an understanding of the good news without its relation to the poor. The gospel and the poor were integrally related in the announcement and activity of Jesus. That

50. Carlos H. Abesamis, S.J., *Backpack of a Jesus-Seeker . . . Following the Footsteps of the Original Jesus* (Quezon City: Claretian, 2004), p. 11.

51. Abesamis, *Backpack of a Jesus-Seeker*, pp. 16-24.

52. Vinay Samuel and Chris Sugden, *Evangelism and the Poor: A Third World Study Guide* (Bangalore: Partnership in Asia, 1983); also Chris Sugden, *Seeking the Asian Face of Jesus* (Oxford: Regnum, 1997).

is why even those who are rich, to whom this good news was announced, had to approximate to the poor to receive it (e.g., the rich young ruler).[53]

The Witness-Reception of Jesus Christ amid Asian Religions

Asia is characterized by a plurality of religions. Asian Christians have need to work out their Christological understanding in plural and diverse religious contexts; Hindu, Buddhist, and Chinese cultural contexts are among the contexts in which this work has to be done. Hindu conceptions of Jesus are more elaborate and diverse than those of many other non-Christian faith traditions. Christological formulations first articulated by Hindus are quite unprecedented in Asia.[54] Indeed, popular Hindu leaders such as Keshab C. Sen (1838-84) and Mohandas K. Gandhi (1869-1948) even professed love for Jesus Christ and saw Christ's lasting importance for India while not renouncing their Hindu way of life.[55] R. S. Sugirtharajah demonstrated personal admiration and fondness for Jesus and his teachings. He appreciatively used *diverse Hindu images of Jesus*, which include:

Jesus as Supreme Guide to human happiness (Rajah Ram Mohum Roy)
Jesus as True *Yogi* and Divine Humanity (Keshub Chendur Sen)
Jesus as *Jivanmukta* (One who has attained liberation while alive) (Vivekananda)
Jesus as the Son of Man, seeking the last, the least, and the lost (Rabindranath Tagore)
Jesus as the Supreme *Satyagrahi* (love and fighter for truth) (Mahatma Gandhi)
Jesus as *Advaitin* (one who has realized destiny with Brahman-God) (Swami Akhilananda)
Mystic Christ (Radhakrishan)[56]

53. Samuel and Sugden, *Evangelism and the Poor*, p. 20.
54. Sugirtharajah, ed., *Asian Faces of Jesus*, p. 57.
55. Sunil Stephens, "The Significance of Jesus Christ in Hindu-Christian Dialogue," in *Naming the Unknown God* (Mandaluyong: OMF Lit. and Asian Theological Seminary, 2006), pp. 114-21.
56. Sugirtharajah, ed., *Asian Faces of Jesus*, p. 3.

Indian Christians later imitated the Hindu approach with their own sketches of Jesus using their own cultural and philosophical resources. For example, Jesus is described this way:

> Jesus as *Prajapati* (Lord of creatures) (K. M. Banerjee)
> Jesus as *Cit* (Consciousness) (Brahmobandhav Upadhyaya)
> Jesus as *Avatara* (Incarnation) (A. J. Appasamy, V. Chakkarai)
> Jesus as *Adi Purusha* (the first person) and *Shakti* (power-strength)
>   (P. Chenchiah)
> Jesus as Eternal *Om* (logos) (S. Jesudasan)[57]

These Hindu and Indian Christian cultural and philosophical images of Jesus are not immune from criticisms even within India. Present-day Indian Christian *dalits* and tribals view these articulations as favoring the Sanskrit tradition, which was the "very system instrumental to their own oppression and marginalization."[58] Lesslie Newbigin, long-time missionary to India, was quite aware of this, and therefore insisted on returning to the Christ of history as the key toward a truly salvific Christology in light of the Hindu and Indian religio-cultural realities.[59]

Buddhist-sensitive conceptions of Jesus Christ favor the image of *Jesus as a poor monk,* where the monastic model approximates Asian aspirations and ideals. Asia is the "oldest and the largest generator of monasticism, besides being the inheritor of the largest portion of the world's poverty."[60] Hence Aloysius Pieris posits the relevance of the image of Jesus as a poor monk for Buddhist settings in Asia. The recovery of the meditative dimension from the monastic influence is something Asian evangelicals could use to enrich and deepen their traditions. Instead, they remain critical of the reduction of evil and sin to mammon and greed and the gospel to liberation from oppression. Evangelicals in the Majority World insist on the fullness of the gospel as ultimately deliverance from sin, evil, and death. Though they do not exclude the bodiliness and materiality of salvation, they resist its reduction to socioeconomic liberation.[61]

57. Sugirtharajah, ed., *Asian Faces of Jesus,* p. 4.
58. Sugirtharajah, ed., *Asian Faces of Jesus,* p. 4.
59. Lesslie Newbigin, *The Gospel in a Pluralist Society* (Grand Rapids: Eerdmans, 1989), pp. 66-79.
60. Pieris, *Asian Theology of Liberation,* p. 57.
61. Simon Chan, "Evangelical Theology in Asian Contexts," in *The Cambridge Com-*

With reference to Islam, one must distinguish Christology in Islamic contexts from Islamic Christology. Christology in an Islamic context is a Christian Christology that developed in a Muslim setting and was addressed to it, while Islamic Christology is a specifically Muslim or Qur'anic view of Christ. Christology in Islamic contexts often makes the doctrine of the Trinity the focal point of Christological reflection. Modalism and Nestorianism are often considered but the ancient Christian churches from the Islamic East in general continue to uphold traditional Christological doctrine following its Chalcedonian or non-Chalcedonian form. However, Muslims find the generational language about Christ as the only-begotten Son of God to be most offensive to their theology. Sura 112 of the Qur'an makes it clear that "God neither begets nor is begotten." Hence, Michael Nazir Ali proposes the language of procession (the Son "proceeding" from the Father, cf. John 8:42) rather than generation as a better point of departure in talking to Muslims about the person of Christ. Qur'anic naming of Jesus also "lends itself more to 'processional' than to 'generational' language."[62] *Jesus as prophet* is the most frequent title ascribed to Jesus in the Qur'an. However, there are other titles for Jesus in the Qur'an that allow an opening for a discussion of Jesus as more than a prophet.[63] *Almasih* (messiah) is applied to *Isa* in the Qur'an, and was blessed by Allah to be such (19:31, also 3:49). Such messiahship is also supported or confirmed by the Holy Spirit (2:253; 5:110). Jesus is also called *Kalimah,* or Word (3:45; 4:171), and *Abd Allah* (servant of Allah, 19:30, also 4:172; 43:57-59).[64]

Christians living side by side with Muslims need to live Christianly and not merely debate or converse with them about Jesus and their religion. Christology is intimately linked with a Christian lifestyle, lived in community. "The compulsion to believe in Jesus being the son from living like Jesus"[65] are closely aligned. If Muslims name Jesus

---

panion to Evangelical Theology, ed. Timothy Larsen and Daniel J. Treier (Cambridge: Cambridge University Press, 2007), p. 230.

62. Michael Nazir Ali, "Christology in an Islamic Context," in *Sharing Jesus in the Two-Thirds World* (Grand Rapids: Eerdmans, 1984), p. 146.

63. Effendy Aritonang and Triawan Wicaksono Kho, "A Study of Jesus' Offices and Roles in the Qur'an," in *Naming the Unknown God,* ed. E. Acoba et al. (Mandaluyong: OMF Lit. and Asian Theological Seminary, 2006), p. 84.

64. Aritonang and Kho, "Study of Jesus' Offices and Roles in the Qur'an," pp. 83-86.

65. David Emmanuel Singh, "Christian Relations with Muslims: Review of Selected Issues and Approaches," *Transformation* 22, no. 1 (January 2005): 59.

as *Almasih,* it is "up to them to choose to enquire more of the Jesus of the Gospel if they are attracted by the life of the Christian."[66] Increasingly, living Christianly is far more effective in reaching Muslims, in achieving Shalom, than evangelism by words alone.[67] The story of the Peacebuilders Community in the southern Philippines is one great example of this.[68]

Chinese Christologies are linked to China's past history of evangelization that goes back to Nestorian Christians arriving in China as early as 635, and then the Franciscans led by John of Montecorvino, who arrived in 1294.[69] A Nestorian Buddhist Christology portrayed the incarnation through "the story of *Avalokitesvara,* a male *bodhisattva* who took on female form and became known to the Chinese as Guan Yin, the goddess of mercy . . . *Jesus is like a bodhisattva* in his mission to save others." Later when the Jesuits arrived in China in 1582, Matteo Ricci and his companions explored missionary strategies that presented Christ gradually to the Chinese so as not to favor premature conversions. In a catechism that Ricci published, *The True Meaning of the Lord of Heaven,* Christ was presented as teacher and performer of miracles. Ricci then compared Christ to China's great teacher, Confucius, concluding that Christ was greater than any king or teacher. A fuller account of the Christ-event was given by Diego de Pantoja, one of Ricci's close companions. He emphasized the salvific value of the passion of Jesus through his elaboration of the *Doctrina Christiana* as well as *The Recitation of the Passion of the Savior,* which Chinese Catholics recited during Holy Week.

After Ricci, other missionaries like Giulio Aleni labored in China from 1582 to 1610. Aleni in particular pushed for greater Christ-centeredness in the missionary approach but informed by extensive knowledge of Chinese culture and language. Aleni used the Chinese language to tell the story of Jesus in publications such as *The Life of Jesus in Words and Images* and *The Life of Our Lord Jesus Christ.* He countered Chi-

---

66. Singh, "Christian Relations with Muslims," p. 60.

67. For a theology of community that thrives on this approach, see Emo Yango, "Toward a Theology of Communities in the Kingdom of God," *Phronesis* 10, no. 1 (2003): 7-27.

68. http://peacebuilderscommunity.org/history/.

69. In what follows I draw from Ary C. Dy, *Building a Bridge: Catholic Christianity Meets Chinese-Filipino Culture* (Quezon City: Jesuit Communications Foundation, 2005), p. 58.

nese objections to the incarnation in his *Learned Conversations of Fuzhou*. Aleni wrote the first Chinese text fully devoted to Christology, *Introduction to the Incarnation of the Lord of Heaven*.

Moving to the present scene, with Chinese culture today increasingly becoming globalized, the search is no longer for a single Chinese Christology but for Chinese *Christologies*. The Chinese classics remain vital dialogue partners in cultural theologizing and apologetics, as in the writings of K. K. Yeo.[70] Ary Dy proposes, however, that the image of the suffering Jesus will continue to speak to the Chinese masses, where suffering remains a prevailing experience. Another possibility is a Christology that draws on the place of words in Chinese culture. One sees this in the film *Hero,* which contains many scenes where a person gazes long and hard on a word or piece of calligraphy, seeking to understand the character of the writer. Such meditative acts can affect one's character and way of life. Presenting Jesus Christ as the Word, then, may be a rich and dynamic way of addressing Chinese culture.[71]

Christ and Supernaturalism in Popular Piety

Jesus as Lord of the Spirits. Pentecostal and Charismatic experience continues to dominate Asian forms of Christianity. One might even say this is Protestantism's dominant worldwide folk religion. Based on the figures from the *World Christian Encyclopedia,* Asia is second only to Latin America in terms of the number of Pentecostal and Charismatic adherents, and it is fast catching up.[72] At least a third of the Asian Christian population is Charismatic or Pentecostal, and the number continues to increase. What is most distinctive about the Pentecostal Charismatic movement is the "strong emphasis of the Holy Spirit as understood in the New Testament."[73] Thus Everett Wilson's statement

70. See, in addition to his essay in this volume, Khiok-Khng Yeo, *What Has Jerusalem to Do with Beijing? Biblical Interpretation from a Chinese Perspective* (Harrisburg: Trinity Press International, 1998).

71. Dy, *Building a Bridge*, p. 65.

72. Allan Anderson, "The Charismatic Face of Christianity in Asia," in *Asian and Pentecostal,* ed. Allan Anderson and Edmond Tang (Oxford: Regnum, 2005), p. 2.

73. Hwa Yung, "Pentecostalism and the Asian Church," in *Asian and Pentecostal,* p. 41.

that "Pentecostalism, the faith of apostolic signs and wonders, represents itself as a self-validating expression of primitive Christianity" is authenticated in the Asian arena.[74] Viewed through the lens of this defining characteristic, the Pentecostal Charismatic movement may be seen as a phenomenon that is indigenous to Asian Christianity and not as an imported movement from North America. The Azusa Street revival in twentieth-century America does not define Asian charismatic Christianity. Various pre-Azusa (nineteenth century) and post–Azusa Street Pentecostal and Charismatic forms abound in Asian Christianity.[75] Central to the Pentecostal movement's Christological practice is a strong, Christ-centered orientation to healing and to confronting demonic spirits, invoking especially the image of *Christus Victor* (the Victorious Christ).[76] The vision of the victorious Jesus (Col. 2:15) serves as a central motif in the formulation of the gospel to Asian peoples.[77]

Jesus among Folk Catholics.[78] The picture of Asian Christologies would be incomplete if we did not include an example of how folk Catholics view Jesus Christ in the Philippines. The prevalence of poverty and suffering makes the *Nazareno* (Nazarene) a favorite image of Jesus among the Filipino masses. The image is that of a life-size portrayal of Jesus clad in a maroon robe, crowned with thorns and carrying a large wooden cross in semi-kneeling position. Tens of thousands line the streets waving white hand towels, chanting "viva señor," and lighting candles. Hundreds of devotees risk life and limb as they jostle their way up to the platform to touch the image.

74. Everett A. Wilson, "They Crossed the Red Sea, Didn't They? Critical History and Pentecostal Beginnings," in *The Globalization of Pentecostalism: A Religion Made to Travel,* ed. Murray W. Dempster et al. (Oxford: Regnum, 1999), p. 110; as quoted in Hwa Yung, "Pentecostalism and the Asian Church," in *Asian and Pentecostal,* p. 41.

75. Hwa Yung, "Pentecostalism and the Asian Church," in *Asian and Pentecostal,* pp. 43-48.

76. Wonsuk Ma, "In Jesus' Name! Power Encounter from an Asian Pentecostal Perspective," in *Principalities and Powers: Reflections in the Asian Context* (Mandaluyong: OMF Lit. and Asian Theological Seminary, 2007).

77. See also Melba Maggay, *The Gospel in Filipino Context* (Manila: OMF Lit., 1987), p. 4.

78. This section is taken from a group project on doing local theology at the Asian Theological Seminary led by Dr. George Capaque and myself, "Poverty, Religion and Culture in the Devotion to the Black Nazarene," in *The Church and Poverty in Asia,* ed. Lee Wanak (Mandaluyong: OMF Lit. and Asian Theological Seminary, 2008), pp. 108-27.

What lies behind this popular devotion? Close analysis of this phenomenon reveals one particular motivation. As Jesus suffered, he understands the sufferings of people, and asks them to carry their own cross. He is no stranger to suffering and this provides a point of identification with the Filipino devotee. Thus, most of the devotees of the *Nazareno* have made *panatas* (lifelong commitments of service) in exchange for a request for healing, good health, work, or other needs. One observer, Teresita Obusan, who has studied this very closely, called this devotion to the *Señor* a faith of basics.

Such faith, stripped of everything but the essential, is less concerned with a good afterlife than it is in receiving assistance now, while one is alive. Another researcher has put it this way: "This is a God whom they understand as somebody who died for them exclusively. So they love, and must love fervently, somebody who is willing to undertake such a sacrifice for them. To the masses, there is no other way to reciprocate."[79]

The people's understanding of what Jesus brings about in their lives (salvation) is closely related to who Jesus is for them (Christology). This translates into the following projective (local) images of Christ among the devotees:

- If Christ is the bringer of *kagalingan* (healing), *himala or milagro* (miracles), then Christ to them is the Wonder-Worker and Healer *(Mapaghimala)*.
- If Christ brings God closer to them in their suffering, then Christ to them is their *Kuya or Amang* (Brother or Father), worthy of their *sakripisyo* (sacrifice) and *pagdamay* (solidarity, feeling-with).
- If Christ grants their requests then Christ for them is *Poon or Panginoon* (Lord), worthy of submission and *panata* (vows).

These local images show the cultural dimensions of Christology as seen from folk religious experiences. There, the longing is for the Christ who heals, who is a divine source of power, a provider, yet one who feels with them in their pain — as their friend. It reveals a longing for salvation that involves the material and the bodily, not just dwelling on the spiritual and the afterlife.

This calls for a rereading of the Bible informed by folk yearnings

79. Karl De Mesa, quoted in *Inside Quiapo* (Manila, n.d.), p. 18.

about Christ and salvation. Rereading Scriptures with these cultural understandings of Christ and salvation, we come to more fully appreciate the fullness of who Christ is and what the Bible really means by salvation. In Asian Christology, reference is often made to Christ as Lord of the spirits as a contextual image.[80] However, Christ as Wonderworker, Healer.[81] Friend and Brother[82] — images often neglected in typical presentations of Christology — are equally important to several Asian contexts.

Concluding Reflections

First, we have emphasized that Christology in light of the Gospels is discipleship-in-context Christology (cf. John 20:30-31). Therefore, the true test of any Christology is in how it assists authentic following of Christ in one's own context. An authentic understanding of Christ's significance draws from the Bible, but is always socially embodied and expressed through a community's engagement with the word in their respective societies and cultures. The practice of articulating Christology is a threefold process of identification of cultural understandings of Christ and salvation, biblical-theological evaluation, and reappropriation in local contexts.

Second, the recovery of the kingdom of God as central to the life and teaching of Jesus Christ continues to revitalize Majority World churches. This is also true in the Asian church with its challenge to live Christianly and do mission holistically. Asia in particular is a setting that calls for cultural rootedness, holistic mission, and social-public transformation.

Third, doing Christology as a missiological act takes account of the social, cultural, and geographic location of Christian communities, and seeks to transform these locations with the light of Christ. Thus, we see the flourishing of indigenous practical Christologies in Asia engaging issues of Asian religiousness and poverty, and reclaiming human and cultural dignity for the sake of Christ and his church.

80. Maggay, *Gospel in Filipino Context*, p. 4.

81. Even the current quest for the historical Jesus sees this image as crucial to the Gospel portrait. A recent restatement of this comes from Ben Witherington III, *The Jesus Quest* (Downers Grove: InterVarsity, 1997), pp. 185-95, 211-12.

82. Witherington, *Jesus Quest*, chapter 7 is suggestive on this point.

Finally, all the above developments witness to the work of the Spirit, as a witness to the reality of Pentecost, where we hear cultures, peoples, tribes, and nations, speaking in their native languages of the great deeds that God has done (Acts 2:8, 11) and continues to do in and through Jesus the Christ.

For Further Reading

Chan, Simon. "Evangelical Theology in Asian Contexts." In *The Cambridge Companion to Evangelical Theology*, edited by Timothy Larsen and Daniel J. Treier. Cambridge: Cambridge University Press, 2007.

De Mesa, José. *Following the Way of the Disciples: A Guidebook for Doing Christology in a Cultural Context*. Quezon City: East Asia Pastoral Institute, 1996.

Gener, Timoteo. "Contextualization." In *Global Dictionary of Theology*, edited by William Dyrness, Velli Matti Kärkkäinen, Simon Chan, and Juan Martinez, pp. 192-96. Downers Grove: InterVarsity, 2008.

Gener, Timoteo. "Re-visioning Local Theology: An Integral Dialogue with Practical Theology, a Filipino Evangelical Perspective." *Journal of Asian Mission* 6, no. 2 (2004): 133-66.

Gener, T. D., L. Bautista, and K. J. Vanhoozer. "Theological Method." In *Global Dictionary of Theology*, edited by W. Dyrness, V. M. Kärkkäinen, S. Chan, and J. Martinez, pp. 889-98. Downers Grove: InterVarsity, 2008.

Greenman, Jeffrey P., and Gene L. Green, eds. *Global Theology in Evangelical Perspective*. Downers Grove: InterVarsity Academic, 2012.

Schreiter, Robert. *The New Catholicity: Theology Between the Global and the Local*. Maryknoll: Orbis, 1997.

Stephens, Sunil. "The Significance of Jesus Christ in Hindu-Christian Dialogue." In *Naming the Unknown God*, pp. 109-26. Mandaluyong City, Metro Manila: OMF Literature and Asian Theological Seminary, 2006.

Sugirtharajah, R. S., ed. *Asian Faces of Jesus*. Maryknoll: Orbis, 1993.

Wanak, Lee, ed. *The Church and Poverty in Asia*. Mandaluyong City, Metro Manila: OMF Literature and Asian Theological Seminary, 2008.

CHAPTER 4

¿Quién Vive? ¡Cristo! Christology in Latin American Perspectives

JULES A. MARTÍNEZ-OLIVIERI

Introduction

Presenting a succinct summary of the ethos of Christian theology in Latin America, and Christology in particular — contextualized in its plurality as well as its common elements — is a difficult task. This chapter aims to present the common threads that shape Latin American Christological reflection. I attend to the major theological movements in the region: Catholic liberation theology and Protestant Christology. The purpose is to survey how each construes Christology as faith seeking *Gloria Dei, vivens homo* (the glory of God is the human fully alive),[1] that is, to engage in theological and historical discourse that strives to articulate the transformation that Jesus, as the Christ of God, brings to human life. In this pursuit, I also highlight the important methodological, hermeneutical, and dogmatic elements that shape the doctrine of Jesus Christ in Latin America.

A Précis of Liberation Theology in Latin America

Background

By 1977, liberation theology had begun to make inroads into academic theological circles. A key aspect that drew attention to this movement

1. A paradigmatic phrase that comes from Irenaeus of Lyons.

was its proposal of an innovative way of doing theology. Christian theology is to be a praxis-oriented and politically transformative discourse, a critical reflection on Christian praxis in light of Scripture and the life of the church.[2] The Conference of Latin American Bishops (CELAM) in Medellín, Colombia, is widely seen as the birthplace of liberation theology. Held in 1968, this Conference constructively engaged the results of Vatican II, suggesting a hermeneutical criterion to guide theological reflection: the perspective of the poor. Hugo Assmann provided a provocative rationale for the emergence of liberation theology:

> If the historical situation of dependence and domination of two-thirds of humanity, with its thirty million per year dying of hunger and malnutrition, does not become the point of departure of any Christian theology — even in the rich and dominating countries — theology will not be able to situate and realize historically its fundamental themes. . . . This is why [it] is necessary to save theology from its cynicism.[3]

The explicit admission and embrace of the locality and environment in which faith is practiced as a *locus theologicus* intends to show the originality of liberation theology in contrast to traditional (classical) theology and modern European theology.[4] Gutiérrez lucidly explains a key factor that spurred the emergence of liberation theology in Latin America. The nonbeliever who questions the logic and structure of the Christian worldview does not pose the main challenge to the Christian faith. Instead, the challenge comes from

> the non-human, that is, from whom is not recognized as a human by the ruling social order: the poor, the exploited, the one who is systematically and legally divested of his being human, the one who hardly knows what it means to be human . . . Therefore, the ques-

2. Gustavo Gutiérrez, "The Task and Content of Liberation Theology," in *Cambridge Companion to Liberation Theology* (New York: Cambridge University Press, 1999), p. 29.

3. Hugo Assmann, *Teología desde la praxis de liberación* (Salamanca: Sígueme, 1973), p. 40.

4. J. Batista Libânio, "Panorama de la teología de América Latina," in *Panorama de la teología Latinoamericana,* ed. Juan J. Tamayo-Acosta (Navarra: Verbo Divino, 2002), p. 60.

tion will not refer to the mode that must be used to talk about God in an adult world, but more so to the way that [God] has to be announced as a Father in a non-human world, [and] to the consequent implications of the fact of saying to the non-human that [he] is a child of God.[5]

Liberation theology is better grasped as a theological movement than one strict mode of doing theology. Though it is true that such theology first emerged from the Roman Catholic quarters in Latin America, the adjective "liberation" has become a way to refer to a range of explicitly contextual theologies that focus their theological concerns on triangulating the world, church, and Scripture in light of the themes of oppression, violence, and discrimination in their respective contexts.[6] To this end, there is a plurality of liberation theologies today. Some of them concentrate on responding to international economic oppression, while others take on issues such as classism, racism, gender, and sexual violence. This also helps us understand why liberation theology is not the only theology in the Latin American region. For although many Roman Catholic and Protestant theologians share some of the fundamental intuitions of the movement, such as the perspective of the poor, many do not identify with liberation theology. Nevertheless, one must grant that some of the most important general contributions from Latin America to Christian theology are embedded within this movement, particularly as it evolved, refined, and broadened its scope in its systematic development.

Theology and Method

The theological method in liberation theology was very early defined around the central political and economic preoccupations that were

5. Gustavo Gutiérrez, "Praxis de Liberación: Teología y anuncio," *Concilium* 96 (1974): 366.

6. A central concern of Gustavo Gutiérrez's critique is the theory of economic dependence of Latin American countries with the United States as a social evil, not only discrimination. This focus on dependence as a social evil distinguishes Latin American theology from African American theology, which focuses primarily on racism as a discriminatory social and ideological structure embedded in the culture. See Gutiérrez *Teología de la liberación: Perspectivas,* Verdad e Imagen (Salamanca: Sígueme, 1990), chapter 1.

affecting the social and ecclesial contexts in which the Christian faith is lived. We can identify fundamental intuitions that shape theological methods in liberation theologies, as well as in Protestant theologies that share liberation priorities. First, the fundamental commonality is a soteriological orientation. The Christian concept of salvation includes not only present communion with God and the hope of life after death; salvation also entails liberation from societal manifestations of sin in present historical experience. Hence, while affirming a final eschatological salvation for humanity and creation with God, Latin American theology insists on the praxis of faith and the active pursuit of justice for the other. As the Catholic Episcopal Conference in Puebla, Mexico, pronounced in 1979, to think of salvation as integral liberation means to stress both the subjective aspect (liberation from personal sin) and the historical aspect (liberation from the actual economic, sociopolitical, and cultural situation), which qualifies as "social sin."

In this vein, the fundamental contribution and continuing relevance of liberation theology lies in bringing the primacy of praxis and the perspective of the poor to the center of theology.[7] These hermeneutical criteria are the pillars of a re-envisioned theology — a theology that is not naïve about the extent of its rootedness in particular contexts and that is explicitly programmatic in its historical and political implications.

Rosino Gibellini considers that liberation theology introduced into theological language a linguistic innovation. For the word "liberation" is infused with a semantic range that surpasses its conventional use.[8] The language of "liberation" refers back to the biblical traditions of the historical dynamism of God's rescue of and restorative justice among his people. Theologically, "liberation" refers to a soteriological category that when applied to the historical experience of the church speaks of God's salvation at three levels: (1) the sociopolitical level: liberation of the oppressed from their oppressors ("exploited classes, marginalized races, despised cultures");[9] (2) the anthropological level: liberation that

7. Antonio González, *The Gospel of Faith and Justice* (Maryknoll: Orbis, 2005), pp. 2-10.
8. Rosino Gibellini, *La Teología del siglo XX*, Coleccion Presencia Teológica (Santander: Sal Terrae, 1998), p. 378.
9. Gustavo Gutiérrez, *La fuerza histórica de los probres* (Salamanca: Sígueme, 1982), p. 243.

allows for the attainment of a society of equals; and (3) the theological level: liberation from sin, which is the ultimate source of all evil and injustice, through a life of communion and participation. Hence, for liberation theologians, the word "liberation" does not merely signify a topic in theology. It does not refer to another theology of the genitive, but to an orientation and manner of doing theology – what Assmann called "a theology from the praxis of liberation."[10]

In order to attend to these dimensions of the concept of liberation, a corresponding methodological approach is employed whereby the aforementioned levels are analyzed. Clodovis Boff articulates these three aspects as the socio-analytical dimension, the hermeneutical mediation, and the mediation of praxis.[11] Using this epistemological analysis, Leonardo Boff states that the goal of liberation theology is "to articulate a reading of reality starting from the poor and from the interest of the liberation of the poor; in function of this, [it] utilizes the human and social sciences, reflects theologically and proposes pastoral actions that alleviate the way of the oppressed."[12] The method presupposes a personal stance that precedes the theological task. Theology is always and strictly a second act of faith. The first act is one of commitment to the Lord Jesus Christ and his work, primarily by adopting his preferential approach toward and treatment of the weakest in society. This is a political, ethical, and evangelical option in favor of the poor. It is a political option in that the theologian must always work within a set of social spaces where she must side with those who are the victims of systemic oppression. It is an ethical option because it is a moral response to the unacceptable reality of material misery and its detrimental effects on the Majority World. And it is an evangelical option because the commitment is based on the eschatological blessings of the Gospels regarding the fate of the poor (e.g., Matt. 25:35-46): "the poor are the eschatological criteria of salvation/perdition."[13] Hence, the impoverished masses are the indispensable theological loci.[14]

10. Assmann, *Teología desde la praxis*, p. 40.
11. Clodovis Boff, "The Method of Theology of Liberation," in *Systematic Theology: Perspectives from Liberation Theology: Readings from Mysterium Liberationis,* ed. Ignacio Ellacuría (Maryknoll: Orbis, 1996), pp. 17-21.
12. Gibellini, *Teología del siglo*, p. 378.
13. Gibellini, *Teología del siglo*, p. 379.
14. Leonardo Boff, *Teología de la político: Sus mediaciones* (Salamanca: Ediciones Sígueme, 1980).

A Précis of Protestant Theology in Latin America

Two Trajectories

One can trace theological production among Protestants according to two different but complementary trajectories. The first trajectory is the one associated with the historically Protestant churches (Lutheran, Methodist, Presbyterian, and Reformed). The key theologians representing these churches are Rubem Alves, Emilio Castro, Julio de Santa Ana, and José Míguez Bonino. The second trajectory is the one associated with the Fraternidad Teológica Latinoamericana (Latin American Theological Fellowship) and is represented by evangelicals such as C. René Padilla, Samuel Escobar, and Emilio Antonio Núñez.

Míguez Bonino offers a helpful typology that identifies the "faces of Protestantism": the liberal face, the evangelical face, the Pentecostal face, and the ethnic face. In terms of theological distinctiveness, the two broader categories are the liberal and evangelical faces – categories that, to some extent, overlap sociologically with one another in the context of an ecclesial family. Still, the distinctions are valuable.

The liberal face of Protestantism refers to church communities that resulted from the missionary efforts of historical or mainline denominations in North America. This tradition is amicable to and promotes many aspects of modernity (e.g., liberal democracy, progress, education, human rights, and freedom). Theologically, the Holiness revival movements in the United States, the social view of the gospel, and liberalism influence it. Traditional theological themes (e.g., the doctrine of God, Christology, ecclesiology, and revelation) are not necessary objects of formal dogmatic elaboration, but we can identify key emphases in regard to the practice of theology. There is an insistence on theological reflection based on concrete historical realities – an explicit effort to locate reflection in context, distancing the theologian from what could be considered *in principio* abstract discussions without historical relevance. To this end, biblical themes such as justice and salvation are treated in light of the experience of pastoral ministry and the meaning of being a church in historical development. The goal is the articulation of "a situated theology, strongly critical in relation to theoretical theological construals," with the aim of achieving a satisfactory relationship between the experience of faith (which implies practical and ethical commitments) and its theory.[15] The role of theology is to provide an orientation and accompaniment in the search for a more humane society.

The evangelical face is also tied to the Latin American situation (poverty, violence, and political oppression). The evangelical face identifies those Christians who receive their heritage from the Holiness and revivalist movements in the United States, but, in contrast with the ecumenically oriented churches, it promotes the experience of salvation on more subjective and individual terms. Evangelicals in Latin America are theologically orthodox but are generally politically liberal since they do not share the conservatism of their counterparts in the United States. For evangelicals, to be liberated from sin is not so much to be freed from the sinful oppression of others but from the experience of personal sin. Life is to be lived in holiness, which often entails not only moral purity but also a tension between the people of God and the rest of society. Evangelicals are also heirs of the Protestant Reformation, with a distinctive emphasis on the paradigmatic *solas* – *sola Scriptura, sola fide, solus Christus,* and *sola gratia.* The Salvadorian theologian Emilio Antonio Núñez characterized *evangélicos* as "theocentric, bibliocentric, christocentric, and pneumatological."[16] In a similar vein, David Stoll identified the *evangélicos* as those who "pursue social issues without abandoning evangelism, deal with oppressive structures without endorsing violence, and bring left- and right-wing Protestants back together again."[17]

Salvation and Liberation

Soteriology in Protestantism emphasizes the theme of Christian salvation as communion with God through Jesus Christ, maintaining that

15. Celina A. Lértora Mendoza, "Teologias latinoamericanistas reformadas y evangélicas," in *Teología en America Latina,* ed. Carmen-Jose Alejos-Grau and Jose-Ignasi Saranyana (Madrid: Iberoamericana, 2002), p. 445.

16. Emilio A. Núñez, "Towards an Evangelical Latin American Theology," *Evangelical Review of Theology* 7, no. 1 (1983): 125-31.

17. As cited in Daniel Salinas, *Latin American Evangelical Theology in the 1970's: The Golden Decade,* Religion in the Americas series (Leiden: Brill, 2009), p. 15. David Stoll, *Is Latin America Turning Protestant: The Politics of Evangelical Growth* (Berkeley: University of California Press, 1990), p. 131.

the God of the Bible is a God who reconciles people and transforms societies.[18] In order to emphasize that the Christian view of salvation from sin is an affirmation of God's kingdom-establishing activity lived in historical reality (a transcendence experienced in history), Protestants have also used the nomenclature of salvation as "liberation." The common denominator is that the concept of liberation-salvation is informed via Christology: Jesus Christ paradigmatically fulfills the Old Testament trajectories of the exodus freedom and the prophetic visions of God's actions to free the people of Israel from internal oppression and the oppression exerted by foreign political powers. In Jesus, the messianic vocation is redefined in terms of liberation of the captives — the sinners, the sick, the afflicted, the poor, and the victims. Hence, since salvation entails liberation from sinful captivities, both personal and societal, it is not a metahistorical concept or experience but "a reality indissolubly tied to the history of human beings."[19]

Jesucristo el Salvador: The Shape of Christology in Latin America

We are now ready to present a concise overview of the emphases of contemporary Christologies in Latin America by providing a summary of Catholic and Protestant approaches. What I am suggesting is that *Christology in Latin America moves from a focus on the history of Jesus and its soteriological significance toward an account of Jesus the Christ who calls for participation in the kingdom of God.*

The most mature treatments of Christology have come from the systematic Christologies of Leonardo Boff and Jon Sobrino. Though a systematic Christology monograph has yet to be produced from within the Protestant tradition, fine introductions are found in Nancy Bed-

18. The formation of the *Fraternidad Teológica Latinamericana* (Latin American Theological Fellowship) in the 1970s began a new evangelical discourse: one lining up with creedal orthodoxy, in line with the Reformation heritage, emphasizing theology as a contextual missional discourse, taking a more sophisticated view of Scripture, promoting an interdenominational ethos, and having social relevance. See José Míguez Bonino, "Las iglesias protestantes y evangélicas en América Latina y el Caribe: un ensayo interpretativo," *Cuadernos de teología* 14, no. 2 (1995): 31.

19. José D. Rodriguez, *Introducción a la teología,* 2nd ed. (Mexico, D.F.: Publicaciones El Faro, 2002), p. 17.

ford's *La porfía de la resurrección: Ensayos desde el feminismo teológico latino-americano*,[20] an exploration of the contributions of feminist theology for Christology; Alberto García's *Cristología: Cristo Jesús: Centro y praxis del pueblo de Dios*, a systematic outline gathering the contributions of both Latino U.S. theologians and Latin American Protestants;[21] Antonio González's *The Gospel of Faith and Justice*, which considers the relationship between Christology, the kingdom of God, and the Trinity on the one hand, and the mission of peace, justice, and reconciliation of the church on the other hand. And most recently Samuel Escobar's *En busca de Cristo en América Latina* traces the history and developments of the doctrine of Christ in evangelical thought.[22]

Access to Jesus

Contemporary Christological method presents two main trajectories for approaching the meaning of the life and work of Jesus as God's Messiah. The first trajectory can be identified as "from above," or "descending." It refers to the way in which the knowledge of Jesus' identity and praxis begins through an epistemic movement from the Trinitarian life to the mediator and herald of the kingdom of God in the power of the *pneuma* (Spirit). Hence, the confession of the Christ, the Son of God, gains its dogmatic priority and intelligibility under the purview of Trinitarian doctrine.

The second trajectory is traditionally identified as "from below," or "ascending." Here the humanity of Jesus is established as the material foundation for Christology. Christology begins with the *facta* and *verba* of Jesus' human life, with the aim of moving toward the confession of his divinity. This approach emphasizes Jesus' human aspects that identify him very early in his life as part of an ethnic minority in Galilee, while also focusing on the actions that portray him as being within the milieu of the expectations of the kingdom of God. Emphasis on the singular humanity of Jesus is one of the distinctive methodological contri-

20. Nancy E. Bedford, *La porfía de la resurrección: Ensayos desde el feminismo teológico latinoamericano*, Colección FTL (Buenos Aires: Kairós, 2008).

21. Alberto L. García, *Cristología: Cristo Jesús: Centro y práxis del pueblo de Dios*, Biblioteca Teológica Concordia (St. Louis: Concordia, 2006).

22. Samuel Escobar, *En busca de Cristo en América Latina* (Buenos Aires: Ediciones Kairos, 2012).

butions of Latin American theology, as the development of Christology in Latin America has centered on paying attention to the historical Jesus.[23] This is the case paradigmatically with liberation theology, but it is also a key aspect of contemporary Protestant Christologies. We begin with an overview of the former.

A Liberation Christology

Leonardo Boff In Christological work in Latin America, Leonardo Boff's contribution in *Jesus Christ Liberator* is a catalyst for reflection on the life and work of Christ.[24] How does one speak about Jesus and his salvation in a way that is relevant to the struggles of a great majority of people who live in subhuman conditions of impoverishment and oppression? In Boff's proposal, this approach to Christology includes at least five constructive elements that speak to the experience of liberation. First, it must give primacy to the anthropological element over the ecclesiastical, for the central issue facing the church is a humanity that needs to be humanized, not a church that needs institutional presence. Second, it must favor the utopian over the factual. The reign of God entails a historical experience of a changed reality in favor of the creation of a new human being after the likeness of Christ and his praxis. Third, a critical rather than dogmatic perspective must be adopted. More specifically, the issue is how one discerns that which is liberative from that which is not. Mere confession of Christ does not provide the criteria to make such a judgment. Doctrinal confessions about Jesus as the Christ of God that begin with the creeds, though emphasizing the New Testament resurrection motif, do not offer a sufficient foundation to inform the praxis of disciples because theological confessions need the historical context of Jesus — namely, his words, actions, and death — to gain coherence and practical relevance. Fourth, the method must prioritize the social-communitarian dimension over the personal. That is, it must create a space to speak to the collective implications of the message of Jesus. Finally, the method must retain the primacy of or-

23. For an introductory survey of these methodological options in Christology and their respective goals, see Wolfhart Pannenberg, *Jesus, God and Man* (Philadelphia: Westminster, 1968).

24. For a succinct summary of the argument, see Leonardo Boff, *Jesus Christ Liberator: A Critical Christology for Our Time* (Maryknoll: Orbis, 1978), pp. 43-48.

thopraxis over orthodoxy, right acting over right dogma, highlighting the praxeological core of Jesus' message.

These priorities allow for a view of Jesus of Nazareth as the "liberator," a contextually relevant way of presenting Jesus in Latin America. Boff explains that such a Christological title highlights the freedom Jesus brings from the conscience of sin and all kinds of alienations, particularly the human condition of broken relations toward each other and God. The praxis of Jesus is both the historical realization of the concrete kingdom of God and the beginning of the process of liberation. Jesus' confrontation with the world and the oppressors of his time, as well as his violent death, must be understood as the reaction to his liberative action. The resurrection is hence the irruption in history of the anticipated and definitive liberation whereby the utopia of the kingdom becomes *topia* in history.[25] The resulting thesis for a liberative Christology focuses on the nature of the reign of God: "the Kingdom, although it might not be of this world by its origin (its origin is in God), it is present in our midst, manifesting itself in processes of liberation."[26] To follow Jesus is to seek after his cause and plenitude.

Jon Sobrino The most complete outline of Christology from a liberation perspective is offered by the Salvadorian theologian Jon Sobrino, beginning with his *Cristología desde América Latina: Esbozo a partir del seguimiento del Jesús histórico* (Christology from Latin America: An Outline Beginning with the Following of the Historical Jesus).[27]

Sobrino's Christology is characterized by an interest in soteriology as it relates to a specific historical and political context in which the existential questions posed to faith do not come from secularism and atheism, but, rather, center on the meaning of the good news of salvation for the impoverished, the violently oppressed, and the excluded of this world. Despite the immense cultural, religious, and ethnic plurality in the continent, it is still true that these groups share common life struggles.

25. Gibellini, *Teología del siglo*, p. 389.
26. Leonardo Boff, *La fe en la periferia del mundo: El caminar de la Iglesia con los oprimidos* (Santander: Sal Terrae, 1981), p. 44.
27. Jon Sobrino, *Cristología desde América Latina: Esbozo a partir del seguimiento del Jesús histórico*, 2nd ed., Colección teologia latinoamericana (Ciudad Mexico: Editiones CRT, 1977). For the English translation, see *Christology at the Crossroads: A Latin American Approach* (Maryknoll: Orbis, 1978).

In this Christology, Jesus' ultimacy and transcendence is established from three basic premises: (1) the aim of liberation theology is the reality of God's kingdom, (2) the ethos of this theology is a critical reflection on praxis, and (3) the *locus theologicus* is the poor of this world. The goal is to provide not only a reorganization of the Christological task, but a reformulation of Christology as the basis of liberation, that is, as salvation from all kinds of evils, especially those that manifest themselves in the perpetuation of poverty, oppression, and violence.

In this vein, Christology has an eschatological structure based on the relationship between the Jesus of history (along the lines of the modern new quest for the historical Jesus) and the dual referents of the kingdom of God and the God of the kingdom. Approving of most modern Christologies' insistence that the final reality for Jesus was not himself, nor God *in directo,* but the kingdom of God, Sobrino argues that we can only come to know it in and through Jesus. For Sobrino, these are "indispensable realities for theology, giving it a basis on which better to organize and grade Jesus' multiple external activities, to conjecture his inner being, and, undoubtedly, to explain his historical fate of dying on the cross."[28] The kingdom is the principal category that provides both direction for Christian praxis and hope for life.

The kingdom of God, as a primary metaphor for God's transcendent activity in history, functions as an organizing category from which this liberation theology claims "a totality from which it can deal with all theological subjects."[29] The "resurrection" event, although embracing all aspects of faith (the ultimate meaning of history, a radical hope, the defeat of death, etc.), is not a clear enough paradigm to inform how we should live and act *now* in history in light of the conditions that negate the very life that the resurrection offers. The kingdom is proposed to have more explanatory power for discipleship.

If the subject matter of Christology is Jesus as the Christ of God, the access to its material content should be "from below," via the close examination of historical accounts in the Gospels. Christology has two fundamental moments: the texts of revelation that speak of the historic presence of Jesus Christ, and the actual reality of Christ's pres-

28. Jon Sobrino, *Jesucristo liberador: Lectura histórico-teológica de Jesus de Nazaret* (Madrid: Trotta, 1991), p. 67.
29. Sobrino, *Jesucristo liberador,* p. 123.

Jules A. Martínez-Olivieri

ence today in which true faith in Christ finds its expression.[30] Hence, the formal presupposition is that Jesus of Nazareth is the Christ of God, whereas the methodological presupposition is that an "ascending" Christology is as valid as, or even more fruitful for discipleship than, the dominant "descending" Christologies that begin with the ultimate realities of the faith: the Triune God and the incarnation of the Son. More so, there are at least *a posteriori* considerations that support the emphasis on Jesus of Nazareth: the historical tendency to ignore Jesus' own historical life and priorities, even where there is a confession of faith in Christ, and the terrible consequences of confessing Christ while using him to legitimize the idols of history, political powers, and inhumane and anti-Christian oppression. The reason for focusing on history is not demythologization, but to move toward the "de-pacification" and "humanization" of Jesus in a way that recovers his historicity as integral for faith and praxis today.

The road that leads to the confession of Jesus as the Christ of God is through Jesus of Nazareth, by considering his concrete history in its totality and recognizing his praxis as central to our understanding of his life and mission. In this sense, liberation Christology attempts to historicize the Christ event and thus follows the path of many modern theologies with their so-called historical turn. The "historical Jesus" represents the point of departure, which is better understood as the practice of viewing the historical Jesus as the history *of* Jesus.[31] Through this history, with faith in his Father, obedience to his mission, in death and resurrection, Jesus is confessed as the Son of God.

Latin American Protestant Christology

The historical consciousness that Christology found in the twentieth century encouraged Protestants to prioritize the historical and political dimensions of theological discourse in order to galvanize Christian discipleship. But it also presents an opportunity to critically bring to the forefront of Christology the role of history, ethics, and ideologies. It is a methodological option that has inspired a renovation of Chris-

30. Sobrino, *Jesucristo liberador,* p. 23.
31. Jon Sobrino, *Jesús en America Latina: Su significado para la fe y la cristología* (Santander: Sal Terrae, 1982), pp. 112-13.

tian discipleship and grounded the work of theology with a deep concern for the praxis of the faith.

In Protestant Christology in Latin America, the confession that Jesus is the one unbegotten Son, the Logos, surely provides the ontological presupposition on which Christian faith delves into the mystery of God, for which creedal orthodoxy serves as the standard. However, the work of Christology in Latin America among Protestant theologians also advances under the methodological proposal that it is equally legitimate, or even more necessary from the systematic perspective, to approach Jesus as the Christ of God via the historical particularity of Jesus as the man from Nazareth. It is the attention to Jesus' historical life that permits the very possibility of his anthropological identification as fully human. The retrieval of the humanity of Jesus in its historical Jewish expression provides the ground for any attempt at ontological reflection on the significance of Jesus' divinity and helps the faith avoid reductionism. This is a general achievement of contemporary Christology that is adopted in Latin America.

The Argentinean Lutheran Guillermo Hansen proposes that to think about Jesus' humanity and divinity is to delve into the notions of transcendence and immanence: the complete otherness of God and the complete presence of God in the dynamism of creative existence. The path toward thinking theologically about Jesus begins with the presupposition that in this human being there is an extraordinary mediation – an irruption of divine transcendence in immanence, which consequently implies that in the person of Jesus we find a projection of immanence into transcendence. This *doble via* (double way) is what allows us to "confess that in Jesus the divine makes itself present, but it is also what allows us to christologize the divine, that is, identify transcendence with Jesus."[32]

Therefore, when Christians assert that Jesus reveals God and *vice versa*, and that in this human being the criterion to discern the ultimate meaning in history is found, theology is claiming to "comprehend the 'ultimate' from a figure that can be historically located and correlated to key social, political and cultural dimensions"[33] – thereby emphasizing

32. Guillermo Hansen, "¿Se conmueven los cimientos de la cristología?: La tercera búsqueda del Jesús histórico y la respuesta 'alquímica' de la teología," *Cuadernos de teología* 25 (2006): 134.

33. Hansen, "¿Se conmueven los cimientos de la cristología?" p. 134.

that in the life events of Jesus one finds the divine reality. That is, in virtue of the only undivided person (e.g., Chalcedon and *the comunicatio idiomatum*) of Jesus, it is possible to attribute to God that which is human. Jesus christologizes divinity itself.[34] Consequently, knowledge of Jesus Christ is both a confession of faith of the highest order – that this man Jesus is truly of God, from God, and very God – and a historical apprehension and affirmation of Jesus as the Nazarene from Galilee. To believe in Jesus Christ is not only a theological confession but also a trust in and will to enter into *secuela Christi* (following of Christ). As Christians, says Nancy E. Bedford, "we believe in God through Jesus by God," and "we recognize in Christ the *deiformity* of Jesus but also the *christoformity* of God."[35] What she means is that in order to understand the person and work of Jesus, we are inevitably referred to God in his life, and when we think about God, we are inevitably drawn to think of God as seen through Jesus. Christian faith results from a historical epistemological access to Jesus, existentially internalized by the Holy Spirit.

Christology in Holistic Perspective Proposing that Christological discourses must be evaluated not only for their coherence but also their material content in accordance with the whole gospel and how they function in concrete situations, Bedford outlines the contours of a Latin American feminist Christology.[36] The goal is constructive: to represent Jesus of Nazareth as the Christ in whom the Triune God acts as God with us and for us, for the sake of justice, righteousness, and transformation. Bedford shares the conviction that Christology must be understood in Trinitarian terms. Analyzing the dominant religious and cultural images of Jesus in Latin America – as the suffering victim or the celestial monarch – she emphasizes that theologians need to avoid "toxic christologies": discourses about Jesus that function as tools for maintaining the status quo and domination of the other, particularly women. In Bedford's judgment, a Trinitarian approach to Christology provides the "pneumatic space" where the continuation of faithful praxis and explication of the meaning and relevance of the gospel of Jesus are realized in the freedom of God's people.[37] That is,

34. Hansen, "¿Se conmueven los cimientos de la cristología?" p. 135.
35. Nancy E. Bedford and Guillermo Hansen, eds., *Nuestra Fe* (Buenos Aires: Instituto Universitario ISEDET, 2008), p. 111.
36. Nancy E. Bedford, "Otra vez la cristología," *Cuadernos de teología* 27 (2008): 39 n. 9.
37. Bedford, "Otra vez la cristología," p. 49.

"when the strength of the Spirit of God acts to overcome the limitations and hierarchies of gender, new spaces are created through the trinitarian economy of God so that the church functions as a home full of life."[38] This approach to Christology has the strength of highlighting the pneumatic dimensions of Christology and ecclesiology, as well as the social implications for gender issues and the integral wellbeing of women and children who fall victim to physical and emotional abuse by men: the logic of patriarchal violence.

Christology and the Limits of Creedal Orthodoxy Latin American theology has an uneasy relation in its reception of the Christological dogma embodied in the Nicene and Chalcedonian Creeds. It affirms the binding nature of the dogma, but questions its relevancy for the contemporary challenges of the church in Latin America. The concentration on the historical dimension of salvation with its focus on recovering the centrality of Jesus' concrete actions aims to fix what are perceived as inherent limitations of the creeds: the emphasis on transcendence at the expense of the historical; the stress on Jesus as divine at the expense of the importance of his historical humanity; and the lack of attention to the ethical dimension of Christology. It is charged that the Christian tradition disassociated the mediation of God's presence in history (Jesus) from the mediation of God's will.

Therefore, although the significance of the creeds is affirmed, the interpretation of the councils — of Chalcedon in particular — reveals a distinction made between the biblical testimony concerning Jesus' identity, and the metaphysical and philosophical mediations that conditioned the theological language of the milieu. Arguably the major difference between classical Christology and the Christologies arising in Latin America is found in the language used to elucidate the mystery of the identity and work of Jesus of Nazareth. It is often argued that creedal Christology in its treatment of the identity and work of Jesus operates with the philosophical terminology of "nature, persons, substance, accident, essence, subsistence, hypostatic union, *communicatio idiomatum,* vicarious satisfaction, etc."[39] This kind of conceptual language did not necessarily diminish the spirituality of the early church

38. Bedford, "Otra vez la cristología," p. 49.
39. Juan-José Tamayo-Acosta, ed., *Diez palabras claves sobre Jesús de Nazaret* (Estella: Verbo Divino, 1999), p. 12.

fathers and Christian communities, but the language became "more technical and abstract, less narrative and experiential," over time, contributing to the eventual bifurcation between the being of Jesus and his salvific work.[40]

Hence, the authority of the creeds is relative to the necessities of their originating context. The contention is that while "the Nicene Creed and the Chalcedonian definition systematized in metaphysical language the biblical data concerning Christ as fully God and fully man and as the indivisible one . . . they lost sight of Jesus's concrete actions in history," obscuring in the process Jesus' life and humanity, as well as his identification with and concern for the poor and the marginalized of his time.[41]

The main limitation of creedal Christology is its tendency toward abstraction consequent upon its use of philosophical conceptuality — making the doctrine of Christ susceptible to historical indifference. The recovery of the history of Jesus in person, practice, options, and destiny is what grants theology the material content to appropriate the work of Jesus of Nazareth as the work of God for the sake of humanity and creation. The creeds need the fundamental corrective of the focus on the good news as an announcement primarily directed toward the victims of institutionalized exclusion and violence, as well as to all who are subject to all kinds of captivities. This critique is of particular importance in evangelical Christianity in Latin America, which despite its acknowledgment of the full humanity of Christ is nevertheless affected by docetism. This influence makes it difficult to establish relationships between doctrine and social ethics because such minimizing of the full humanity of Jesus as compared to his divine identification functionally rejects the materiality of the incarnation.[42]

Catholic and Protestant Christologies locate in the history of Jesus the arrival of the *eschatón*. At the center of the Christian confession of Jesus is his mission, his preaching, his relationship with his *Abba*,

40. Bedford and Hansen, eds., *Nuestra Fe*, p. 122.

41. C. René Padilla, "Toward a Contextual Christology from Latin America," in *Conflict and Context: Hermeneutics in the Americas* (Grand Rapids: Eerdmans, 1986), p. 81.

42. Padilla, "Towards a Contextual Christology," p. 83. Docetism refers to a Christology in which Jesus' humanity is conceived as an apparent quality of his personhood. That is, Jesus only appears to be fully human.

and the Spirit revolving around the proclamation of the arrival of the kingdom of God. The death and resurrection of Jesus are understood not only in the context of the grand biblical narrative of God's redemptive work and in the paradigm of his divine and human identity, but in light of the actions of Jesus of Nazareth, the history of Israel, and God's identification with those actions. The liberation of the masses subjected to sin in its personal, collective, and structural manifestations depends on the cross and resurrection of Jesus, as he is the representative of both the true human and the victims who long for God's ultimate justice.

In the royal announcement of the fulfillment of this reign, Jesus Christ is analytically indispensable to comprehension of it because to announce the kingdom is to announce Jesus Christ, and to announce Jesus Christ is to announce the kingdom.[43] The theological inseparability of Jesus and the kingdom is due to the Gospels' datum that "the function of Jesus after paschal consists in introducing and exercising God's reign in history: 'God was in Christ reconciling the world to himself.'"[44] Antonio González summarizes the relationship between Christology and the kingdom as follows: "The reign of that king is none other than the reign of God. Precisely for that reason, the separation of the proclamation of the Christ, that is, of the Messiah or the anointed one, from the proclamation of the reign of God makes no sense at all. There is not, nor can there be, a Christ without a reign."[45] In emphasizing Jesus' integral historical personhood and the presupposition of the presence of transcendence (i.e., God was in Christ), theology in Latin America hopes to discern a pattern and content for theological ethics. As C. René Padilla argues: "If the Christ of faith is the Jesus of history, then it is possible to speak of social ethics for Christian disciples who seek to fashion their lives on God's purpose of love and justice concretely revealed."[46] The ethical dimensions of Christological discourse give rise to an exercise in faithful creativity where con-

---

43. Antonio González, *El evangelio de la paz y el reinado de Dios,* Colección FTL (Buenos Aires: Ediciones Kairos, 2008), p. 51. The English translation of chapters 2 through 5 can be found in González, *Gospel of Faith and Justice,* chapters 2, 3, 4, 7.

44. González, *El evangelio de la paz y el reinado de Dios,* p. 52. Other cited passages include Mark 1:14-15; Acts 28:31; Rom. 1:4; 14:17; 1 Cor. 4:20; Phil. 2:9-11; Col. 4:11. See also chapters 2-3.

45. González, *Gospel of Faith and Justice,* p. 72.

46. Padilla, "Towards a Contextual Christology," p. 89.

temporary Christians seek to prolong the logic of Jesus' praxis in their different cultural and political settings.

Christology and the Cross Theologians in Latin America approach the soteriological question of Jesus' death on the cross with both historical and theological emphases. Theologically, the death of Jesus is central to the intelligibility and power of the gospel. Jesus redeems from sin, is a substitution for sinners, conquers death, defeats Satan, brings reconciliation and forgiveness, justifies and makes people just, and provides hope for the victims of sin by shining the light of love and justice for the liberation of humanity.

In terms of the reality of history, the death of Jesus is seen as the historical outcome of his confrontation with political and religious authorities: suffering for the sake of justice and calling his disciples to follow his example of sacrifice. Liberation theology places strong emphases on the historical causes of the crucifixion. The death of Jesus was a political murder, a fate sealed by the conflictive religious and political nature of his message and the kind of life he lived and expected others to live. The life of Jesus cannot be relativized, and the question "why was he killed?" needs to be anchored in a material reality. The danger of decontextualizing and relativizing the life of Jesus is that the political conditions of the cross event are lost, and the main addressees of his message – the humble, the poor, women, and other marginalized groups – therefore become invisible both in the testimony in Scripture and in our societies.[47]

Bedford shares this concern and believes that in the historical conditions of the cross we can "find, therefore, the truth about the system in which we live" – with its systemic violence against those made weak in society, particularly women – and "the way in which the triune God proceeds, whose fidelity to his creation we confess and in whose mercy we are immersed in following Jesus."[48] In the historical and theological density of the cross, there is healing for victims and transformation for victimizers. To avoid an abstract conception of salvation and to protect the integrity of Christology, theology needs to affirm that the death of Jesus was the consequence of his announcement that the kingdom of God had arrived.

47. Padilla, "Christology and Mission," p. 28.
48. Bedford, *La porfía*, p. 142.

Conclusion

Amid the legacy of violent colonialism, political Christendom, dictatorships, civil wars, discrimination, exclusion, and poverty, the person of Jesus Christ becomes in his historicity and humanity the Lord and Son who ushers in the kingdom of God and calls on all men and women to follow him. The one who calls is the Jesus who reaches the poor, who calls for universal repentance, and who heals victims and transforms victimizers. His gospel is the announcement of the arrival of the reign of his Father present in his words, actions, and choices. His ethos is shaped by a life filled and moved by the power of the Spirit to bring life. The cross is the result of Jesus' mission confronting a world of violence, idolatry, and evil. It is also the way in which God's self-giving stands as an event for us who believe, but also against the anti-kingdom of corruption and injustice. Salvation is in history but is not limited to history. Christology from a Latin American perspective is an ascending Christology elaborated on the historical self-abasement of the Christ of God and the hope of his salvific global will.

The aforementioned proposals are in a continual process of development, as theologians are working on a series of challenges. An explanation is needed regarding how to define the nature of history with a concomitant account of divine action. If God's action in history is understood — as Míguez Bonino, Bedford, and González argue — as the action of the Trinitarian God, accounts of Jesus as the Trinitarian Son and of his salvific mission in relation to the revelation of the Father and the activity of the Spirit are needed. Moreover, we still need to better elucidate the impact of a recovery of the Jesus of history on our understanding of the presently reigning eschatological Jesus, a reigning that finds its elaboration through pneumatology. Also needed is a theological elaboration of the nature and use of Scripture as an authoritative source for epistemic access to the carpenter from Nazareth and the *norma normans* for orthopraxis.

It is notable that the common aim of Latin American Christologies is to articulate a transformative Christology that avoids the practical and discursive dualisms between a heavenly savior and an earthly liberator. The unity of Jesus Christ — avoiding the dichotomy of the Jesus of history and the Christ of faith — and of exegesis and dogmatics is a challenge too. This unity is sought between ethics and ontology, between a social and an individual vision of salvation.

Jules A. Martínez-Olivieri

The task is to relocate the history of Jesus Christ at the beginning of Christology. The burden is to provide an account of how the history of Jesus offers people a vital and indispensable foundation for love, life, and hope.

For Further Reading

Escobar, Samuel. *En busca de Cristo en América Latina*. Buenos Aires: Ediciones Kairos, 2012.

González, Antonio. *The Gospel of Faith and Justice*. Maryknoll: Orbis, 2005.

Lois, Julio. "Christology in the Theology of Liberation." In *Mysterium Liberationis*, edited by Ignacio Ellacuría and Jon Sobrino, pp. 169-94. Maryknoll: Orbis, 1993.

Míguez Bonino, José. "Latin America." In *Introduction to Third World Theologies*, edited by John Parratt, pp. 16-43. Cambridge: Cambridge University Press, 2004.

Padilla, C. René. *Mission Between the Times: Essays on the Kingdom*. Rev. ed. Carlisle: Langham Monographs, 2010.

Sobrino, Jon. *Christ the Liberator: A View from the Victims*. Maryknoll: Orbis, 2001.

PART II

BIBLICAL EXPLORATIONS

CHAPTER 5

Reading the Gospel of John through Palestinian Eyes

YOHANNA KATANACHO

Introduction

There is no doubt in my mind that all of us read the Gospel of John from a particular perspective.[1] We are all shaped by our social, political, cultural, and religious assumptions. This is very true in Israel-Palestine. For example, some Messianic Jews in Israel-Palestine believe that Jesus is the Jew par excellence who lived in a Jewish culture.[2] They read the Gospel of John from this point of view.[3] Other Jews are troubled by the

1. For a survey of approaches to the Gospel of John, see Frank Pack, "The Gospel of John in the Twentieth Century," *Restoration Quarterly* 7 (1963): 173-85; Harold Songer, "The Gospel of John in Recent Research," *Review and Expositor* 62 (1965): 417-28; Robert Kysar, "The Gospel of John in Current Research," *Religious Studies Review* 9 (1983): 314-23; Mark Stibbe, *The Gospel of John as Literature: An Anthology of Twentieth-Century Perspectives* (Leiden: Brill, 1993).

2. It is important to keep in mind that first-century Judaism is neither equivalent to the Old Testament nor identical with twenty-first-century Judaism. The Jewishness of the first-century Jesus is not like the Jewishness of contemporary Jews. Sadly, the Jewishness of Jesus seems to be highlighted in Israel in a way that alienates him from Palestinians and alienates Messianic Jews from the global church. It becomes a barrier instead of being a channel in which the blessings of God are brought forth. In addition, it is important to note that the Gospel of John uses the label "Jew" in a context of hostility. We need to keep in mind that John himself is a Jew and that the word "Jew" in the Gospel of John does not represent the position of all the Jews in the first century, let alone the Jews throughout history.

3. Messianic Jews have a spectrum of views concerning Jesus Christ. Some accept the traditional Christian views while most of them refuse the language of the Nicene Creed and prefer to express the identity of Jesus in Jewish categories. Few refuse the

103

Jesus presented in the Gospel of John since he describes some Jews as "unbelieving descendants of the devil (8:44), blind, sinful, and incapable of understanding their own scriptures."[4] Further, some Israeli Jews are not interested in Jesus Christ at all. They call him "Yshu," which is a Hebrew acronym that means "may his name and memory be obliterated!"[5] Others in Israel-Palestine emphasize that there is a continuum between the native people of the land throughout the centuries. Consequently, Jesus and contemporary Palestinians share the same geopolitical location.[6] The geographical and sociopolitical continuity makes Jesus not only a Palestinian but also a Palestinian identification figure. The identity and actions of Jesus embody the hopes of Palestinians and represent them, more so than other nations. Many Palestinian Muslims see him as a Palestinian prophet and some of them believe that the Gospel of John predicted the coming of Muhammad, the prophet of Islam.[7] On the other hand, many Palestinian Christians see Christ as the Son of God who was born in the Palestinian town of Bethlehem. Several Palestinian liberation theologians affirm that the Palestinian Jesus is again facing Herod, but this time it is an Israeli Herod.[8]

---

theology of the Nicene Creed. For a detailed discussion on Messianic Jewish Christology, see Richard Harvey, *Mapping Messianic Jewish Theology* (Milton Keynes: Paternoster, 2009), pp. 96-139.

4. Adele Reinhartz, "A Nice Jewish Girl Reads the Gospel of John," *Semeia* 77 (1997): 179. See also Adele Reinhartz, *Befriending the Beloved Disciple: A Jewish Reading of the Gospel of John* (New York: Continuum, 2001).

5. See, for example, the Jesus Boat Museum on the Sea of Galilee; the English explanation about the first-century boat uses the label "Jesus" but the Hebrew text uses "Yshu." I complained to the administration of the museum but they insisted on using what is common in Israel.

6. Mitri Raheb, "Toward a Hermeneutics of Liberation: A Palestinian Christian Perspective," in *The Biblical Text in the Context of Occupation: Towards a New Hermeneutics of Liberation*, ed. Mitri Raheb (Bethlehem: Diyar, 2012), pp. 11-27.

7. Some Muslims believe that the Paraclete in the Gospel of John points to Muhammad the prophet of Islam. For further details, see the following Arabic resources: Ahmed Hijazi Al-Saqa, *Paraclete: It Is the Name of the Prophet of Islam in the Gospel of Jesus* (Cairo: Al-Muty'y, 1972), pp. 4, 29. Cited July 31, 2012. Online: www.al-maktabeh.com/ar/play.php?catsmktba=12. See also the Arabic book of Faruq Abed Al-salam, *Muhammed, Peace Be Upon Him, in the Gospel of John* (Cairo: Markaz Al-salam lltjhyz Al-fani, 2006). Cited July 31, 2012. Online: www.al-maktabeh.com/ar/play.php?catsmktba=2182.

8. Some examples of Palestinian liberation theology are Naim Ateek, *Justice and Only Justice: A Palestinian Theology of Liberation* (Maryknoll: Orbis, 1989); Naim Ateek, A *Palestinian Christian Cry for Reconciliation* (Maryknoll: Orbis, 2008); Mitri Raheb, *I Am a*

It seems that many who pay attention to Jesus are far from the Chalcedonian Christ who is an inclusive figure that embodies all of humanity.[9] Instead, a particular Christ is conceived who is exclusive by definition. Consequently, the ontological Chalcedonian reality that Christ is fully human is lost in the mix. While the Chalcedonian Definition makes an indispensable ontological contribution to our Christology, it does so while sidestepping any functional dimension.[10] Another problem is that the connection between Christ's full humanity and his particular ethnicity are not addressed. The notion that Christ is the Jewish peacemaker, not only between humanity and God but also between the Jews and the nations, is not developed. It does not define the Jewishness of Jesus at all. In short, the need for studying Jesus Christ beyond Chalcedonian expressions is clear.[11] The Scriptures no doubt are able to enrich our understanding of Chalcedonian Christology; they can help us focus on concerns that have not been addressed before. Consequently, I propose reading the scriptural story of Jesus of Nazareth combining the human and divine spatiotemporal realities from a functional point of view. How can the Jewish Jesus who is born in Palestine and is fully human be a peacemaker or a liberator? How can he represent both Palestinians and Jews as the humble and suffering servant as well as be the resurrected Christ? How can the Gospel of John help us unpack the concept of the full humanity of Jesus in the context of the Palestinian-Israeli conflict? The Gospel of John is a fruitful place to contemplate the inclusive reality that Christ brings forth.

Palestinian Christian (Minneapolis: Fortress, 1995). For further details about mapping Palestinian theology, see Yohanna Katanacho, "Palestinian Protestant Theological Responses to a World Marked by Violence," *Missiology: An International Review* 36 (2008): 289-305.

9. For understanding Chalcedonian Christology in the context of nineteenth- and early twentieth-century discussions, see Mark Nestlehutt, "Chalcedonian Christology: Modern Criticism and Contemporary Ecumenism," *Journal of Ecumenical Studies* 35 (1998): 175-96. See also James Moulder, "Is a Chalcedonian Christology Coherent?" *Modern Theology* 2 (1986): 285-307. For understanding the context and theology of the Chalcedonian Creed, see Frances Young, "The Council of Chalcedon 1550 Years Later," *Touchstone* 19 (2001): 5-14.

10. William Baker, "The Chalcedonian Definition, Pauline Christology, and the Postmodern Challenge of 'From Below' Christology," *Stone-Campbell Journal* 9 (2006): 81-82.

11. In suggesting the need to move "beyond Chalcedon" in this way, I do not suggest contradicting Chalcedonian Christology or denigrating its contribution.

Yohanna Katanacho

The exclusive particularism that is rooted in national and ethnic visions of the identity of the Christ is in tension with the depiction of Christ in the Gospel of John. John is advocating a Christocentric worldview in which important particulars of Pharisaic Judaism are deconstructed, making way for an inclusive vision of Christ and his kingdom. As John deconstructs major elements of Pharisaic Judaism, his new world order reorganizes the world in relation to Christ. In the following paragraphs I discuss the "new beginning" in the Gospel of John, holy space, holy time, holy experience, holy community, and holy land. These components are not only important in the Gospel of John but are also foundational for Pharisaic Judaism.[12] They shape the new world order presented in John. Limits of space prevent me from going into great detail, but my analysis of the dominant conceptual structures in the Gospel of John has implications for the Palestinian-Israeli conflict — one marked by strong theopolitical patterns — that I draw out.[13] I also reflect, from a Palestinian point of view, on the Chalcedonian Christology that avers that Jesus is "fully human."

A New Beginning

Scholars agree that the beginning of the Gospel of John echoes the beginning of the book of Genesis.[14] It starts with the phrase "in the beginning"; there are references to life and light as well as creation in

12. I am simply reading John in its final canonical form from a literary point of view. I agree with Craig Blomberg that "recent scholarship has adequately demonstrated that the canonical form of John is replete with thematic unity, literary artistry and intentional characterization." Craig Blomberg, "The Globalization of Biblical Interpretation: A Test Case John 3–4," *Bulletin of Biblical Research* 5 (1995): 3. See also E. Ruckstuhl, *Die literarische Einheit des Johannesevangeliums* (Göttingen: Vandenhoeck & Ruprecht, 1987); R. Alan Culpepper, *Anatomy of the Fourth Gospel* (Philadelphia: Fortress, 1983).

13. For an introduction to the Palestinian Israeli conflict, see Alex Awad, *Palestinian Memoirs: The Story of a Palestinian Mother and Her People* (Bethlehem: Bethlehem Bible College, 2012). See also Salim Munayer and Lisa Loden, eds., *The Land Cries Out* (Eugene, Ore.: Wipf & Stock, 2012). The former resource is clearer and more specific in presenting the Palestinian side of the story but the latter resource presents both Palestinian and Jewish points of view.

14. See, for example, George Beasley-Murray, *John* (Dallas: Word, 2002), p. 10.

both passages. Some would even see seven days recast in John 1–2.[15] In the Gospel of John a new stage is clearly initiated in which Christ is all in all. Christ, the God-man person, is not only the transcendent reality, but is also the immanent eschatological reality. Through his presence the divine reality is revealed, touched, heard, and seen. The heavens open and the Spirit of God appears (1:32-34). The invisible God becomes visible (1:14, 18). The full union between God and humanity becomes a reality that bursts forth with grace and truth (1:14, 17). The God-man is not only with God but is also with humanity. He is not only in heaven but he is also humble enough to be found in Nazareth, a small backwater town.[16]

The incarnation is a central theme in chapter 1, but alone is not sufficient to mark this new beginning. After the Son entered the world and the Spirit appeared, pilgrims were able to see heaven open while the angels of God were ascending and descending over Jesus Christ (1:51). This angelic scene, along with the phrase "a true Israelite without deceit" (1:47), echoes the story of Jacob when he received the promises of God and when he had the vision of the gate to heaven (Gen. 28:17). Genesis tells us that through Jacob's descendants all the nations will be blessed and he and his descendants will inherit the land (28:13-14). Jesus applies these verses to himself, in his own first-century context. Jesus is making the assertion here that the King of Israel has been revealed and he will establish the kingdom of God on earth. The words "from now" (John 1:51) bring to a close the chapter that starts with the phrase "in the beginning" (1:1). It paves the way for anticipating a new world and world order in which heaven and earth are connected. Heaven is open through Jesus and the secrets of the Father are revealed through him. As John 1:18 sums it up, Jesus is the only perfect exegete of the Father and of the divine realities. The Greek word "exēgēsato" that is used in John 1:18 means make fully known or give a description or a detailed report. John uses the medium of signs that point to Jesus Christ to give content to this description.

The first sign (2:11) illustrates the new beginning mentioned in

15. D. A. Carson, *The Gospel According to John* (Grand Rapids: Eerdmans, 1991), p. 168. See also Stephen Kim, "The Relationship of John 1:19-51 to the Book of Signs in John 2–12," *Bibliotheca Sacra* 165 (2008): 323-37.

16. James Strange informs us in the *Anchor Bible Dictionary* that Nazareth was a small agricultural village with 480 residents only (Strange, "Nazareth," in *Anchor Bible Dictionary*, ed. David Noel Freedman [New York: Doubleday, 1992], vol. 4, p. 1050).

the previous paragraph. It is important to notice that John is speaking about signs, not miracles or wonders.[17] Signs are supposed to lead us to something else. John informs us that the signs should lead us to believe that Jesus is the Messiah and the means to life (20:31). The wedding at Cana is the beginning of a series of signs. It is the first sign. God started his work in the first Testament with a couple, and now he starts a new work with another couple in a wedding. Weddings in first-century Jewish culture symbolized God's relationship with Israel. It is worth taking time to notice a couple of things about this story.

First, water is important in the Gospel of John. In chapter 1, we see the waters of baptism. In chapter 2 we encounter water being transformed into wine. In chapter 3 Nicodemus had to be born from the water and the spirit-Spirit. In chapter 4 Christ gives the Samaritan woman water that springs with eternal life. In chapter 5 another sign is connected to water. In chapter 6 we see Jesus walking on the water. In chapter 7 Jesus talks about the living water (i.e., the Holy Spirit). In chapter 9 Jesus asks the blind man to wash in Siloam, another water scene. In John 11:55 we are reminded of the importance of water to cleansing. However, in chapter 13 Jesus states that water does not guarantee cleansing. Last, in John 19:34 water is mentioned yet again. To say the least, it seems that John is really interested in using water as a motif. The water in chapter 2 was needed for cleansing.[18] Religious people had to ritually cleanse themselves in order to keep the requirements of first-century Judaism. The text implies that all the water jars are filled with water. In other words, Jesus resolves the problem of not having wine and creates a new problem. There is no longer water at the wedding. People no longer have any ritual means to cleanse themselves.

This leads me to my second observation. What is the means of cleansing if there is no water? The Gospel of John is like a tapestry; certain themes or words run through it. One of these important words is "hour." Jesus told his mother that his hour had not yet come. At the

17. The term "Book of Signs," now widely accepted by most Johannine scholars in reference to John 1:19–12:50, is usually associated with C. H. Dodd, see C. H. Dodd, *The Interpretation of the Fourth Gospel* (Cambridge: Cambridge University Press, 1953), p. x.

18. For further details, see Wai-Yee Ng, *Water Symbolism in John: An Eschatological Interpretation* (New York: Peter Lang, 2001).

same time he performed the sign. Jesus is pointing out that the basis of the coming messianic age that is full of joy is not miracles but is the hour. He clarifies that the hour has not come. The " 'hour' becomes a theological leitmotif that encapsulates Jesus' passion, his glorification, and human redemption."[19] John uses the label "hour" in 7:30, 12:23, 12:27, 13:1, and 17:1. Taken together, these texts clarify that John uses the word "hour" to refer to the cross and glorification of Jesus Christ. Put differently, the hour becomes the indispensable foundation for the new world order, or the messianic age. It is associated with all the elements of the new world order and it is the means by which the elements of Pharisaic Judaism are transformed and integrated into a Christocentric reality. The cleansing water of Judaism cannot be transformed into the messianic wine without the hour and all the meaning it carries. The Christ event centered on the hour becomes the starting point for reading the main elements of Judaism, that is, holy space, holy time, holy experience, holy community, and holy land. The hour becomes the lens in which we see the incarnation.[20] This eschatological reality is the hermeneutical lens for interpreting not only the signs of Christ but also his identity. We cannot understand the humanity of Christ only from the perspective of his birth or the incarnation. We also need to understand his humanity from the perspective of the cross. Jesus is not only a Jew but he is also the Savior of the nations. While his Jewishness makes it possible for him to embody the hopes of biblical Israel and fulfill its destiny, his identity as the Savior of the world highlights a reality that transcends exclusive attitudes toward the nations. Both Jews and Gentiles are equally the objects of God's salvation. His humanity is the means of full redemption and reconciliation with God, humanity, and the cosmos. His humanity is the space in which we can touch God and be in fellowship with him. It is an inclusive humanity, not a form of exclusive Jewishness. It is appropriate now to move to my second concern, that is, Christ as the true temple (John 2:19-21).

---

19. Craig Morrison, "The 'Hour of Distress' in Targum Neofiti and the 'Hour' in the Gospel of John," *Catholic Biblical Quarterly* 67 (2005): 590.

20. This approach is clear in the works of medieval Arab theologians. See, for example, the Arabic texts of chapters 6, 7, and 8 of *Summa Theologiae Arabica* as found in Joshua Blau, *A Handbook of Early Middle Arabic* (Jerusalem: Hebrew University, 2002), pp. 73-82.

Holy Space

Holy space plays a central role in second temple Judaism, as the temple is the center of religious life in first-century Judaism. Interestingly, the Gospel of John places the cleansing of the temple right after the wedding at Cana, continuing to develop the Johannine theme of a new world order. John tells us that Jesus refers to himself as the temple (2:21). This is significant in light of the new realities centered around Jesus Christ, but also significant in light of the fact that John places the cleansing of the temple with Jesus entering Jerusalem. Unlike the Synoptic Gospels, which put the cleansing of the temple at the end of the ministry of Jesus, John presents it between the wedding at Cana and meeting Nicodemus in order to highlight the new world order in which Christ replaces the temple.[21]

The section from John 2:1 that ends with 4:54 has several clues about how John treats "space" as we compare the stories of Nicodemus and the Samaritan woman. John 3 showcases a man, a Jewish religious leader,[22] while John 4 narrates a conversation between Jesus and a despised Samaritan woman, someone who would have been seen as a second-class citizen in first-century Israel. The Jewish leader comes at night (usually a negative in the Gospel of John) while the woman

21. The issue of replacement theology has been polarized and politicized to the extent that people are usually misunderstood whenever they use the word "replace" in my context. Many have associated replacement theology with anti-Semitism and consequently it is very difficult to address the pertinent theological issues without encountering *ad hominem* arguments. I simply reject the view that the church replaces the Jews because they are condemned by God (punitive replacement theology). In using the word here, I am simply stating that Jesus Christ embodies the hopes of biblical Israel and fulfills them. All the nations, including the Jews, are called to join the community of Jesus Christ who is the only Savior of the world. The society of Christ does not replace the society of Israel but Christ transforms the latter society into the church. Further, the church, or the society of Christ, existed in the society of Israel but became visible and able to fulfill its calling through Jesus Christ.

22. See, for example, Blomberg, "Globalization of Biblical Interpretation," p. 4. Carson says, "John may intend a contrast between the woman of this narrative and Nicodemus of chapter 3. He was learned, powerful, respected, orthodox, theologically trained; she was unschooled, without influence, despised, capable only of folk religion. He was a man, a Jew, a ruler; she was a woman, a Samaritan, a moral outcast. And both needed Jesus." Carson, *Gospel According to John*, p. 216. See also Mary Pazdan, "Nicodemus and the Samaritan Woman: Contrasting Models of Discipleship," *Biblical Theology Bulletin* 17 (1987): 145-48.

comes during the day.[23] The leader perceives Christ in a limited and distorted way while the woman is able to confess not only that Jesus is the Christ but also that he is the Savior of the world. Clearly the author of the Gospel of John prompts a comparison of these two figures. The comparison will not be complete if we ignore the idea of holy space, which is central in John 4:20-25. In chapter 3 Jesus tells Nicodemus that the presence of the Spirit of God is not limited to a specific place (3:8). The work of the Spirit of God might be everywhere and those who are born of the Spirit might be everywhere.

This idea is expanded in Jesus' conversation with the Samaritan woman. Here Jesus says that the temple of Jerusalem is no longer needed for worshiping the Father. Jesus denies the monopoly as to the true place of worship to the Pharisaic Judaism of his day because true worshipers do not emphasize the place of worship but the nature of worship. Worshipers cannot please God more when they pray on the temple mount. True worship is defined by the nature of God as revealed in Jesus Christ, not by the place of worship. Indeed, John has already pointed out this divine reality in John 1:14. This verse states that Jesus became a tabernacle in our midst.[24] The concept of connecting Jesus to the house of God is further seen in John 1:51, where we are reminded of the ladder of Jacob and the house of God, Beit El (Bethel). Jesus is the true house of God and the true temple.[25] This assertion is a challenge both to Judaism and to Islam. Any perception that the temple mount, with or without the temple, is the place in which God is found or will be found in the future is undermined by what Jesus says in John. In short, the humanity of Jesus is the space in which all humanity meets God. It is a space of reconciliation between God and human beings. Divinity and humanity are fully reconciled in Jesus Christ. Humanity cannot be fully reconciled with itself

---

23. John does not want us to forget that Nicodemus came at night. See John 3:2; 19:39. Several important manuscripts will add that Nicodemus came at night in John 7:50. For further details, see Nestle-Aland, *Novum Testamentum Graece* (Stuttgart: Deutsche Bibelgesellschaft, 1994), p. 273.

24. We can translate the first part of John 1:14 in the following way: "and the Word became human and dwelt among us." The verb "dwelt" is related to the concept of pitching a tent or a tabernacle and one of its compound forms is used in the Septuagint to refer to the tabernacle. This verb might be perceived as a figure of speech connected to God's abiding and gracious presence.

25. For further details, see Paul Hoskins, *Jesus as the Fulfillment of the Temple in the Gospel of John* (Milton Keynes: Paternoster, 2007).

without Jesus Christ. The house of God is a human being. God, through Christ the temple, is accessible to every human being who believes in Jesus Christ. There is thus no room for ethnic pride or exclusiveness.

Holy Time

As with holy space, a concept the Gospel of John deconstructs only to reconstruct it in his Gospel Christologically, John similarly deals with another central element in Judaism, holy time. Israel's worship has always been centered on one specific religious calendar. The most prominent element of Israel's calendar is the Sabbath day. As Adele Reinhartz reminds us, the Sabbath is a foretaste of the world to come.[26] John mentions two signs that happened on a Sabbath: healing of the crippled person in chapter 5 and healing of the blind man in chapter 9. He informs us that Jesus healed a crippled man on a Sabbath (5:9) and asked him to carry his mattress. Consequently, the Jews were upset because they are not allowed to carry anything on a Sabbath (Neh. 13:15-23; Jer. 17:21-22). They were angry with Jesus because he healed a man on a Sabbath (John 7:23) and because he made mud to heal the blind person on a Sabbath (9:14). In fact, John informs us that the Jews wanted to kill Jesus because he broke the Sabbath (5:16). Jesus responds with an interesting explanation. He claims that God works on the Sabbath (5:17). The signs that Jesus performs are actually the work of God himself since the Son cannot do anything apart from the Father and can do everything the Father does. Furthermore, if the Jews accept circumcision on Saturday, why would they not accept salvific healing on the same day? Jesus thus challenges the Jews not to be satisfied with superficial interpretations of their Jewish faith (7:22-24). The Sabbath is associated with the work of God in his creation. It is associated with the rest of God in the unspoiled world of Genesis 1 and it is associated with eschatological rest. In a fallen world, the Sabbath becomes an eschatological reality. On the Sabbath human beings rest from their works and hope for the full restoration (cf. Heb. 4:9). The eschatological Sabbath cannot be found apart from the work of Christ, who is fully God and fully human. Christ himself embodies our Sabbath, being the first signpost and the first fruit of the coming age.

26. Reinhartz, *Befriend the Beloved Disciple*, p. 117.

Holy Experience

Jesus not only deconstructs the rituals in the wedding at Cana, replaces the temple in John 2, and fulfills the Sabbath in John 5, he also recapitulates one of the most important traditions in Judaism: the exodus and the wilderness traditions. In John, Jesus is the new Moses.[27] Jacob Enz explains that both Jesus and Moses were unrecognized deliverers (Exod. 2:11; John 1:11), and both are connected to the sign of the serpent (Exod. 4:4; John 3:14).[28] Both the Gospel of John and the book of Exodus are built around a series of signs, both mention hardening of hearts (Exod. 14:8; John 12:37-40), and both have prayers of intercession (Exod. 32–33; John 17).[29] Enz demonstrates that many other similarities between Moses and Jesus can be found. For example, both Moses and Jesus are connected to manna (Exod. 16:4, 15; John 6:35) and to light (Exod. 13:21-22; 14:20; John 8:12).[30] Though Enz may overstate his case, he is right about seeing a connection between Moses and Jesus, between the Gospel of John and the book of Exodus (see especially John 6–8). Jesus is the bread in chapter 6, the water in chapter 7, and the light in chapter 8. He is thus not only the center of Passover but also the center of the wilderness experience.

There is no doubt that Israel's Passover is important in the Fourth Gospel. Israel's Passover is a reminder of at least four things: (1) God rescued Israel from death (Exod. 12:12-13) and the angel of death passed over the homes of the children of Israel. (2) God is holy and hates evil; so Israel is not to have any yeast (which symbolizes evil). (3) The Passover is the beginning of a new calendar in which God brings forth life. (4) The Passover is the feast of liberty. John connects the Passover (6:4) to the wilderness experience (6:31). He declares that Jesus is the sacrifice of the Passover (6:53-58) and is the true manna or bread that comes down from heaven. John is again reconstructing Israel's experience in a Christocentric way. John also describes Jesus as the source of living water. This descriptor alludes to Israel's experience in the wilderness when God gave them water out of the rock. This reconstruction of the exodus runs even deeper. John names Jesus as the light. As Israel went

27. Jacob Enz, "The Book of Exodus as a Literary Type for the Gospel of John," *Journal of Biblical Literature* 76 (1957): 208-15, 209.

28. Enz, "Book of Exodus," pp. 209-10.

29. Enz, "Book of Exodus," pp. 210-12.

30. Enz, "Book of Exodus," p. 213.

out of Egypt, received the manna, drank the water from the rock, and was led by a pillar of fire, so Jesus is the manna, the water, and the light. These are all visible images that hark back to Exodus. However, in each case, John expands the target audience beyond the limits of Israel. The bread is for the world (6:33), the water is for anyone who is thirsty (7:37), and the light is for the whole world (8:12). In John, Jesus is the source of life, whether the life of liberation from Egypt or the life that is associated with maintaining Israel in the wilderness. Jesus is also the source of guidance since in John's presentation, Israel's experiences are meaningless without Christ. This radical reconstruction leads to a dangerous tension as Jesus questions the absoluteness of the identity markers of the children of Abraham in John 8.

Holy People

The identity of ancient Israel is rooted in father Abraham as well as in their liberation from Egypt.[31] Their liberation is the consequence of their unique identity and connection to Abraham, who is chosen by God. When God elected Abraham, he also elected his seed to rule the Abrahamic kingdom and endowed them with a unique status. They are considered God's firstborn son (Exod. 4:22-23). Rabbi Akiva said, "Even the poorest in Israel are considered as freemen who had lost their estates, for they are the sons of Abraham, Isaac, and Jacob."[32] Jesus deconstructs both the concept of liberation as understood by his audience as well as their connection to Abraham and the God of Abraham. First, he claims that true Abrahamic sonship-daughtership is intimately related to the works of Abraham. It is not defined by descent but by faith commitments that are revealed in works. To be part of the "seed" of Abraham does not make one a child of Abraham.[33] The work

31. It is interesting that Egypt is often called the house of the slaves (Exod. 13:3, 14; 20:2; Deut. 5:6; 6:12; 7:8; 8:14; 13:6; Josh. 24:17; Judg. 6:8; Jer. 34:13; Mic. 6:4). Paul Hoskins argues that in John's typology sin corresponds to the Egyptians who are holding the children of Israel in bondage. Paul Hoskins, "Freedom from Slavery to Sin and the Devil: John 8:31-47 and the Passover Theme of the Gospel of John," *Trinity Journal* 31 (2010): 47-63, 56.

32. This quotation is found in Stephen Motyer, *Your Father the Devil?: A New Approach to John and the "Jews"* (Carlisle: Paternoster, 1997), p. 173.

33. Elsewhere I have argued that DNA cannot be the identity marker of biblical

of Jesus' Jewish opponents, however, reveals a satanic dimension for they are seeking to kill Jesus Christ, who is greater than Abraham. In fact, Abraham believed in Jesus (John 8:56) for he is the Great I AM! John is claiming that one cannot accept Abraham and refuse Jesus. One cannot benefit from Abraham's blessing without Jesus Christ. Christ has to be at the center of the identity of Abraham's true children. In John's perspective, Abraham's seed cannot see the kingdom of God if they do not accept Jesus Christ and live as his disciples. When Jesus reached out to the Samaritan woman, he was enlarging the scope of the Abrahamic blessings. Stated differently, no one can claim Abrahamic benefits without acting like Abraham. If John's Jesus preached today, he would claim that no Israeli Jews can be children of Abraham until they act like Abraham and stand with oppressed Palestinian refugees. Similarly, John's Jesus would challenge that no Palestinians can be true followers of Jesus unless they identify and empathize with the survivors and victims of the Holocaust.[34] God's design includes both Palestinians and Israeli Jews. The Jesus of John makes this a reality we dare not ignore.

Second, the followers of Jesus Christ are the community of the free ones. Establishing the community of Christ is a clear concern in the Gospel of John. The children of God are those who accept Jesus Christ (1:12) and are born of the Spirit (3:6). They are not necessarily members of the synagogue (9:34). John argues that the path to freedom is the liberation that comes from Jesus Christ. In chapter 12, John elaborates the theme of freedom. This chapter discusses the entry into Jerusalem. Unlike the Synoptic Gospels, John explicitly mentions the palm branches, which were the symbol of freedom since the Maccabean revolt.[35] He presents the entry into Jerusalem in the midst of a big demonstration. Members of Jewish religious communities were laying out the palm branches and even chanting provocatively. Their cries were quoting Psalm 118:26, with a twist, since they were adding to it the phrase "king of Israel." They were ready to overturn Rome if Jesus

---

Israel. See Yohanna Katanacho, *The Land of Christ: A Palestinian Cry* (Bethlehem: Bethlehem Bible College, 2012).

34. I have been influenced by the statement of Frederick Herzog, "No man can see the kingdom of God unless he becomes black," which is quoted in Blomberg, "Globalization of Biblical Interpretation," p. 11.

35. It is interesting to note that the current 10 shekel coin in Israel has a palm tree.

were willing to be their leader. In contrast, John describes Jesus riding into Jerusalem on colt, a symbol of peace. John then quotes Zechariah, also with a minor twist. John uses the words "fear not" instead of "rejoice." Then he adds "behold your King." The first step toward freedom is looking at Christ without fear. John pairs Jesus' entry into Jerusalem with the desire of the Greeks to see Jesus. When Judah the Maccabean cleansed the temple in 167 BCE he kicked out the Gentiles from the temple. The Synoptic Gospels show Jesus cleansing the temple but not from Gentiles. Rather, the cleansing is from some Jews who abused the temple. John, on the other hand, openly discusses including Gentiles in the community of God. Stated differently, for John, the path to freedom is not lined with palm branches or heard in the militant ethnocentric approach. Rather, freedom occurs when the seed of wheat will die and the plant is the new community where the enemy becomes a brother. The community of Jesus Christ is not any parochial ethnocentric community. The community of Jesus Christ is composed of those who, like the seed of wheat, die and are reborn into the community of peace and brotherhood. This is the way of freedom and the way to create a new community. It is the path of the Jewish Jesus — the Savior of the whole world.

In short, this community appears in its embryonic form in the part of the Gospel some scholars refer to as the "Book of Glory" (13–20:31).[36] In this book, Christ calls his disciples "my children" (13:33) as a sign of creating his community. It is a Jewish community but with a Christocentric understanding of Jewishness. The children of Christ (13:33) are the children of God (1:12). Christ informs his children that he will not abandon them or leave them as orphans. The new community of God envelops the ones who abide in the vine (15:1-5) and are led by the Spirit (16:13).

Holy Land

After (1) restructuring the concept of the cleansing water in the wedding at Cana, (2) replacing the temple with Jesus in chapter 2, (3) pointing out that Jesus is the Sabbath in chapter 5, (4) rebuilding our percep-

---

36. For further details about the Book of Glory, see Raymond Brown and Francis Moloney, *An Introduction to the Gospel of John* (New York: Doubleday, 2003), pp. 307-15.

tion of the exodus and wilderness traditions in a Christocentric way, and (5) reshaping the major markers of being the children of Abraham and consequently the children of God, John then leads us to reconsider the concept of the holy land from a Christocentric point of view.[37]

In John 10, Jesus declares that he is the good shepherd and the door. The good shepherd is described as leading the going in and out of the sheep and finding pasture. It's plausible that the image of the good pasture refers to the Promised Land. This claim gains strength in light of the way John develops his theology of the new world order. John's treatment of the temple, the Sabbath, prominent experiences in the wilderness, and the sonship-daughtership of Abraham all contribute to understanding the tension between the synagogue and the followers of Christ in chapter 9. This undergirds how we understand what John is saying about the holy land in chapter 10. A new exodus is happening and a more fulfilling holy land is given. The connection of John 10 to the Promised Land can also be seen in the similar expressions found describing the Promised Land in the book of Numbers. The book of Numbers discusses the topic of entering into the Promised Land and asserts that ancient Israel needed a shepherd. Moses prays, saying, "May the LORD, the God of the spirits of all mankind, appoint a man over this community to go out and come in before them, one who will lead them out and bring them in, so the LORD's people will not be like sheep without a shepherd" (Num. 27:16-17). The thematic and linguistic similarities suggest reading these texts together in a canonical context. Further, it is interesting that both leaders, Jesus and Joshua, have the same name in Hebrew. Jesus is the New Testament Joshua who will not kill the local inhabitants of Palestine but will destroy the wolf by offering himself as a sacrifice. These declarations are discussed in the context of the Feast of Dedication (John 10:22), which highlights liberty; the Maccabean revolution discussed earlier also lends background and credence to this reading. Jesus is not only interested in the land but is also interested in the people of the land. Instead of killing the inhabitants of the land he is willing to die in order to save them. His identity as the Savior of the world shapes his behavior toward the inhabitants of the land.

---

37. In response to Christian Zionism, I have argued elsewhere that Christ, not Israel, is the owner of the Land. See Yohanna Katanacho, "Christ is the Owner of Haaretz," *Christian Scholar's Review* 34 (2005): 425-41.

Second, the concept of the holy land in John 10 is also related to the concept of a good shepherd in the Old Testament. The Old Testament is full of places where God is described as the good shepherd. One passage that contains several similarities with John 10 is Ezekiel 34. I have discussed elsewhere the centrality of this text as it relates to the Arab-Israeli conflict.[38] I focus here on the biblical connection between the two texts. The flow of the text in Ezekiel is extremely important. The literary unit, which starts from Ezekiel 33:21 and ends in 37:28, opens with a clear discussion of Abraham and inheriting the Promised Land (33:24). Then Ezekiel talks about the bad shepherds of Israel, pointing out that God will bring a new David who will be the good shepherd (34:23-24). The theme of the new David is also found at the end of the literary unit where we also encounter the themes of one people and one shepherd. There will no longer be any division. David will be the one shepherd who will lead the people into the Promised Land (34:24-25). This time there will not be another exile. Obviously, the book of Ezekiel is not talking about the historical David who died hundreds of years before the times of Ezekiel. Ezekiel is talking about a Davidic figure. This David will be the good shepherd who will unify the people of God, lead them into the Promised Land, and fulfill the Abrahamic promises. Simply put, Jesus claims that he is this good shepherd. John is rethinking the theme of the Promised Land in a Christocentric way. No one can truly enter this land without Christ as the door. Christ is not only the door; he is also the way (John 14:6). Unless he washes our feet we cannot be on the way to life and we cannot find the door that leads to life. This leads me to my final point in the Christocentric world order, that is, new creation.

A New Creation

Many scholars have pointed out the similarities between John 1 and Genesis 1–2. Jeannine Brown, however, adds important insights related to the theme of new creation in the Gospel of John.[39] Jesus blew the Spirit on his disciples in John 20:22. This is reminiscent of Genesis 2:7,

38. Katanacho, *Land of Christ,* pp. 58-65.

39. Jeannine Brown, "Creation's Renewal in the Gospel of John," *Catholic Biblical Quarterly* 72 (2010): 275-90.

when God blew his breath into Adam and Eve.[40] Both scenes are set in a garden (cf. John 18:1, 26; 19:41; 20:15). In the first garden Adam fell; the curse as well as death entered our world. In the second garden the second Adam was able to overcome any temptations. He transformed the graveyard into a spring of life. This life will change the whole world. John includes the need to accept Jesus (1:12) and accept the Spirit (20:22). This is the path that brings life. This is the path of the new world order and John's way of restructuring Pharisaic Judaism. It is not an approach that replaces the Jewish people or claims that they are cursed because of the crucifixion of Christ. It does not seek to exclude any ethnicity, but to highlight the centrality of Jesus Christ, the Savior of the world. Christ does not reject Israel but embodies its deepest hopes and is the climax of its restoration.

Concluding Remarks

John presents a new world order in which he deconstructs major elements in Pharisaic Judaism and reconstructs them in relation to Christ. There are several implications of this insight that relate to the Palestinian-Israeli conflict. First, Jews and Palestinians need to resist the temptation of exclusive contextualization. Christ is fully human and he can represent both Palestinians and Jews. Christ's humanity cannot be defined in an exclusive way. This is the way of the Chalcedonian Definition and is our way. It is indeed important to understand the kind of Christ that we follow. He is not the Christ who refuses Palestinians or Jews or anyone else. He is not the Christ who excludes others from dialogue.[41] All people are equally loved by God, created in his image, and so we value all human beings without exception. Every human being is a gift from God. In addition, the value of humanity is

40. Most commentators connect John 20:22 with Genesis 2:7. See, for example, Beasley-Murray, *John*, pp. 380-81; Thomas Brodie, *The Gospel According to John: A Literary and Theological Commentary* (Oxford: Oxford University Press, 1993), p. 569; Carson, *Gospel According to John*, p. 651; Andreas Köstenberger, *John* (Grand Rapids: Baker, 2004), p. 575; Andrew Lincoln, *The Gospel According to Saint John* (Peabody: Hendrickson, 2005), p. 499.

41. Based on studying John 1, Rafiq Khoury, a Palestinian theologian, affirms that the Christ in whom we believe is a servant and is the Christ of dialogue. See *For the Sake of Open Borders between Eternity and Time: Towards an Incarnational Theology on the Soil of Our Country* (Bethlehem: Al-Liqa' Center, 2012), p. 145. The book is in Arabic.

not only related to being created in the image of God but is also related to the incarnation in which God became human, elevating the value of humanity and transforming the fallen creation into a glorified one. The Christ event is the means of transforming us into the children of God. Jesus indeed was born in a Jewish culture, but his human identity redefines Jewishness in inclusive ways. Put differently, in Jesus Christ historical Jewishness cannot be separated from eschatological Jewishness. Jesus is not only a historical Jew but he is also the eschatological Jew par excellence, who redefines Jewishness in inclusive ways and embodies its deepest hopes. He is indeed fully human and can represent all human beings.

Second, our perception of holy space and the promises of land should not be divorced from a Christocentric worldview. Any credible interpretation of the Old Testament must take into consideration the New Testament *relecture* (rereading) of Pharisaic Judaism, and its major components as they are represented in the Gospel of John. Our perception of the temple, the Sabbath, the exodus and wilderness traditions, the sonship-daughtership of Abraham, and holy land needs to be influenced and perhaps redefined by a Christocentric worldview. John's *relecture* is possibly the best way forward. The Chalcedonian Christ must be restored to the hermeneutical center. Jesus is fully human. Both Palestinians and Jews can see him as their hero and Savior.

For Further Reading

Abed Al-salam, Faruq. *Muhammed, Peace Be Upon Him, in the Gospel of John.* Cairo: Markaz Al-salam lltjhyz Al-fani, 2006.

Ateek, Naim. *Justice and Only Justice: A Palestinian Theology of Liberation.* Maryknoll: Orbis, 1989.

Ateek, Naim. *A Palestinian Christian Cry for Reconciliation.* Maryknoll: Orbis, 2008.

Awad, Alex. *Palestinian Memoirs: The Story of a Palestinian Mother and Her People.* Bethlehem: Bethlehem Bible College, 2012.

Beasley-Murray, George R. *John.* Nashville: Thomas Nelson, 1999.

Blau, Joshua. *A Handbook of Early Middle Arabic.* Jerusalem: Hebrew University, 2002.

Brown, Raymond, and Francis Moloney. *An Introduction to the Gospel of John.* New York: Doubleday, 2003.

Carson, D. A. *The Gospel According to John.* Grand Rapids: Eerdmans, 1991.

Culpepper, R. Alan. *Anatomy of the Fourth Gospel.* Philadelphia: Fortress, 1983.

Dodd, C. H. *The Interpretation of the Fourth Gospel.* Cambridge: Cambridge University Press, 1953.

Enz, Jacob. "The Book of Exodus as a Literary Type for the Gospel of John." *Journal of Biblical Literature* 76 (1957): 208-15.

Harvey, Richard. *Mapping Messianic Jewish Theology.* Milton Keynes: Paternoster, 2009.

Hijazi, Ahmed. *Paraclete: It Is the Name of the Prophet of Islam in the Gospel of Jesus.* Cairo: Al-Muty'y, 1972.

Katanacho, Yohanna. "Christ is the Owner of Haaretz." *Christian Scholar's Review* 34 (2005): 425-41.

Katanacho, Yohanna. *The Land of Christ: A Palestinian Cry.* Bethlehem: Bethlehem Bible College, 2012.

Katanacho, Yohanna. "Palestinian Protestant Theological Responses to a World Marked by Violence." *Missiology: An International Review* 36 (2008): 289-305.

Khoury, Rafiq. *For the Sake of Open Borders between Eternity and Time: Towards an Incarnational Theology on the Soil of Our Country.* Bethlehem: Al-Liqa' Center, 2012.

Köstenberger, Andreas. *John.* Grand Rapids: Baker Academic, 2004.

Kysar, Robert. "The Gospel of John in Current Research." *Religious Studies Review* 9 (1983): 314-23.

Lincoln, Andrew. *The Gospel According to Saint John.* Peabody: Hendrickson, 2005.

Motyer, Stephen. *Your Father the Devil? A New Approach to John and the "Jews."* Carlisle: Paternoster, 1997.

Moulder, James. "Is a Chalcedonian Christology Coherent?" *Modern Theology* 2 (1986): 285-307.

Munayer, Salim, and Lisa Loden, eds. *The Land Cries Out.* Eugene, Ore.: Wipf & Stock, 2012.

Ng, Wai-Yee. *Water Symbolism in John: An Eschatological Interpretation.* New York: Peter Lang, 2001.

Pack, Frank. "The Gospel of John in the Twentieth Century." *Restoration Quarterly* 7 (1963): 173-85.

Pazdan, Mary. "Nicodemus and the Samaritan Woman: Contrasting Models of Discipleship." *Biblical Theology Bulletin* 17 (1987): 145-48.

Raheb, Mitri. *I Am a Palestinian Christian.* Minneapolis: Fortress, 1995.

Raheb, Mitri. "Toward a Hermeneutics of Liberation: A Palestinian Christian Perspective." In *The Biblical Text in the Context of Occupation: Towards a New Hermeneutics of Liberation,* edited by Mitri Raheb, p. 7. Bethlehem: Diyar, 2012.

Reinhartz, Adele. *Befriending the Beloved Disciple: A Jewish Reading of the Gospel of John.* New York: Continuum, 2001.

Reinhartz, Adele. "A Nice Jewish Girl Reads the Gospel of John." *Semeia* 77 (1997): 177-93.

Songer, Harold. "The Gospel of John in Recent Research." *Review and Expositor* 62 (1965): 417-28.

Stibbe, Mark. *The Gospel of John as Literature: An Anthology of Twentieth-Century Perspectives.* Leiden: Brill, 1993.

CHAPTER 6

From Artemis to Mary: Misplaced Veneration versus True Worship of Jesus in the Latino/a Context

AÍDA BESANÇON SPENCER

Introduction

The Chalcedonian Definition amplified the Nicene Creed, in response to such persons as Nestorius, who (probably) argued that God cannot have a mother. The Definition added that Jesus Christ had two natures without confusion: "because of our salvation begotten from the Virgin Mary, the *Theotokos*, as regards His manhood."[1] Evangelical Hispanics[2] agree that Mary was *Theotokos*, mother of God, literally, "God-bearing," implying that Jesus was God even in the incarnation. According to Justo González, Nestorianism is not a temptation for Hispanic Christians because Hispanics, who themselves suffer, "feel the need to assert that the broken, oppressed, and crucified Jesus is God" and, yet, Jesus must be divine "for otherwise his suffering has no power to redeem."[3] Veneration of Mary was not a major concern during the early church years. Ironically, though, as time developed, what was intended to affirm Jesus' deity and humanity and Jesus' ability to promote human salvation instead came to affirm Mary as almost a semi-god, one without sin, who had the power of special

1. J. N. D. Kelly, *Early Christian Doctrines,* 2nd ed. (New York: Harper & Row, 1960), pp. 311-12, 318, 339-40.
2. "Latinos" is used to represent Spanish- and Portuguese-speaking men and women in the Americas. "Hispanic" is used when primarily Spanish-speaking people in the Americas are indicated.
3. Justo L. González, *Mañana: Christian Theology from a Hispanic Perspective* (Nashville: Abingdon, 1990), pp. 148-49.

mediation. This, then, lessened Jesus' humanity and ability to mediate directly on behalf of humans.

This chapter seeks to approach the topic of Christology from a Latina feminist evangelical perspective and, therefore, focuses on the relationship of Mary and Jesus and intercession. The challenge is to esteem Mary but not deprecate Jesus.

Some biblical themes are highlighted in Latin American Christian culture, such as the priority of the (Christian) family and the importance of one's mother. Four main topics are covered in this chapter. (1) Originally, devotion to Mary appeared to replace devotion to mother goddesses, especially Artemis of Ephesus. (2) Veneration of Mary is not necessary because Jesus is the sympathetic and unique intercessor, as explained especially in 1 Timothy 2:5-7. God can appeal to males and females. In contrast, focusing on Mary's feminine attributes and Jesus' masculine attributes is more akin to pagan worship of female and male deities. Jesus can represent all humans effectively. (3) Mary is an example of a humble disciple with limitations. (4) Authority is key in this discussion. Nevertheless, aside from intercession, different aspects of Mary's character have been highlighted through the years in Latino/a cultures. These bring out different aspects found in her Magnificat (Luke 1:46-55): the conquering Mary, the suffering Mary, and the liberating Mary.

Veneration in the Latino/a Context

"Meanwhile, standing near the cross of Jesus were his mother, and his mother's sister, Mary the wife of Clopas, and Mary Magdalene. When Jesus saw his mother and the disciple whom he loved standing beside her, he said to his mother, 'Woman, here is your son.' Then he said to the disciple, 'Here is your mother.' And from that hour the disciple took her into his own home" (John 19:25b-27 NRSV).

With this event, Jesus began what would become one of the blessings in the Latino/a culture and, for some, a snare. Normally, a widow would live with the former husband's family, if we agree with the tradition that Mary was now a widow.[4] His family legally had the obliga-

---

4. Joseph is active in the early years of Jesus' life and ministry, but there is no mention of him later (Matt. 1:18-25; 2:13-15, 19-23; 13:55; Luke 2:4, 16, 33, 43; 4:22; John 1:45; 6:42).

tion to maintain the husband's former wife (*Mishnah Ketub.* 4.12; 12.3). Mary could also have lived with one of her other sons, such as James, Judas, Joseph, or Simon (Matt. 13:55-56). Instead, with this event, Jesus has established the priority of the Christian family over the blood family. Jesus had already prepared the disciples in many ways, for example, when he responded to the woman in the crowd who said to him, "Blessed is the womb that bore you and the breasts that nursed you" with "Blessed rather are those who hear the word of God and obey it!" (Luke 11:27-28 NRSV), or when his mother and siblings are identified as whoever does the will of God (Mark 3:31-35). When they stood watching Jesus' crucifixion John tells us that from that hour "the disciple took [Mary] as his own into his own home" (John 19:27b). John must first have brought her back to Galilee. Eventually, John brought Mary to Ephesus in Asia Minor.[5] And, in this region, the misunderstandings about Mary began to occur. Part of the over-the-line veneration may have arisen from the very area where John and Mary lived, Ephesus in Anatolia of Asia Minor.

The Latino/a culture emphasizes the family. Christians not related by blood can become welcomed into a blood family. Latinos also emphasize devotion to one's mother. Even when I worked at the maximum security state prison of New Jersey (Trenton State Prison), the male Latino inmates included in their own publication poems dedicated to their mothers, for example:

> Cuando digo que lloramos por la mujer,
> yo me refiero a mi viejecita Santa,
> la mujer que me dio el ser, que soy,
> yo lloro por esa mujer,
> por mi madre, compañeros.

("When I say that we should weep for womankind, I refer to my dear elderly Saint, the woman who gave me being, I am, I weep for that woman, for my mother, my companions.")[6]

---

5. The early church had firm traditions of John's movement to Ephesus. The Council of Ephesus (431) affirmed that Mary was in Asia with John (Eusebius, *Church History* 3.20, 23, 31; 4.14; 5.8, 24; F. W. Farrar, *The Early Days of Christianity* [New York: Funk & Wagnalls, 1883], pp. 379, 393).

6. Raul Acosta Jr., "La celda #34," *El Mensaje: Trenton State Prison News* 1, no. 1 (February–March 1974): 25.

But Latinos also emphasize devotion to Mary, which is some-times helpful, and sometimes harmful. For instance, in a lovely song dedicated to the Virgin of Rocío, Isabel Pantoja in her album *Desde Andalucía* (RCA 1988) sings of the miraculous virgin as "la más bonita, la más guapa, la más bella" (the most beautiful) in the world, who came from heaven to stay in Isabel's own country, Spain, "madre mía del cielo" (my heavenly Mother). She lives in Andalucía, "Viva la madre de Dios!" Such passionate devotion to Mary, celebrating her beauty and thus her feminine qualities, combines with nationalistic pride and an appealing melody to make the "Vírgen del Rocío" attractive to many.

In popular Roman Catholicism of today, especially in Spanish-speaking countries and in churches and homes across the world, some-times adherents feel more comfortable praying in intercession to Mary than to Jesus.[7] (1) What are some of the reasons for venerating Mary? (2) Why should it not happen? (3) How does Mary's own example en-courage us to honor Mary but venerate and employ the intercession of Jesus? (4) After addressing these questions I will summarize the various Latino/a views on Mary.

Why Venerate Mary?

The renowned Williston Walker in his standard *A History of the Christian Church* explains, "There seems little doubt that the cult of the Virgin originally attracted and replaced the devotion that had been offered to the 'mother goddesses' of Egypt, Syria, and Asia Minor; at the same time, however, it was her role as the chosen vehicle of the Incarnation which set her, in Christian eyes, above martyr or apostle as the noblest and holiest of human persons."[8] The veneration of Mary in Asia Minor may be seen in such evangelists as Gregory Thaumaturgus (born ca. 213) who

---

7. Sixto J. García agrees: Mary has played a "traditionally seminal role . . . through the centuries in Hispanic prayer and liturgy." "A Hispanic Approach to Trinitarian The-ology: The Dynamics of Celebration, Reflection, and Praxis," in *We Are a People! Initiatives in Hispanic American Theology*, ed. Roberto S. Goizueta (Minneapolis: Fortress, 1992), p. 121.

8. Williston Walker, Richard A. Norris, David W. Lotz, and Robert T. Handy, *A History of the Christian Church*, 4th ed. (New York: Charles Scribner's Sons, 1985), p. 192. John Mc-Guckin mentions the context of Isis, a great Mother, combined with Artemis. "The Early Cult of Mary and Inter-Religious Contexts in the Fifth-Century Church," in *Origins of the Cult of the Virgin Mary*, ed. Chris Maunder (New York: Burns and Oates, 2008), pp. 10-11.

claimed that the apostles and the Virgin appeared to him and guided his work.[9] In particular, Ephesus in Asia Minor became a crucial place for exaltation of Mary. A basilica was dedicated to the Mother of God when the ecumenical council of 431 met there.[10] A sanctuary dedicated to Artemis in Ephesus was rededicated to Mary.[11] This church is said to be the first of its kind dedicated to the Virgin. The original building was built ca. 117-138. There are remains of the building that can be seen even now.[12] The veneration of Mary appears to have developed first in Asia Minor and Palestine and then spread to the West after the close of the sixth century with a wave of Christian refugees fleeing from the Islamic invasions.[13] In a time of "obscurantism, superstition, and credulity," Pope Gregory the Great of Rome (540-604), in contrast to earlier Christian teachers who had sought to preserve Christian faith free of popular superstition, "readily accepted the stories circulating at this time as if they were simple and direct confirmation of Christian faith."[14] When Pope Gregory observed the Feast of the Assumption (August 15), he informally recognized Mary's resurrection.[15] Popular Christianity became institutionalized. But not until the 1800s and 1900s did some of these popular teachings become dogma. In 1854, Pope Pius IX's bull *Ineffabilis Deus* officially declared that the Virgin Mary, "in the first instant of her conception," was "preserved untouched by any taint of original guilt."[16] In 1950, Pope Pius XII concluded that

9. Justo L. González, *The Story of Christianity I* (San Francisco: Harper & Row, 1984), p. 99; Henri Daniel-Rops, *The Book of Mary*, trans. Alastair Guinan (New York: Hawthorn, 1960), p. 92.

10. Walker et al., *History of the Christian Church*, p. 192.

11. Leonardo Boff adds, "When the pagan devotees of the goddesses and virgins were converted, they simply substituted Mary for the goddess known by such and such a title, often retaining the corresponding ritual forms and even the statue of the goddess or virgin in question, with just a change of name." *The Maternal Face of God: The Feminine and Its Religious Expressions*, trans. Robert R. Barr and John W. Diercksmeier (San Francisco: Harper & Row, 1987), p. 218.

12. Fatih Cimok, *A Guide to the Seven Churches* (Istanbul: A Turizm Yayinlari, 1998), p. 43.

13. Walker et al., *History of the Christian Church*, p. 192. For example, a basilica was built at Gethsemane at the possible place of Mary's burial to commemorate the "falling asleep" and later assumption of the Virgin. A church in Jerusalem marked the nativity of Mary. See also Farrar, *Early Days of Christianity*, p. 379.

14. González, *Story of Christianity I*, p. 247.

15. Daniel-Rops, *Book of Mary*, p. 110.

16. Walker et al., *History of the Christian Church*, p. 351.

the majestic Mother of God, from all eternity united in a mysterious way with Jesus Christ . . . , immaculate in her conception, in her divine motherhood a most unspotted virgin, the noble ally of the Divine Redeemer . . . should be carried up, in body and soul, to the celestial glory of Heaven, to reign there as Queen at the right hand of her Son, the immortal King of the ages . . . Therefore we . . . declare . . . as dogma revealed by God, that the Immaculate Mother of God, ever-Virgin Mary, on the completion of the course of her earthly life, has been taken up, in body and soul, to the glory of heaven.[17]

From humble believer, Mary had now become the Queen of heaven, able to intercede with a believer's petition to the more remote Jesus and the most remote Father.

How might this dogma about Mary have been related to the original context of Ephesus where Mary had lived with John? There were four groups of pagan cults in ancient Anatolia: Zeus, the Mother goddesses, Mēn, and the champions of divine justice and vengeance.[18] The most widely worshiped god in Central Asia was Zeus. According to Stephen Mitchell, "The gods of pagan Anatolia were not abstract and remote. At Lystra they could walk among their people and make themselves seen or heard. After centuries of Christian or Christianizing thought, entangled in attempts to articulate the ineffable, the problems of understanding paganism do not lie in penetrating its mysteries but in perceiving the obvious, the gods made manifest."[19] The pagan gods were plain for all to see. The organization called the *Xenoi Tekmoreioi* worshiped Artemis in particular. There were many shrines to the Mother of the gods. Zeus and his mother were worshiped. Zeus was remote, although awesome, and to be reached through the agency of divine intermediaries. The Phrygians in general were orgiastic worshipers of the Mother of the gods. Syncretization was common. The heresy of Montanism began in Anatolia in 170. Celibate asceticism had great appeal. By the end of the third century Christians outnumbered the rest of the population. Belief in a remote and rarified Zeus transferred to belief in a remote highest God of the Jews and Christians.

17. Henry Bettenson, *Documents of the Christian Church*, 2nd ed. (New York: Oxford University Press, 1963), p. 281.

18. Stephen Mitchell, *Anatolia: Land, Men, and Gods in Asia Minor* (Oxford: Clarendon, 1993), pp. 19, 28.

19. Mitchell, *Anatolia*, p. 11.

How better to reach Zeus than through his mother, and then how better to reach God than through his mother, Mary?[20]

Why Should Veneration of Mary Not Happen?

An important key for transformation may be to refocus from Mary to Jesus, as the sympathetic intercessor, the only mediator, a human for humans. Vatican II repeated that Christ is the one Mediator.[21] This is the same message that Paul emphasized when writing Timothy, who was serving at Ephesus in the first century: "For God (is) one, one (is) also a mediator between God and humans, human Christ Jesus, the One having given himself (as) a ransom in behalf of all, the witness to (his) own times, for which I myself was appointed a preacher and apostle (I speak truth, I do not lie), a teacher of Gentiles in faith and truth" (1 Tim. 2:5-7).[22] The first two clauses (v. 5) have two key theological ideas. A Jew would heartily affirm the first clause, as Moses summarizes: "Hear Israel, (the) Lord our God *(elohim),* (the) Lord (is) one" (Deut. 6:4). According to Deuteronomy, believers are to love the Lord with their whole being (vv. 5-6). Jews were renowned in ancient times for their belief in one God, symbolized, for example, by Judith's proclamation to the Gentile magistrates: We "acknowledge no god but the Lord" (Jdt. 8:20 REB). The Roman historian Tacitus describes the Jews as despising the gods, having "a purely spiritual monotheism . . . for them, the Most High and Eternal cannot be portrayed by human hands and will never pass away" *(Hist.* 5.5). Judaism had been prominent in Asia Minor. God-fearers who were attracted to Judaism's monotheism were ready to accept Christianity.[23] Why did Paul include the clause "God is one" in 1 Timothy 2? He appears to imply that God is unique in that God genuinely wants people to be saved (v. 4). God also is the only being capable of saving people and the only deity before whom a human needs approval. God is also able to accomplish salvation completely within the Godhead. The One who requires purity from humans and the One who can accomplish that purity

20. Mitchell, *Anatolia,* pp. 12, 16, 18-20, 22, 28, 30, 37-44, 48-51, 57, 63, 114.

21. Walker et al., *History of the Christian Church,* p. 699; Vatican II, Dogmatic Constitution on the Church, no. 62.

22. Unmarked translations are by the author when necessary to reflect the literal Greek or Hebrew of the original Bible.

23. Mitchell, *Anatolia,* pp. 32-33, 35-36, 43.

are the same. Later in 1 Timothy, monogamous marriage or a *one*-flesh union will reflect humans being created in the image of *one* God.[24]

The pagan Gentiles might find several offensive aspects in Paul's statement. First, many would believe in a variety of gods for a variety of purposes and peoples. As Artemidorus explained, "What the gods signify for men, goddesses signify for women. Gods are more auspicious for men than goddesses; goddesses are more auspicious for women than gods" (*Onir.* 4.75). Similarly, some today find the female Mary more approachable than a male Jesus. Andrew M. Greeley, for instance, explains that "Mary reveals the tender, gentle, comforting, reassuring, 'feminine' dimension of God." He describes her also as "the only mother goddess currently available."[25] For example, one man mentions that he used to pray to Mary instead of God when he was really desperate: "I felt that as a woman she would be more compassionate than God the Father. Now that my image of God has both male and female attributes, I find God more approachable."[26] At Ephesus, many would place the gods in a hierarchy with Artemis at the top. Pausanias summarizes the ancient sentiment: "All cities worship Artemis of Ephesus, and individuals hold her in honour above all the gods. The reason, in my view, is the renown of the Amazons, who traditionally dedicated the image, also the extreme antiquity of this sanctuary. Three other points as well have contributed to her renown, the size of the temple, surpassing all buildings among men, the eminence of the city of the Ephesians and the renown of the goddess who dwells there."[27] The temple was one of the Seven Wonders of the Ancient World. When Antipater saw the temple "that mounted to the clouds," the other wonders lost their brilliancy for, "Lo, apart from Olympus, the Sun never looked on aught so grand!"[28]

Artemis was often pictured with bow and arrow and stag. The priestesses and priests of the Ephesian Artemis would model a celibate reli-

24. For example, 1 Tim. 3:2, 12; 5:9. See also Aída Besançon Spencer et al., *Marriage at the Crossroads: Couples in Conversation about Discipleship, Gender Roles, Decision Making and Intimacy* (Downers Grove: InterVarsity, 2009), pp. 28-30.

25. Andrew M. Greeley, *The Mary Myth: On the Femininity of God* (New York: Seabury, 1977), pp. 17, 123.

26. Aída Besançon Spencer et al., *The Goddess Revival: A Biblical Response to God(dess) Spirituality* (Eugene, Ore.: Wipf & Stock, 1995), p. 127.

27. Pausanias, *Description of Greece* 4.31.8 (Loeb Classical Library).

28. *Greek Anthology* 9.58 (Loeb Classical Library); Epigrams of Saint Gregory 8.177.

gious lifestyle in honor of the virgin goddess.[29] The temple of Artemis at Ephesus was also renowned as an asylum for the innocent, yet simultaneously Artemis could be a slaughterer.[30] She could use her arrows to protect, but also to attack. One etymology for her name was "slaughterer, butcher."[31] Artemis could protect mothers and kill them. Many considered her the "mediator," capable of saving "all" (cf. 1 Tim. 2:4-5). In addition, Ephesus had shrines sacred to Zeus, Cybele, Demeter (Mother of the gods), Apollo (Artemis's brother), Asclepius (god of healing), Aphrodite, Dionysus, Hygeia, Pan, Isis, Hecate, Marnas (river god), Leto (Artemis's mother), Athena, Serapis, Eros, and deified emperors such as Augustus.[32] The Bible, in contrast, asserts that there is only one God who can serve all needs, including salvation, for all people.[33]

The pivotal teaching in Deuteronomy 6:4 also contains an allusion to plurality within the one God. "One" can refer, for example, to two people united in marriage (Gen. 2:24) or to all humans when they have one language (Gen. 11:1, 6). *Elohim* is an abstract plural word for "God" but it uses a singular verb when referring to the unique living God (e.g., Gen. 1:26-28). The Lord has *one* "name," but three persons ("the Father and the Son and the Holy Spirit").[34] Thus, after God's revelation to Paul[35] and his own reflection, Paul can assert that God is one but yet that one God has three persons.[36]

29. "Virgin" may simply refer to being unmarried and at the temple sex is prohibited between husband and wife (W. M. Ramsay, *The Cities and Bishoprics of Phrygia* 1 [Oxford: Clarendon, 1895], pp. 95, 136).

30. See Acts 19:27; Jerome Murphy-O'Connor, *St. Paul's Ephesus: Texts and Archaeology* (Collegeville, Minn.: Liturgical, 2008), pp. 26, 44, 123-24, 135-36, 150-51. See further, Aída Besançon Spencer, "Setting. Temple of Artemis," in *The Pastoral Letters*, New Covenant Commentary series (Eugene, Ore.: Cascade, 2013).

31. N. G. L. Hammond and H. H. Scullard, eds., *Oxford Classical Dictionary*, 2nd ed. (Oxford: Clarendon, 1970), p. 126; H. G. Liddell and R. Scott, *A Greek-English Lexicon*, rev. H. S. Jones and R. McKenzie (Oxford: Clarendon, 1968), p. 248; Martin P. Nilsson, *1 and 2 Timothy and Titus*, African Bible Commentary Series (Grand Rapids: Zondervan, 1971), p. 509; Euripides, *Iphigenia in Tauris* 35, 40, 381-84, 1458-61. Another etymology is "safe and sound" (Artemidorus Daldianus, *Onirocriticon* 2.35; Strabo, *Geography* 14.1.6).

32. Peter Scherrer, ed., *Ephesus: The New Guide*, trans. Lionel Bier and George Luxon (Selçuk, Turkey: Graphis, 2000), pp. 58-61, 70, 80, 86-87, 92-94, 134-35, 151, 170-71, 188, 198-201, 209-13.

33. E.g., Spencer et al., *Goddess Revival*, pp. 81-85.

34. Matt. 28:19. See Spencer et al., *Marriage at the Crossroads*, pp. 28-29.

35. Acts 9:4-5; Gal. 1:11-12, 16-17; 1 Thess. 2:13.

36. See also, for example, 2 Cor. 13:13.

Christ Jesus is the only mediator between God and humans. Paul places in juxtaposition the terms "humans" and "human" in 1 Timothy 2:5. Even though Jesus was born a male, Jesus only uses the generic self-description "human" (*anthrōpos*, not *anēr*),[37] because if Jesus is to represent humans (male and female) he himself must be "human" first of all. He is the counterpart to "the *Adam*," "humanity" (made of male and female; Gen. 1:26-28). A "mediator" *(mesitēs)* is in a middle *(mesos)*[38] position between several parties (Gal. 3:20), in this case two: God and humans. Job cried out to God the dilemma: "If I wash myself with soap and cleanse my hands with lye, yet you will plunge me into filth, and my own clothes will abhor me. For [God] is not a mortal, as I am, that I might answer him, that we should come to trial together. There is no *umpire* [or mediator, *mesitēs*] between us, who might lay his hand on us both" (Job 9:30-33 NRSV). But Jesus is this unique "umpire" or "mediator" (God *and* human). As Paul also explains to the Corinthians, God is "the one reconciling [humans] to himself through Christ" (2 Cor. 5:18). Humans did not obey God's first covenant. Jesus set them free from the sins committed under the first covenant so that they could become heirs under a new covenant.[39]

What kind of "mediator" is Jesus? He is "the One having given himself (as) a ransom *(antilutron)* in behalf of all, the witness to (his) own times" (1 Tim. 2:6). *Antilutron* hearkens back to Jesus' words to his disciples: "the Son of Humanity did not come to be served but to serve and to give his life a ransom for many."[40] In that context, Jesus uses his own example as a model for servant as opposed to tyrant leadership (Matt. 20:25-27). In 1 Timothy 2, Paul uses the concept as an explanation of the means by which God saves all people. Salvation has already been done willingly by Jesus. Jesus has given his life in exchange for[41] and on behalf of all people to save them. His function as a ransom was displayed in Jesus' lifetime, the

---

37. Not *anēr*, "male." Spencer et al., *Goddess Revival*, pp. 99-101. See also Mark Strauss, "Linguistic and Hermeneutic Fallacies in the Guidelines Established at the 'Conference on Gender-Related Language in Scripture,'" *Journal of the Evangelical Theological Society* 41 (1998): 246-47.

38. Joseph Henry Thayer, *Thayer's Greek-English Lexicon of the New Testament* (Marshallton: National Foundation for Christian Education, 1889), p. 401.

39. Heb. 8:6–9:15; 12:24.

40. Matt. 20:28 (*lutron anti*). See also Mark 10:45.

41. Thayer, *Lexicon*, p. 50.

"lamb" who was sacrificed.[42] Thus, in the syncretistic culture and times of Asia Minor that eventually affected even the church, Paul has reiterated monotheism, the uniqueness of God who alone is able to save and cleanse men as well as women. Today, however, some Spanish and English translations of 1 Timothy 2:5 mute Jesus' humanity:

> "un solo mediador entre Dios y los hombres: Jesucristo hombre" (Reina-Valera 1995, La Biblia de las Américas, Nueva Versión Internacional)

> "one mediator between God and men (man), the man (Man) Christ Jesus" (KJV, NKJV, RSV, NEB, REB, TEV 1966, NIV 1984, ESV).

In 1 Timothy 2:5, *anthrōpoi* is in the plural to refer to all humans, while Jesus is described as *anthrōpos* (singular). Even though Jesus may have been a male, Paul here describes him as a "human," even placing the two instances of *anthrōpos* next to each other ("mediator between God and humans, human Christ Jesus") to highlight the humanity of Jesus. If Paul had emphasized Jesus' *maleness,* then women might wonder if Jesus was an apt representative or mediator for women. But, for their salvation, Jesus must be representative of women *and* men, as inclusively human.[43] As a matter of fact, in the New Testament Jesus never once uses *anēr* ("man") as a self-description.[44] Thus, translations such as the following render best the generic meaning and language of the original Greek:

> "God and humankind, Christ Jesus, himself human" (NRSV) or

> "God and humanity, the human Christ" (CEB)[45]

Rendering the original generic Greek should also serve as a basis to satisfy those who seek a female, racial, or cultural deity figure.

---

42. For example, 1 Cor. 5:7.
43. See also John 10:33; 11:50; 1 Cor. 5:21; Phil. 2:8.
44. Spencer et al., *Goddess Revival,* pp. 99, 253 n. 13.
45. See also NIV Inclusive Language ed., CEV, NCV. See Aída Besançon Spencer, "Exclusive Language − Is It Accurate?" *Review and Expositor* 95 (1998): 383-95. In Spanish, Jesus could be described as "un ser humano," as in "los seres humanos: el ser humano Jesucristo," or "la humanidad: humano Cristo Jesús." See *Palabra de Dios para Todos* and *Biblia la Palabra Hispanoamericana.*

Jesus as "human" is representative of women and men and is over all cultures.

The author of Hebrews also writes of Jesus' ability to be the perfect mediator between God and humans. While Jesus is the heir of all things and very God, creator, superior to angels, priest forever, and high priest in heaven,[46] he offered his own blood for eternal redemption that results in outer and inner cleansing and an eternal inheritance for humans set free from sins (9:12-18). He is the one perfect sacrifice (9:27; 10:14). However, Hebrews also explains the full identification of Jesus with humans. The one who sanctifies and those who are sanctified have one Father. They are brothers and sisters. Both have flesh and blood. Because Jesus and humanity are like siblings in every respect, Jesus becomes a merciful and faithful high priest, a sacrifice for atonement for sins. Jesus was tempted so he can help humans who are tempted. Jesus is both forerunner and high priest. Jesus is able to save completely those who come to God through him because he always lives to intercede for them. Therefore, humans can draw near to God, without any additional intercessor.[47]

Mary may have been an empathetic human, but she does not have the power of God to succeed fully in her intercession. If God is not remote, God, the Trinity, can serve as God's own intercessor. Elizabeth A. Johnson summarizes that the growth of Mary's mediation stemmed partially from "a deficient Christology." The divinity of Jesus Christ was stressed "to the point where his real humanity slipped from view or seemed unreal. In this situation the simply human Mary seemed more approachable. In addition, the gracious mercy of God in Christ had been partially eclipsed by emphasis on God's just judgment."[48]

---

46. Heb. 1:2-14; 3:1; 7:17, 21, 24; 8:1; 10:21-22.

47. Heb. 2:11-18; 7:25; 10:21-22. Antonio González reiterates the importance of Jesus as the only mediator between God and humans in order to promote "an egalitarian community" free of all domination where "no messianic figure" with "theocratic authoritarianism" can govern in God's place and where no priest other than Christ is necessary. *The Gospel of Faith and Justice* (Maryknoll: Orbis, 2005), pp. 84-85.

48. The post-Reformation growth of Mary's mediation might be attributed to "a deficient pneumatology." Action universally attributed to the Holy Spirit was attributed to Mary. Elizabeth A. Johnson, "Mary as Mediatrix," in *The One Mediator, the Saints, and Mary: Lutherans and Catholics in Dialogue VIII*, ed. H. George Anderson, J. Francis Stafford, and Joseph A. Burgess (Minneapolis: Augsburg, 1992), p. 324.

*How Does Mary's Example Encourage Us to Honor Mary
but Venerate and Employ the Intercession of Jesus?*

Mary as a thinking (Luke 1:29, 34; 2:51) and faithful believer should be honored. Her humility is laudable. Even though she could not fully comprehend what would be happening to her, and despite the stigma and her possible execution, she agreed with the angel: "Behold the Lord's slave, let it be with me according to your word" (1:38). She believed the angel's word to her would be fulfilled (1:45). She comprehended and welcomed the fact that God, the Mighty One, was doing great things for her (1:48-49). At Cana, she was willing to let Jesus handle the problem in his own way, even if she had not understood that his time had not yet come (John 2:1-4). She was present with others at the crucifixion of her own son, even though by facing this horror "a sword would pierce" her own soul (Luke 2:35; John 19:25). She, along with her family, were devoted to prayer, waiting in Jerusalem with the other disciples for the coming of the Holy Spirit (Acts 1:14). Her praise to God is also exemplary. Her song of praise in Luke 1:46-55 has been studied by many for its emphasis on the liberation of the oppressed, God as Savior, the favorable position of the humble (especially the slave and hungry and poor), and the irony of life, with God reversing positions so the result is joy. Her appropriation of God's message in the Old Testament affected Jesus, James, and eventually Paul.[49]

Nevertheless, because of her humility, I think she would be horrified to discover the undue attention she has received from some replacing veneration due to her son, Jesus, Son of the Most High, Emmanuel, God with us, the Lord (Matt. 1:23; Luke 1:31-32, 35; 2:11). She was blessed among women, but blessed because of "the fruit of her womb."[50] She was not blessed in herself. The role of Mary is a difficult problem for ministry in Latin America. Do we emphasize her so much that she becomes an intercessor replacing even popular devotion to Jesus, or do we ignore her so as not to confuse anyone? God's action toward her and her response remind us of our great loss if we ignore her. Mary reminds us to pay attention to those who look least significant. They may very well be

49. See also Aída Besançon Spencer, "Position Reversal and Hope for the Oppressed," in *Latino/a Biblical Hermeneutics: Problematic, Objectives, Strategies*, Semeia Studies (Atlanta: SBL Publications, 2013).

50. Luke 1:42: the second clause ("blessed [is] the fruit of your womb") explains the first clause ("blessed [are] you among women").

God's channel of work and the cornerstones of God's work and models for all of us. However, the lowly are human too. The lowly are sinners also. Even Mary probably had doubts about Jesus when the family went to restrain him, for they were saying, "He has gone out of his mind" (Mark 3:20-22, 31-35).[51] She also did not understand how he could stay behind in Jerusalem at age twelve: "Did you not know that I must be in my Father's house?" But Mary and Joseph "did not understand what he said to them" (Luke 2:49-50). Jesus himself, although concerned for care of his mother, saw that priority toward the Christian community and obedience to him superseded the importance of his own family: "'Who is my mother and who are my brothers and sisters?' And, after having looked around at the crowd sitting around him, he says, 'Behold my mother and my brothers and sisters, for whoever may do God's will, that person is my brother and sister and mother.'"[52]

Summary and Survey of Latino/a Views of Mary

One might not consider that the treatment of Mary would affect one's understanding of Jesus. However, in predominantly Roman Catholic countries of Latin heritage, such as those where Spanish, Portuguese, and Italian are spoken, emphasis on Mary is highly stressed, sometimes to the detriment of attention toward Jesus himself as God and the perfect intermediary between God and humans. According to Diego Irarrazabal, even many Catholic "pastoral theologians claim that (Marian devotion) takes the place of prayer to God."[53] Over-exaltation of Mary can approach or become a kind of goddess worship.[54] Latin Americans adhere to Mary as "the Life-Mother," the maternal face of God. In some other contexts, in reaction, Mary can become completely ignored.[55]

51. Possibly because Jesus was not eating and was accused of being demon possessed, his family was concerned for him.

52. Mark 3:33-35. See also Matt. 12:46-50; Luke 8:19-21. See also Eric D. Svendsen, *Who Is My Mother? The Role and Status of the Mother of Jesus in the New Testament and Roman Catholicism* (Amityville: Calvary, 2001).

53. Diego Irarrazabal, "Mary in Latin American Christianity," in *The Many Faces of Mary*, ed. Diego Irarrazabal, Susan Ross, and Marie-Theres Wacker (London: SCM, 2008), p. 102.

54. Spencer et al., *Goddess Revival*, pp. 34-35.

55. Jeannette Rodriguez, "Tonanzin Guadalupe: From Passion, Death, to Res-

In early Christian worship up to the fourth century, the place accorded to Mary was minimal. No Marian liturgy has been found up to that point, although some apocryphal writings, such as the Gospel of James, exhibit an independent interest in Mary.[56] When the fifth-century church strived to explain Christ's nature, to combat Nestorius the Council of Ephesus highlighted that "the Holy Virgin is the Mother of God" (*Theotokos,* or "God-bearer"), the "mother of him who is Emmanuel," not "the mother of God the Word" nor the "Mother of Christ" *(Christotokos).*[57] After the Council of Ephesus succeeded in its proclamation of Mary as the "Mother of God," Christians sang about the triumph of the "God-bearer."[58] Henri Daniel-Rops concludes that the later dogmas about Mary are not based on any New Testament text but are implied by it. By the sixth or seventh century these dogmas of Mariology were held by many Christians and eventually recognized by many Roman Catholic theologians and religious leaders. Dogma developed to follow practice. Divine revelation was not seen as confined to Scriptures, but it "extends itself and shows itself through the Church."[59] Authority for dogma is a key difference between believers: is the locus of authority Scripture only or Scripture plus?

All believers point to similar scriptural passages to understand Mary. However, different aspects of the same larger passage (Luke 1:46-55) may be emphasized in different times and by different readers. Possibly, Luke 1:51-52 and Revelation 12:1 and Mary as Queen of heaven might

---

urrection," in *Many Faces,* ed. Irarrazabal, Ross, and Wacker, pp. 108, 113; Irarrazabal, "Mary in Latin American Christianity," in *Many Faces,* ed. Irarrazabal, Ross, and Wacker, p. 104; Nora O. Lozano-Díaz, "Ignored Virgin or Unaware Women: A Mexican-American Protestant Reflection on the Virgin of Guadalupe," in *Blessed One: Protestant Perspectives on Mary,* ed. Beverly Roberts Gaventa and Cynthia L. Rigby (Louisville: Westminster John Knox, 2002), pp. 86, 89.

56. Daniel-Rops, *Book of Mary,* pp. 82-83; Raymond E. Brown, Karl P. Donfried, Joseph A. Fitzmyer, and John Reumann, eds., *Mary in the New Testament: A Collaborative Assessment by Protestant and Roman Catholic Scholars* (Philadelphia: Fortress, 1978), pp. 248, 293; Beverly Roberts Gaventa, *Mary: Glimpses of the Mother of Jesus* (Minneapolis: Fortress, 1995), pp. 133-45, has the Protevangelium of James.

57. Philip Schaff and Henry Wace, eds., *Nicene and Post-Nicene Fathers,* Second Series (Peabody: Hendrickson, 1900), vol. 14, pp. 206-10.

58. Among others, Richard M. Price notes that Marian piety "received a powerful spur from the defeat of Nestorius and the definition at the Council of Ephesus that Mary is rightly styled *Theotokos.*" "The *Theotokos* and the Council of Ephesus," in *Origins of the Cult of the Virgin Mary,* p. 99.

59. Daniel-Rops, *Book of Mary,* pp. 113, 93-94, 98, 100, 102, 109-10.

be emphasized by nations who want to use Mary as their patron: God "hath shewed strength with his arm; he hath scattered the proud in the imagination of their hearts. He hath put down the mighty from their seats" (KJV) ("Quitó de los tronos a los poderosos" [Reina-Valera 1995]). Even though the woman probably represents Israel giving birth to the new Israel in Revelation 12,[60] some equate the woman with "a crown of twelve stars" (v. 1) with Mary who was assumed into heaven.[61] This is the triumphant Mary, the patron of Catholic Christendom, the general of the conquering army fighting infidels. Mary has become "Our Lady of Liberation." In Constantinople, according to Clodovis Boff, the Mother of God became the patron of the imperial capital, replacing the old goddesses Rea and Fortuna. In the liberation of Mexico, *La Morenita* (an Indian version of Mary) was the symbol of the liberating army.[62]

Other readers might emphasize Luke 1:48: "For (God my Saviour) hath regarded the low estate of his handmaiden: for, behold, from henceforth all generations shall call me blessed" (KJV). Mary is "the slave" ("la sierva") of God. This view might highlight Mary as a model of submissive, obedient, passive, self-sacrificing motherhood. Such thinking produced a parallel culture of *marianismo* that gave space for androcentrism with expectations for women such as: (1) do not forget a woman's place; (2) do not forsake tradition; (3) do not be single, self-supporting, or independent-minded; (4) do not put your own needs first; (5) do not wish for more in life than being a housewife; (6) do not forget that sex is for making babies – not for pleasure; (7) do not be unhappy with your man or criticize him for infidelity, gambling, verbal and physical abuse, alcohol or drug abuse; (8) do not ask for help;

---

60. The seed of the woman refers to believers in Jesus (Rev. 12:10, 17; 14:12). Thus, the woman appears to represent Israel birthing the new Israel, where her twelve stars represent the twelve tribes. Zion, the old Jerusalem, births the church, the new Jerusalem, who appears in its glory in Revelation 21:2. The vision of Revelation 12 alludes to numerous Old Testament imagery: Israel as a woman in travail who hides to escape anger and is pursued by a dragon (Isa. 26:17–27:1); Zion or Jerusalem has travailed (Isa. 66:7-13); the Sinai wilderness as a place Israel was brought by God to escape Egypt (Exod. 19:1-6); wrath as a river (Isa. 59:19); believers as ruling with a rod of iron (Ps. 2:9; Rev. 2:26-28; 19:15).

61. For example, Bonaventura Rinaldi, *Mary of Nazareth: Myth or History?* (Westminster: Newman, 1966), pp. 153-56.

62. Clodovis Boff, "Toward a Social Mariology," in *Many Faces,* ed. Irarrazabal, Ross, and Wacker, pp. 44-46, 48; Irarrazabal, "Mary in Latin American Christianity," in *Many Faces,* ed. Irarrazabal, Ross, and Wacker, p. 99.

(9) do not discuss personal problems outside the home; and (10) do not change those things that make you unhappy that you can realistically change.[63] *La Madre Dolorosa,* the suffering Mary as a mother with seven swords piercing her heart, is symbolic of this view of Mary.[64]

Since Vatican II, the Magnificat has become instead the emblem of a social Mariology, "Our Lady of Liberation," a Mary who is prophetic and liberating but usually nonviolent.[65] For example, María Pilar Aquino says, "In the base communities [of Latin America] Mary is seen in terms of commitment to the restoration of justice and the affirmation of hope. She gives new meaning to the existence of the people of God, because in her own person she ratifies God's compassion and power to turn the suffering of the poor and oppressed into joy and abundance." Some Latin Americans observe that there is a gap between popular devotion and the New Testament biblical sources. A new figure of Mary is emerging, "one that is prophetic and liberating, committed to the struggle for justice, faithful to her God and her people."[66] The reversal of positions in Luke 1:52-53 might be emphasized: God put down the mighty but also "exalted them of low degree. He hath filled the hungry with good things; and the rich he hath sent empty away" (KJV). Mary has always been a symbol of public charity, but now she is a proponent of social change as well, especially of improvement of the poor, and, if necessary, restriction of the rich.[67]

Mary is loved and ever-present in the lives of women in Latin America. Every Catholic schoolgirl is exposed to at least one of the

---

63. Lozano-Díaz, *Blessed One,* pp. 90-91; Irarrazabal, "Mary in Latin American Christianity," in *Many Faces,* ed. Irarrazabal, Ross, and Wacker, pp. 97-98, 100; Rosa Maria Gil and Carmen Inoa Vazquez, *The Maria Paradox: How Latinas Can Merge Old World Traditions with New World Self-Esteem* (New York: Putnam's, 1996), p. 8.

64. Rodriguez, "Tonanzin Guadalupe," in *Many Faces,* ed. Irarrazabal, Ross, and Wacker, p. 106.

65. Boff, "Toward a Social Mariology," in *Many Faces,* ed. Irarrazabal, Ross, and Wacker, pp. 44, 48, 50-51.

66. María Pilar Aquino, *Our Cry for Life: Feminist Theology from Latin America,* trans. Dinah Livingstone (Maryknoll: Orbis, 1993), pp. 172, 175.

67. Boff, "Toward a Social Mariology," in *Many Faces,* ed. Irarrazabal, Ross, and Wacker, pp. 45-46; Irarrazabal, "Mary in Latin American Christianity," in *Many Faces,* ed. Irarrazabal, Ross, and Wacker, p. 100; Rodriguez, "Tonanzin Guadalupe," in *Many Faces,* ed. Irarrazabal, Ross, and Wacker, p. 113; C. Hugo Zorrilla, "The Magnificat: Song of Justice," in *Conflict and Context: Hermeneutics in the Americas,* ed. Mark Lau Branson and C. René Padilla (Grand Rapids: Eerdmans, 1986): 220-37.

many Marian images or apparitions. Even Protestants recognize Guadalupe (the Mexican Mary) as a cultural symbol. Mary is a symbol especially for women and mothers in their daily life in Latin America.[68] An interpreter's emphasis affects her or his differences in understanding Christ. Mary may be construed as the liberator, as was her Son; the suffering servant, as was her Son; the conqueror, as was her Son; but *not* as the intercessor, as is her Son.

For Further Reading

García, Alberto Lázaro. *Cristología. Cristo Jesús: Centro y Praxis del Pueblo de Dios.* St. Louis: Editorial Concordia, 2006.

Gaventa, Beverly Roberts, and Cynthia L. Rigby, eds. *Blessed One: Protestant Perspectives on Mary.* Louisville: Westminster John Knox, 2002.

Geisler, Norman, and Ralph E. MacKenzie. "Mariology." In *Roman Catholics and Evangelicals: Agreements and Differences,* pp. 299-330. Grand Rapids: Baker, 1995.

González, Antonio. *The Gospel of Faith and Justice.* Maryknoll: Orbis, 2005.

González, Justo L. *Mañana: Christian Theology from a Hispanic Perspective.* Nashville: Abingdon, 1990.

Irarrazabal, Diego, Susan Ross, and Marie-Theres Wacker, eds. *The Many Faces of Mary.* Concilium 2008/4. London: SCM, 2008.

Johnson, Elizabeth A. "Mary as Mediatrix." In *The One Mediator, the Saints, and Mary: Lutherans and Catholics in Dialogue VIII,* edited by H. George Anderson, J. Francis Stafford, and Joseph A. Burgess, pp. 311-26. Minneapolis: Augsburg, 1992.

Some New Testament passages on contemporary Christology significant for Latin American scholars:

Jesus Christ as mediator: 1 Timothy 2:5-6
Jesus Christ as liberator of the oppressed and promoter of God's reign: Gospel of Luke 4:18-19; 5:29-32, 36-39; 6:20-26; 7:36–8:1

---

68. Carmiña Navia Velasco, "Mary of Nazareth Revisited," in *Many Faces,* ed. Irarrazabal, Ross, and Wacker, p. 19; Rodriguez, "Tonanzin Guadalupe," in *Many Faces,* ed. Irarrazabal, Ross, and Wacker, p. 106; Irarrazabal, "Mary in Latin American Christianity," in *Many Faces,* ed. Irarrazabal, Ross, and Wacker, pp. 97-98.

CHAPTER 7

Christology and Cultus in 1 Peter: An African (Kenyan) Appraisal

ANDREW M. MBUVI

Introduction

Several cultic images are used in 1 Peter — sacrifice, temple, priest-hood — to present the person and work of Jesus in relationship to the Petrine community.[1] Indeed, 1 Peter begins with a sacrificial expression of defining the believers as having been "sprinkled" with the blood of Jesus Christ (1:2). One question that could be asked is how the Petrine community would have understood the person and the work of Jesus given the letter's rather strong use of cultic imagery and language. Related to this would also be how this Petrine perspective would fit with Chalcedon's formulations of the person and work of Jesus Christ.

This language of blood and sacrifice, and its related aspects of purity, is sprinkled throughout the letter of 1 Peter and practically begs to be read in tandem with cultures where the notion of animal (and in some instances human) sacrifice played (and continues to play) a significant role in religious rites.[2] Many African communities practiced (and some

---

1. By cultic I mean the sacrificial system of animals that used to take place in the temple in Jerusalem. Without the temple, which was destroyed by the Romans in 70 CE, there were no more sacrifices but the language that had been used about it was transformed to talk about spiritual sacrifices (e.g., 1 Pet. 1:2; 2:8-12).

2. Gerhard Lindblom, *The Akamba of British East Africa: An Ethnological Monograph*, 2nd ed. (New York: Negro Universities Press, 1969).

My colleague at Shaw, Mike Broadway, read an earlier draft of this essay and gave very insightful responses and suggestions.

continue to practice today) animal sacrifices for various religious purposes, including prayer, cleansing and purification rites, thanksgiving,
protection from malevolent spirits, and birth rites. With these elements
in mind, one wonders whether beginning the presentation of the gospel
message, as most Western missionaries did in sub-Saharan Africa, with
the assumptions of the Chalcedonian Creed, created a "biased" perspective about how to understand the person and work of Jesus Christ.[3]

When foreign missionaries failed to understand African religious
cosmology (much less to regard it positively), and to incorporate African idioms that could communicate the gospel message of Jesus Christ
in ways relevant to the African mindset, they imposed culturally Western idioms that never fully embraced the totality of African religious
reality.[4] This was perhaps motivated in part by a European sense of
superiority based on the racist evolutionary science of the day, but
also by a certain interpretation of such a texts as 1 Peter 1:18-22: "For
you know that it was not with perishable things such as silver or gold
that you were redeemed from *the empty way of life handed down to you
from your forefathers/ancestors*" (NIV).[5] Yet African converts to Christianity, especially those with no formal Western education, automatically
interpreted their new religion through the lens of their African cosmological reality and not the Neoplatonic thought embedded in Western
Christian creeds.[6]

Perhaps a more fruitful endeavor would be using such cultic connections already established and intricately developed in such works
as 1 Peter, which find strong parallels in some African communities. I
am careful not to simply point an accusatory finger at the missionaries
because, in spite of what one may consider their shortcomings, the
vibrancy of African Christianity today owes a lot to those men and
women who left family, friends, and homes, and sometimes sacrificed

3. Robert Schreiter, *Constructing Local Theologies* (Maryknoll: Orbis, 1985), p. ix.
With emergence of non-Western theologies, "Western theologians came to the realization that their own theology has just as much sociocultural bias as any other."
4. This is a point that has been made in virtually all studies of the role of missionaries in sub-Saharan Africa.
5. A simplistic equation of the African religions with the Greco-Roman religion
that most likely formed the background of this passage would be misleading and
shortsighted, as it would fail to appreciate that other perspectives on the backgrounds
of converts are also present in the New Testament (e.g., Acts 17).
6. J. N. K. Mugambi, *Christianity and African Culture* (Nairobi: Acton, 1989), p. 50.

their lives to be buried in African soil, in order to bring the gospel message to the African continent.[7] Nevertheless, one cannot overlook the fact that an overarching condemnation of *religio Africana* as heathenish and devilish and, therefore, subject to obliteration and replacement with culturally Western Christian notions, was a byproduct of Western missionary hubris that was part and parcel of the European colonialism enterprise in Africa.[8]

Kwame Bediako points to two aspects of African missionary encounter that created a theological quandary for the African convert to Christianity: (1) European ethnocentrism that denigrated the African religion, worldview, and culture, and (2) the resultant eradication of religious tradition, memory, and identity. To find their identity, African Christians would have to reconnect with their past.[9] And in order to have a relevant African theology and Christology, they would have to construct them within an African idiom and religious reality.[10] The result has been a concerted cry for the redemption of the African religious reality, by African scholars, as a legitimate storehouse of spirituality that *complements* rather than *contradicts* the biblical worldview.[11]

---

7. See Lamin Sanneh, *Translating the Message: The Missionary Impact on Culture* (Maryknoll: Orbis, 1989), who shows that Christianity in Africa only thrived after the Bible had been translated into African languages and was then fully embraced by those communities as an expression of their own religion in their own idiom.

8. Albert Schweitzer, the eminent German scholar, doctor, and missionary to Lambaréné Gabon, Central West Africa, in the early part of the twentieth century probably typifies the European missionary attitudes to Africa and Africans. In spite of his sacrificial humanitarian and medical services in Lambaréné, Schweitzer's attitude toward the African people he came to serve was pejorative and racist ("The African is my brother — but he is my younger brother by several centuries," *The Observer* [1955]: 10-23). While Schweitzer is known to have assailed colonialism for its mistreatment of the colonized on the basis of difference (cultural or skin color) before leaving Germany for Lambaréné as a medical missionary, these remarks about Africans as "younger brothers" were made only after he had spent considerable time with the Africans in close proximity. He is also said to have repudiated these remarks later.

9. Mercy A. Oduyoye, *Hearing and Knowing: Theological Reflections on Christianity in Africa* (New York: Orbis, 1986), p. 10, agrees when she states that "Any theology that hopes to be relevant [in Africa] will have to take into account the theological presuppositions that underlie the African worldview and social organization." For this to happen, "the people's primal religion has to be related to and grounded in the community's daily life" (pp. 23-24).

10. Sanneh, *Translating the Message*, pp. 172-90.

11. Mugambi, *Christianity and African Culture*, pp. 33-34.

Andrew M. Mbuvi

Colonial and Postcolonial African Response
to the Western Missionary Enterprise

I can delineate in a continuum at least three primary reactions to missions in Africa. First, initial African converts to Christianity, in their zeal to please their Western "masters," totally rejected their African religion and culture. But since the religious aspect of life in African spirituality cannot be conveniently demarcated from other aspects of life, permeating virtually every aspect of life, this initial radical rejection of their past would hound the African converts, many of whom in times of crisis would find themselves reverting to African religious rituals and practices.[12]

Second was the formation of African initiated churches (AICs) in reaction to perceived significant contradictions between their interpretation of the Bible, when they read it for themselves, and how the Western missionaries interpreted it.[13] The biggest concern for such groups was that they observed within the biblical narratives and teachings aspects and elements that were fairly closely aligned to their African worldview but which either the missionaries interpreted differently or failed to mention at all (e.g., polygamy).[14]

The third line of response was the largely postcolonial scholarly rejoinder by African Christian theologians. They have sought to counter

12. African novels are an excellent resource for stories that depict this transition and subsequent struggles. See especially the Heinemann's African Writers series published in London with such works as Chinua Achebe's *Things Fall Apart* (1958), *No Longer at Ease* (1960), and *Arrow of God* (1964); Ngugi wa Thiongo's *The River Between* (1965), *Weep Not Child* (1964), and *A Grain of Wheat* (1967); and Mongo Beti's *Le Pauvre Christ de Bomba* (1956) (English translation: *The Poor Christ of Bomba*).

13. Perhaps this instance would clearly explain the conflicting perception of Western missionaries. The Africans who ended up forming the independent churches were able to read the Bible in their languages because the missionaries had labored to do the translations and to teach them how to read. They could only criticize and disagree with the missionaries' perspectives because they had benefited from the missionary education and translation projects. The same is true for African novelists and theologians.

14. While a subject like polygamy did become a hot button subject between Western missionaries and African Christianity, the practice of polygamy was hardly as widespread as the attention it garnered. It was probably the easiest way to show the clear contrast of a Western worldview that was so radically monogamist emerging out of Victorian conservatism and an African culture that seemed to reflect the polar opposite.

the missionary caricature of African religious reality by publishing their own research, which has argued that the African religious past was not only compatible with biblical teachings and worldviews, but may even have been complex enough to serve as a sufficient platform in preparation for the gospel message that would eventually be brought by Western missionaries.[15] They have also sought to expose the missionaries' complacency, duplicity, and collusion with the racially and economically motivated European colonizing of Africa.

More recently, the African theological scenario can be characterized as pluriform and dynamic, guided by a desire to respond to the politico-socio-economic-cultural concerns of the African community. There is, for example, a growing body of theological reflection championed by Musa W. Dube that has focused on providing an African biblical premise for doing theology in the midst of the AIDS epidemic in Africa.[16] Other studies have explored the theological implication of AICs, the growth of Pentecostal churches, the emergence of the prosperity gospel, and the phenomenon of mega-churches in Africa.[17] Emmanuel Katongole's African Theology Today series and M. Dube, A. M. Mbuvi, and D. Muwayesango's *Postcolonial Perspectives in African Biblical Interpretations* showcase this growing diversity.[18]

How Does Christology Figure in This African Scenario?

A quick survey of African theological scholarship reflects that Christology has undoubtedly been the central subject of the mod-

15. John S. Mbiti's *"Preparatio Evangelica"* concept. See also E. Bolaji Idowu, *Olodumare: God in Yoruba Belief* (London: Longmans, 1962), and Mbiti, *African Traditional Religion: A Definition* (London: SCM, 1973); Mbiti, *African Philosophy and Religion* (London: Heinemann, 1969).

16. Musa W. Dube, *The HIV and AIDS Bible: Selected Essays* (Scranton: University of Scranton Press, 2008); Dube, *Theology in the HIV and AIDS Era Series* (Geneva: World Council of Churches, 2007).

17. Introduction to *A Study of African Independent Churches* (Gweru, Zimbabwe: Mambo, 1987); John S. Pobee and Gabriel Ositelu II, *African Initiatives in Christianity* (Geneva: World Council of Churches, 1998).

18. Emmanuel Katongole, ed., *African Theology Today*, vol. 1 (Scranton: University of Scranton Press, 2002), especially chapter 1, Chris Ukachukwu Manus, "Methodological Approaches in Contemporary African Biblical Scholarship: The Case of West Africa," pp. 1-22.

ern African theological discourse of the past quarter century or so.[19] However, it bears reminding that African connections with Christianity go all the way back to the New Testament itself (Acts 8:26-40), and claims can be made to such historical figures as Origen, Clement of Alexandria, Tertullian, Cyprian of Carthage, and Augustine of Hippo as African theologians.[20] However, their theological trajectory contributed to much of what is today Western theology and not necessarily to recent sub-Saharan African theological development.[21] One may distinguish at least three trends that have characterized Christological conversation in African beginning with writings from the 1960s (the period of independence from colonialism for most African nations) to the present.

The initial phase starting in the 1960s was largely characterized by theology proper, where the concern was to redeem the African conception of God that had essentially been demonized and tarnished in the wake of the Western missionary enterprise in sub Saharan Africa.[22] Works of such luminaries of African theology as John Mbiti of Kenya, Bolaji Idowu of Nigeria, J. B. Danquah of Ghana, Harry Sawyerr of Sierra Leone, Mulago gwa Cikala of the Democratic Republic of Congo, G. M. Setiloane of South Africa, and Kwame Bediako of Gha-

19. C. U. Manus, "African Christologies: The Centrepiece of African Christian Theology," *Zeitschrift für Missionswissenschaft und Religionswissenschaft* 82 (1998): 3-23; Charles Sarpong Aye-Addo, "Akan Christology: An Analysis of the Christologies of John S. Pobee and Kwame Bediako in Conversation with the Theology of Karl Barth" (Ph.D. diss., Drew University, 2011).

20. C. F. Hallencreutz, "From Julius Africanus to Augustine the African: A Forgotten Link in Early African Theology," *Zambezia* 15 (1988): 1-25.

21. Thomas C. Oden, *How Africa Shaped the Christian Mind: Rediscovering the African Seedbed of Western Christianity* (Downers Grove: InterVarsity, 2007). Coptic and Ethiopic traditions are African and originated in the same region and may have influenced some of these early theologians.

22. This is not a naïve and blanket statement of blame on missionaries as it is clear to any observant person that the diverse characteristics of Western missionaries and their sending organizations produced different results in different African communities. Indeed, one of the major writings that on the whole defended a positive assessment of African religious worldview – no matter its shortcomings of trying to place African (Bantu) religions within a Western philosophical framework – was the work of the Belgian missionary to Congo Placid Tempels's *La Philosophie Bantoue* (Paris: Présence Africaine, 1949). See also John Mbiti's assessment of the impact of Western missionaries in Africa, both positive and negative: *African Religions and Philosophy* (London: Heinemann, 1969), p. 236.

na, just to name a few, played key roles in legitimizing conceptions of deity by African Christian scholars, making them, at once, African and Christian.[23] Even though his major works are from the 1980s and 1990s, I place Bediako here since he explains that his perception of African theology in the post-missionary era "is as much a response to missionary underestimation of the value of African pre-Christian tradition, as it is an *African* theological response to the specific and more enduring issues of how the Christian Gospel relates to African culture."[24]

The second stream was Christology proper. Following John Mbiti's lament four decades ago that there was a lack of distinctly African Christology, the following three decades saw an explosion of Christological studies that sought to give a uniquely African image of Jesus.[25] The focus was largely on the study of AICs, which prompted analysis of their distinct appropriations of the words and works of Jesus.[26] Kofi Appiah-Kubi of Ghana identifies what he sees as the three central Christological functions in these communities: Jesus as mediator between humans and God, much in the same way African ancestors and spirits were; Jesus as liberator from oppression; and Jesus as healer of sicknesses.[27] Robert Schreiter, in *Faces of Jesus in Africa,* has gathered together, under the broad topics of enculturation and liberation,[28] Christological perspectives that include Master of Initiation,[29] Elder

23. John S. Mbiti, *Concepts of God in Africa* (London: SPCK, 1970); Idowu, *Olodumare;* Harry Sawyerr, *Creative Evangelism: Towards a New Christian Encounter with Africa* (London: Lutterworth, 1968); J. B. Danquah, *The Akan Concept of God* (London: Frank Cass, 1968); Mulago gwa Cikala, *Un Visage Africain du Christianisme, l'Union Vitale Bantu Face À l'Unité Vitale Ecclésiale* (Paris: Présence-Africaine, 1965); G. M. Setiloane, *The Image of God among the Sotho-Tswana* (Rotterdam: A. A. Balkema, 1976).

24. Kwame Bediako, *Theology and Identity: The Impact of Culture upon Christian Thought in the Second Century and Modern Africa* (Oxford: Regnum, 1992), p. xvii.

25. John S. Mbiti, *Bible and Theology in African Christianity* (Nairobi: Oxford University Press, 1986), pp. 176-227.

26. Cf. Pobee and Ositelu II, *African Initiatives in Christianity* .

27. Kofi Appiah-Kubi, "Jesus Christ: Some Christological Aspects from African Perspectives," in *African and Asian Contributions to Contemporary Theology,* ed. John S. Mbiti (Geneva: World Council of Churches, 1976), pp. 51-65.

28. Robert Schreiter, ed., *Faces of Jesus in Africa* (Maryknoll: Orbis, 1991).

29. A. Sanon, "Jésus, Maître d'initiation," in *Chemins de la Christologie Africaine,* ed. F. Kabasélé, J. Doré, and R. Luneau (Paris: Desclée, 1986), pp. 143-66; Sanon, *Enraciner L'évangile: Initiations Africaines et Pédagogie de la Foi* (Paris: Cerf, 1982).

Brother,[30] Great Ancestor,[31] Great Chief,[32] Ideal Elder,[33] Liberator, Mediator, King,[34] and Healer.[35] Thus, the struggle had commenced to make the person of Jesus relevant to the everyday realities of Africans. Diane Stinton, who adds the categories of Jesus as life-giver and Jesus as leader (chieftaincy) to the list, concludes in her study that the notions of health, mediation, and liberation stand as the central elements in African Christology.[36] It follows that Jesus has been understood in light of societal roles that would make him more relevant to the worldviews of the various African communities.

A third, and more conservative African response has been driven by Western evangelicalism's strong influence on church leadership as reflected in Byang Kato's work, and reprised but better grounded

30. François Kabasélé, "Christ as Ancestor and Elder Brother," in *Faces of Jesus in Africa*, ed Schreiter, pp. 116-27.

31. Charles Nyamiti, *Christ as Our Ancestor: Christology from an African Perspective* (Gweru, Zimbabwe: Mambo, 1984). Bénézet Bujo, *African Theology in Its Social Context* (Maryknoll: Orbis, 1992), uses the term "Proto-Ancestor" since for him, there should not be assumption of any equality of Jesus with ancestors but Jesus is the ancestor par excellence. Rodney Reed and Gift Mtukwa, "Christ Our Ancestor: African Christology and the Danger of Contextualization," *Wesleyan Theological Journal* 45, no. 1 (2010): 144-64, point out concerns about this Christological category: (1) there is a danger that conceiving of Christ as an Ancestor may actually encourage people to think of their ancestors as intermediaries, while the Scriptures clearly teach that we have just one mediator between God and humanity – Jesus Christ; (2) Africans may be encouraged to actually worship the ancestors and place them in a position that only God should hold by offering to them sacrifices and oblations; (3) it seems to make Jesus just another human being rather than God-incarnate; (4) the Scriptures clearly condemn necromancy (consulting the dead) and that is precisely what happens in much focus on the ancestors. To all these challenges, Oduyoye, *Hearing and Knowing*, 9, poses this question: "Why is the relationship of the African with the "living-dead" any more idolatrous than the observances of All Souls Day and All Saints Day?"

32. J. S. Pobee, *Toward an African Theology* (Nashville: Abingdon, 1979), pp. 94-98. Bujo, *African Theology in Its Social Context*, uses the term "Proto-Ancestor" to dispel any possibility that the ancestors and Jesus could be equals. Jesus as the proto ancestor not only *precedes* but also *supersedes* the "ancestors."

33. P. N. Wachege, *Jesus Christ Our Muthamaki (Ideal Elder): An African Christological Study Based on the Agikuyu Understanding of Elder* (Nairobi: Phoenix, 1992).

34. Chris U. Manus, *Christ, the African King: New Testament Christology* (Frankfurt am Main: Peter Lang, 1993).

35. Cécé Kolié, "Jesus the Healer?" in *Faces of Jesus*, ed. Schreiter, pp. 128-50.

36. Diane Stinton, *Jesus of Africa: Voices of Contemporary African Christology* (Maryknoll: Orbis, 2004). Cf. also Clifton R. Clarke, *African Christology: Jesus in Post-Missionary African Christianity* (Eugene, Ore.: Pickwick, 2010).

in Kombo's Trinitarian reflection.[37] However, this response has been heavily criticized, especially by Bediako.[38]

This essay makes initial forays into the topic of Christology with the hope of enriching our understanding of 1 Peter's use of cultic language through comparison with select African cultic practices. This involves analysis of how 1 Peter uses the Jewish *cultus* within a first-century Christian context to relate it to the religious life of the Gentile believers to whom the letter is addressed.[39] So where cultic language is used, these passages will be read in light of some pre-Christian cultic religious practices of the Akamba of Kenya, the community to which I belong. The cultic traditions make a comparative and analytical study between the cultic language in 1 Peter and that of the Akamba on practice of sacrifices, a tantalizing prospect. As Mercy Amba Oduyoye and others have pointed out, there is a need to relate the Christian message to the traditions and indigenous religions of recipient African communities.[40]

Christology and *Cultus* in 1 Peter

I have argued elsewhere that 1 Peter's prevalent vocabulary of holiness (*hagiasmos* — 1:2, 15-16; 2:5, 9; 3:5-7), with its close link to the *cultus*, calls for every facet of life to be subject to holiness since the premise of holiness is God who calls *all* to holiness in *all* aspects of life.[41] "It is a holiness that is grounded in their involvement in this world which must find its outworking in the midst of all the challenges of pilgrim life."[42] This all-encompassing understanding fits well with the African

37. Byang Kato, *Theological Pitfall in Africa* (Nairobi: Evangel, 1975). See also Trinitarian studies by Mika Vähäkangas in *African Theology Today*, ed. Katongole, pp. 69-84; James H. Kombo, *The Doctrine of God in African Christian Thought: The Holy Trinity, Theological Hermeneutics, and the African Intellectual Culture* (Leiden: Brill, 2007).

38. Bediako, *Theology and Identity*, pp. 387-425.

39. In line with most of the recent scholarship on 1 Peter, I hold the position that the original audience is Gentile, but probably made up largely of initial converts to Judaism who elsewhere in the New Testament are referred to as "god-fearers" (Acts 10:2, 22; 13:36; 17:4, 17). Cf. Andrew Mbuvi, *Temple, Exile and Identity in 1 Peter* (London: T&T Clark, 2007), p. 6.

40. Oduyoye, *Hearing and Knowing*, p. 23.

41. Mbuvi, *Temple, Exile, and Identity*, pp. 80-83.

42. Mbuvi, *Temple, Exile, and Identity*, p. 82.

religious perspective, which assumes that everything that happens in life has a spiritual cause.[43] Indeed, Mbiti's famous maxim that "Africans are notoriously religious" would then be a welcome perspective for reading 1 Peter's injunctions to holiness since it seems to have similar expectations of its readers.[44]

Second, Western individualistic understanding of salvation "in the heart" contrasts with the African notion of salvation in the community by overcoming the spirit world.[45] As Edward Fasholé-Luke points out, sacrifice in Africa, as a means of atonement, necessitates communal allegiance that is inseparable from the cultic exercise.

> The object of ritual and cultic acts is to sustain the social and the cosmic order — the two can hardly be separated. So the means of fellowship are not meant to provide for the communion with the gods but to enlist these powers in support of the community. Rituals are primarily of two kinds: sacrifices and magic. Sacrifices and libations are meant to appeal to the goodwill of the gods or spirits; magic (both white and black) seeks to manipulate in more mechanical ways forces that cannot be dealt with by appeal.[46]

For this reason, the book of Hebrews has attracted significant attention from African theologians because it provides readymade cultural and religious categories that align fairly well with those found in African communities: high priest-priests, angels-spirits, ancestors, sacrifices, and the like.[47] However, a book such as 1 Peter, which also shares some elements with Hebrews, has hardly been explored for its distinct elements that could serve as grounds for developing a theological framework that is consistent with African

43. Bolaji Idowu, *African Traditional Religion: A Definition* (London: SCM, 1973).

44. Mbiti, *African Religions and Philosophy*, p. 1.

45. William A. Dyrness, *Learning about Theology from the Third World* (Grand Rapids: Zondervan, 1990), p. 165.

46. Dyrness, *Learning about Theology*, p. 51.

47. Peter Nyende, "Hebrews' Christology and Its Contemporary Apprehension in Africa," *Neotestamentica* 41 (2007): 361-81. See also a distillation of his dissertation from University of Edinburgh: Nyende, "Why Bother with Hebrews? An African Perspective," *Heythrop Journal* 46 (2005): 512-24. David Ekem, "The Author of Hebrews: A Great Dialogue Partner and Interpreter of the Gospel," *AICMAR Bulletin* 3 (2004): 1-25; Kwame Bediako, "Jesus in African Culture: A Ghanaian Perspective," in William A. Dyrness, *Emerging Voices in Global Theology* (Grand Rapids: Zondervan, 1994), pp. 93-126.

religiosity. First Peter itself cannot be said to have a Christology that can be easily labeled, but it does develop "cultic images" that foreground the work of Jesus and that can allow for a formulation of a Petrine Christology.[48]

As Paul Achtemeier points out, "the Christology in 1 Peter is better conceived of as a series of images than a coherent disquisition on the nature of Christ,"[49] and therefore it is important to look at all the passages that paint a picture of Jesus in cultic terms to get a more complete sense of Petrine Christology.[50] The different first-century contexts of recipient communities in the New Testament evoked different images of Jesus. In the Gospels, for example, Jesus is the Good Shepherd, Son of God, Son of Man, and the Vine, just to name a few. All these metaphors try to contextualize for the audiences what might be otherwise too complex or foreign to grasp.[51] In 1 Peter, one can delineate some images of Jesus as the "perfect sacrifice" (1:2-3; 2:18-22), the "chief cornerstone-capstone" (2:4-10), "the divine warrior" or "triumphant victor" (3:18-19), and the "shepherd and overseer of souls" (3:25; 4:4). We will look at some of these passages more closely.

1 Peter 1:2

The metaphor of blood sprinkling in 1 Peter 1:2 evokes Old Testament sacrificial practices where animal blood was sprinkled for diverse reasons, including protection from calamities such as the blood on the doorposts to stop the angel of death (Exodus 12), establishing a covenant with God (Exodus 24), purification of the people (Numbers 19), or as part of an annual tradition at *Yom Kippur* (Day of Atonement) in which blood was sprinkled on the mercy seat or atonement cover of

---

48. Paul Achtemeier, "Christology in 1 Peter: Some Reflections," in *Who Do You Say That I Am? Essays on Christology,* ed. Mark Allan Powell, Jack Dean Kingsbury, and David R. Bauer (Nashville: Westminster John Knox, 1999), p. 141.

49. Achtemeier, "Christology in 1 Peter," in *Who Do You Say That I Am?* ed. Powell, Kingsbury, and Bauer, p. 140.

50. Leonhard Goppelt, *A Commentary on 1 Peter,* trans. J. E. Alsup (Grand Rapids: Eerdmans, 1993), p. 247. Goppelt identifies at least four passages in 1 Peter that are clearly Christological in nature (1:18-21; 2:22-25; 3:18-22, 4:6). I would like to add 1:2, 3 and 2:4-10 to this list.

51. Dyrness, *Learning about Theology,* pp. 164-65.

the ark of the covenant (Lev. 16:11-19).[52] While libations of beer, water, and other drinks were common in most African communities, blood sprinkling was generally rare and usually preserved for more serious situations afflicting the community, including droughts, floods, and plagues.[53]

In such cases, the community elders or spiritual leaders would sprinkle a domestic sacrificial animal's blood at the deity's shrine or a designated location. In addition, blood sprinkling was sometimes done by priests, medicine men, or medicine women during healing sessions.[54] Since the notion of sin in African religious thought is primarily from the vantage point of relational and moral offense to others or to the deity than it is legal, the necessity of Jesus' human sacrifice would communicate the gravity of the offense against God that needed to be appeased.[55]

Similarities are doubtless present in Israelite and African understandings of sacrifice.[56] For example, both used animal blood offerings, plant or grain offerings, and even human sacrifice. The idea that sacrifices are a means of interceding with the divine when the community is facing a catastrophe is true for both communities and would be fertile ground to explain the need for the sacrificial death of Jesus in cultic terms that would be familiar to the African religious outlook.[57] Perhaps more jarring for a Western individual in the nine-

52. Joseph Gutmann, "The Strange History of the *Kapporet* Ritual," *Zeitschrift für die Alttestamentliche Wissenschaft* 112 (2000): 624-26.

53. Lindblom, *Akamba*, pp. 224-25: "Krapf tells how the Akamba said that on account of his arrival [a strange pale-colored individual], the rains would not come, for which reason they killed a sheep and sprinkled the path with its blood."

54. I remember witnessing a special ceremony for my grandfather to bless his children, grandchildren, and great-grandchildren. He drank water and sprayed (sprinkled) it from his mouth to eagerly waiting kin who, owing to the number, scrambled to get the drops of water.

55. J. Omosade Awolalu, "Sin and Its Removal in African Traditional Religion," *Journal of the American Academy of Religion* 44 (1976): 275-87.

56. Christopher Simon Mngadi, *The Significance of Blood in the Old Testament Sacrifices and Its Relevance for the Church in Africa* (Pretoria: University of South Africa, 1981); Knut Holter, "The First Generation of African Old Testament Scholars: African Concerns and Western influences," in *African Identities and World Christianity in the Twentieth Century*, ed. Klaus Koschorke and Jens Holger Schjørring (Gottingen: Ottoharassowitz GmbH & Co. KG Weisbaden, 2005), pp. 149-65.

57. Justin S. Ukpong, "The Problem of God and Sacrifice in African Traditional Religion," *Journal of Religion in Africa* 14 (1983): 187-203; Ukpong, *Sacrifice: African and*

teenth century would have been encountering the existence of human sacrifice during extreme calamities in some African communities like the Akamba. However, the *Akedah* (Abraham's "sacrifice" [binding] of Isaac) in Genesis 22, or even such commands about "passing over to YHWH the first born" as found in Exodus 13:12 perhaps capture remnants of the practice of human sacrifice in early Israelite cult.[58] In fact, a recent study concludes that "human sacrifice in the Israelite cult . . . functioned . . . as a means of capital punishment through which the land and nation were cleansed."[59]

Such an understanding would have facilitated drawing on these existing connections to articulate in familiar terminology the once-and-for-all human sacrifice of Jesus. In a passage like this it would have helped the community to come to an understanding of the need to forgo the practice while maintaining the efficacy of the event by substituting Jesus.[60] Jesus is the "perfect sacrifice," requiring no further sacrifices![61] What makes him perfect? First Peter 2:20-22 explains that he was sinless, without defect, and so, a perfect gift.[62]

Biblical: A Comparative Study of Ibibio and Levitical Sacrifices (Rome: Urbaniana University Press, 1987).

58. Jason Tatlock, "The Place of Human Sacrifice in the Israelite Cult," in *Ritual and Metaphor: Sacrifice in the Bible,* ed. Christian Eberhart (Atlanta: SBL, 2011), pp. 33-48. In 1 Peter 3:21 Noah's flood pre-figures the resurrection of Jesus Christ, but it is peculiar that after using all the sacrifice language, 1 Peter does not turn to the *Akedah* as a sure connection for the interpretation of Jesus' sacrificial death.

59. Tatlock, "Place of Human Sacrifice," in *Ritual and Metaphor,* ed. Eberhart, pp. 47-48.

60. Jon Levenson, *The Death and Resurrection of the Beloved Son: The Transformation of Child Sacrifice in Judaism and Christianity* (New Haven, Conn.: Yale University Press, 1993) p. x: "In point of fact, those roles [sage and prophet], even if real, have historically been vastly less important in Christian tradition than Jesus' identity as sacrificial victim, the son handed over to death by his loving father or the lamb who takes away the sins of the world."

61. Dyrness, *Learning about Theology,* p. 165, laments that "My students in North America have always had a hard time understanding why God had to send his Son to die as blood sacrifice for sins, but they are drawn to images that portray Jesus as healing our estrangement from God. Students in Africa, by contrast, have no trouble with the idea of sacrifice, and they readily see Christ's death as placing him in the position of power with reference to God — death being commonly understood this way in Africa."

62. This was probably the reason that a child was the one sacrificed among the Akamba since not only was a child still connected to the spirit world, but she or he had not lived long enough to have failed in any responsibilities and so was perfect.

When connected to his role in the afterlife (3:18-20) the stakes are raised since now, Jesus in his post-death state, has entered the realm of the spirits and ancestors. Talking of Bantu communities, of which the Akamba are a part, François Kabasélé argues that "Christ is the Elder Brother *par excellence:* it is to him alone that offering must be made. Or again: once we know Christ, all of the offerings must henceforth be made through him. It is the eldest brother who makes an offering to the Ancestors and to the Supreme Being on behalf of the rest."[63] The shortcoming of this analysis is that it fails to incorporate the cultic elements well-developed in 1 Peter — that of Jesus himself as the perfect sacrifice. He is not simply the conduit through whom sacrifices are made. Instead, he is the perfect sacrifice that nullifies all others.[64]

1 Peter 1:18

Comparison with the lamb may more closely align this text with Exodus 12 and the Passover, which could find parallels in African animal sacrifice that were (and are) a common part of African religious practice. Certain specifications, just like the spotlessness of the Passover lamb, also accompany these sacrifices. However, reference to Jesus' precious blood would conjure thoughts of human sacrifice that was formerly practiced only in times of severe visitations, when it was necessary to propitiate the creator deity, to whom all life belongs, in an exceptional manner.[65] Among the Akamba, the child required for the

---

63. François Kabasélé in *Faces of Jesus,* ed. Schreiter, p. 122.

64. Resurrection from the dead (1 Pet. 1:3) has no African parallel. Death is transition to the spirit world with both advantages and disadvantages. Death may be salvation for the individual but not the society. Going on to the land of the dead, especially as an old person, was a good thing. Not so for a young person, which prompted reincarnations or haunting by the dead person's spirit. Names such as Musyoka and Kasyoka ("one who returns") still persist even though many people would identify with Christianity today; the notion of reincarnation still undergirds the naming. In some communities, naming after a dead relative, usually one that was beloved, anticipates that his or her spirit would be present in the newly born child. Whether the new baby counts as the same exact person that had died is unclear. Also, among the Akamba, a child is referred to a *keimu* ("little spirit") for at least about six months after birth because children originate from the spirit world and may choose to return to that world (probably a view prompted by the high mortality rate of infants).

65. Lindblom, *Akamba,* p. 224.

purpose was kidnapped, usually from the neighboring Kikuyu country. In the region around Machakos, Kenya, a child was taken from the rain clan *(mbaa-mbua),* and the mother received goats in compensation for her loss. The child was smeared with fat and buried alive with a goat at the *ithembo* (altar). Atoning sacrifice was already present in the Akamba worldview — the death of one person for the sake of the many![66] Jesus' sacrifice has to be understood within this framework in order to gain full appreciation within the Akamba cosmology.

This understanding then makes perfect sense of referring to Jesus in sacrificial terms in 1:2 and 1:18. The sacrifices made to appease or seek favor from the spirits would be here replaced by Jesus, the "human" sacrifice that appeases the spiritual world and inoculates the threat that it poses to those in the world of the living. It is true that the parallels here between the Akamba sacrificial system and the biblical text are not without exception. For example, Jesus' sacrifice does more than appease the spirit world, it triumphs over it (3:18-22), and Jesus is a willing participant, which is not the case in the Akamba sacrifice. Jesus' sacrifice, however, can be understood as a certain restoration of harmony between the spiritual and the physical worlds that installs Jesus as the ultimate authority and the perfect conduit between the realms. As such, the difference is that while the sacrifices offered had temporary effect, Jesus' personal sacrifice — a once and for all act — holds until the time will come to give account before God (4:5).

1 Peter 3:18-22; 4:6

Karen Jobes notes that this passage is considered one of the most challenging to interpret in the whole of 1 Peter and possibly in the New Testament.[67] Even the reformer Martin Luther seems to have thrown his arms up in despair, noting that "I still do not know for sure what the apostle meant."[68] Ancient reference to the passage as *descensus ad inferos* ("harrowing of hell") by Clement and Origen and attributed to the Apostles' Creed, has no historical basis since the phrase first appeared in Rufus

---

66. Lindblom, *Akamba,* p. 120.
67. Karen Jobes, *1 Peter* (Grand Rapids: Baker, 2005), p. 236.
68. Jobes, *1 Peter,* p. 236.

(400) replacing the original "and was buried."[69] This may suggest a later Greco-Roman interpretation of the understanding of the passage that has subsequently remained enshrined in today's version of the creed.

William J. Dalton's groundbreaking study of this passage undermined the *descensus* interpretation and the other ancient interpretations of the passage that had maintained that a "pre-incarnate Christ," through Noah (e.g., Augustine), had preached the "good news" to the people who died during Noah's flood.[70] Dalton instead argued for the Christological understanding of this passage that portrays Jesus as *Christus Victor* ("Victorious Christ"), who conquers the disobedient spirits (in upper heavens) and proclaims victory and their subjection in his ascension to the right hand of God in heaven.[71] Using Jewish literary background, especially 1 Enoch, Dalton equates the disobedient spirits with the fallen angels on Genesis 6 and not with human spirits.[72]

Nevertheless, the phrase "dead in the flesh, alive in spirit" has remained a *crux interpretum* for the majority of Western commentators of 1 Peter.[73] There seems to be a lot of exegetical gymnastics to align the part of being "alive in the spirit" with Jesus' *bodily* resurrected form or divine nature,[74] which is itself a problem since the phrase says "alive in the spirit" *(zōiopoieō tō pneuma)* and not "alive in the body" *(zōiopoieō tō soma),* and as such has influenced how the whole section is interpreted.[75] However, in contrast to J. S. Feinberg, who understands the phrase to mean Christ's bodily resurrection, an Akamba reading would understand the reference to mean simply that, even after going through death, Jesus was still alive in the "spirit world," where he made proclamation.[76] In the Akamba cosmology the physical and the spirit worlds interact seamlessly, and this makes such a reading quite sensible.[77]

69. Jobes, *1 Peter,* p. 241.

70. William J. Dalton, *Christ's Proclamation to the Spirits* (Rome: Pontifical Biblical Institute, 1965), p. 18.

71. Dalton, *Christ's Proclamation,* p. 118.

72. Dalton, *Christ's Proclamation,* p. 118.

73. Dalton, *Christ's Proclamation,* pp. 19-20.

74. Dalton, *Christ's Proclamation,* p. 19.

75. John H. Elliott, *1 Peter: A New Translation with Introduction and Commentary,* Anchor Bible 37B (New York: Doubleday, 2000), p. 647.

76. J. S. Feinberg, "1 Peter 3:18-20: Ancient Mythology, and the Intermediate State," *Westminster Theological Journal* 48 (1986): 315.

77. This perspective is also distinct from the early church's notion of *triduum mortis* (separation of soul and body), as the whole person can exist in the spiritual state.

Such a reading, however, remains in contrast with that of most Western scholars for whom the passage, according to Jobes, refers "either to the two spheres of Christ's existence (the earthly sphere versus the eschatological) or to two modes of his personal existence (in human form before his death and in glorified form after his resurrection)."[78] Western perspectives seem to generally perceive death as a *negative* state that has to be countered by a *positive* state of being alive in the flesh, and so they posit the resurrection or glorification as the interpretation of the phrase.[79]

In contrast, among the Akamba, vocabulary for death includes such euphemisms as *kwitwa* ("to be summoned or called" presumably by the deity or the ancestors and spirits) or *kuthumuwa* ("to rest" from earthly labors). Parallels in the Hebrew Bible include, for example, the euphemism, "resting with the fathers" (e.g., 1 Kings 2:10; 11:43; 2 Chron. 32:33). In essence then, death is not a disappearance into nothingness but a transition into a different state of being. It is a transformation from the physical (not in the Platonic sense) to a spiritual state that is in a spiritual world, very much a reflection of the physical world we live in, but invisible to the human eye. These worlds are connected not vertically but horizontally, and the boundary is porous where the ancestors and spirits (themselves really also human spirits whose identities have long been forgotten)[80] can traverse between the two worlds.[81]

Therefore, in light of how verses 18 and 19 are laid out, it makes complete sense if understood in light of the African worldview that perceives death as a *transition* to a new state of being that is neither negative nor positive, but simply different: a "spiritual" existence that can still incorporate the physical.[82] As verse 19 announces, it is in this state (spiritual state) that Jesus preached to the spirits that were in prison, following his death in the body. It is not in his resurrected state, but in his "spiritual state" that he goes (not descends) into the spiritual world of spirits and ancestors to preach.[83] Appeals to the Jewish no-

78. Jobes, *1 Peter,* p. 242. See also Elliott, *1 Peter,* pp. 650-51.

79. Achtemeier, "Christology in 1 Peter," in *Who Do You Say That I Am?* ed. Powell, Kingsbury, and Bauer, p. 141; Elliott, *1 Peter,* p. 686.

80. Mbiti, *African Religions,* p. 26.

81. Mugambi, *African Culture,* p. 51.

82. Mugambi, *African Culture,* p. 51.

83. Elliott, *1 Peter,* pp. 650-51. Diane Stinton also points out that a Christological

tion of seven heavens in order to resolve the issue are still focused on where Jesus went and not on what the spiritual state is.[84]

From an African perspective, it is Jesus "who has gone into heaven and is at God's right hand — with *angels, authorities,* and *powers* in submission to him" (v. 22). He goes into this sphere with God's power; he is able to overcome triumphantly all the threats of this world of spirits and to establish his reign even in this realm.[85] A realm that is recognized by the African worldview as source for both fortune and misfortune has been accessed by Jesus who is able to bring his message to it.[86] It is a world of "living-dead" ancestors and spirits whose intrusion into the world of the living is an accepted reality of a porous divide that was managed by sacrifice as a means to appease any perceived infringements or to seek favors. Jesus establishes authority over all spheres of life, the physical and the spiritual, making proclamation of his gospel and authority and sits on the "male hand" side of God,[87] a place of power![88] So, in this passage alone, 1 Peter has combined the images of Jesus as liberator and *Christus Victor.*

---

category such as "Christ the Ancestor" may be more popular in academic circles than it actually is on the local church level.

84. See, Dalton, *Christ's Proclamation,* and Elliott, *1 Peter,* pp. 658-60. This is not to ignore the connection of the Noah story in the passage, but maintains that the spirits there referenced are not simply angels as most scholars argue, but include the spirits of people who rebelled too. (So Wayne Grudem, *The First Epistle of Peter* [Grand Rapids: Eerdmans, 1998], pp. 215-17.)

85. Thus, Bediako, "Jesus in African Culture," in *Emerging Voices,* ed. Dyrness, p. 103: "But if Jesus has gone to the realm of the 'spirits and the gods,' so to speak, he has gone there as Lord over them in much the same way that he is Lord over us. He is therefore the Lord over the living and the dead, and over the 'living-dead,' as the ancestors are also described. He is supreme over all the 'gods' and authorities in the realm of the spirits. So he sums up in himself all their powers and cancels any terrorizing influence they might be assumed to have upon us."

86. Daniel Kasomo, "An Investigation of Sin and Evil in African Cosmology," *International Journal of Sociology and Anthropology* 1 (2009): 145-55: "In nearly all African societies, it is thought that the spirits are either the origin of evil or agents of evil. When human spirits become detached from human contact, people experience or fear them as 'evil' or 'harmful'. . . . Mystical power is neither good nor evil in itself: but when used maliciously by some individuals it is experienced as evil" (p. 147).

87. For the Akamba and most Bantu communities, the right hand is the "male hand," while the left hand is the "female hand." The Akamba traditionally buried the men lying on the right side and the women on their left. Lindblom, *Akamba,* p. 224.

88. Bediako, "Jesus in African Culture," in *Emerging Voices,* ed. Dyrness, p. 103.

Such a reading then makes sense of the reference to "spirits in prison" (v. 19) if understood in light of 4:5-6: "But they will have to give account to him who is ready to judge *the living and the dead*. For this is the reason the *gospel was preached even to those who are now dead*, so that they might be judged according to men in regard to the body, but live according to God in regard to the spirit." This would be a reference to the human spirits of ancestors, in which case the proclamation is for those who died before having a chance to hear the gospel message preached (the "living-dead" ancestors), and thus giving them an opportunity to accept the message.[89] This was a vexing concern for most early African converts to Christianity. This passage provides the possibility of comfort in knowing that the ancestors, who died before the advent of the modern missionary endeavor in Africa, still have the chance to hear the gospel of Jesus Christ.[90]

The one critique that such a reading raises for those who want to interpret Jesus in the model of ancestor is that Jesus goes into this spirit world not to dwell but to "preach" and then come back to life and into heaven. By not remaining in the spirit realm he cannot be classified as ancestor in the same respect that an African ancestor is.[91] While the ancestor can return to the physical realm only in spirit-form and in dreams, Jesus' return is in body and spirit, and in full subjugation of all spirits, angels, ancestors, and powers.

Christological images are quite variegated in 1 Peter. Nevertheless, this brief survey has shown that those images, when interpreted from an African perspective, can be fruitfully understood while being appropriated differently from the common Western readings.

---

89. So Goppelt, *1 Peter*, p. 289: "proclamation of the gospel is encountered by the dead when they are dead and that their death here, as in v. 5, is *literal*" (emphasis added). *Contra* Elliott, *1 Peter*, p. 650, who argues the spirits are "angels."

90. Interestingly, a parallel perspective could be said to have been maintained by the early church, including Cyril of Alexandria, Origen, Clement of Alexandria, Athanasius, and Gregory of Nazianzus.

91. Fergus J. King, "Angels and Ancestors: A Basis for Christology?" *Mission Studies* 11 (1994): 10-26.

Chalcedonian Definition Revisited:
Where Do the Creeds Fit in All This?

Creeds mostly seem to function simply as part of the recitation in worship among the Western missionary–planted churches in Africa, but do not seem to hold much sway beyond that.[92] By giving prominence to the Bible itself (the *word* of God), the creeds have been generally relegated to a non-influential category with the exception of perhaps the Roman Catholic Church.[93] Treating the creeds as sealed documents has meant there has not been any push to develop other elements of Christology.[94] Seen from the list of African Christological concerns outlined in this essay, it is clear that issues central to the Chalcedonian Council (the relationship of the divinity and humanity of Jesus) hardly ever show up.

For the most part, Christological writing in Africa seems to be intent on finding and creating Christological categories and issues that are pertinent to African religious concerns. Even in a passage like 3:18-22, which may invite such a conversation, the African focus instead turned to the movement of Jesus between the spiritual and the divine spheres. While it is true that the Chalcedonian Definition builds on the Nicene Creed, which does highlight the cultic aspect of Jesus being "crucified under Pontius Pilate," even there it does not explicitly connect Jesus' crucifixion to any other cultic imagery. As Clifton Clarke points out,

> The ecumenical councils, such as the ones held at Nicea AD 325 and Chalcedon AD 451, had on this basis of preserving Christian orthodoxy sought to establish a single faith throughout the empire. This,

92. John H. Leith, *Creeds of the Churches: A Reader in Christian Doctrine from the Bible to the Present*, 3rd ed. (Nashville: Westminster John Knox, 1982), p. 555.

93. Clarke, *Christology*, p. 5. The effort of those on the side of "orthodoxy" to castigate any challenges to the creeds with pronouncement of "heterodoxy" or even "heresy," has meant that these culturally limited creeds have often assumed a universal authority in Christian communities, yet may not have found much relevance in how different local communities do theology or Christology. This rigidity and resistance to interrogation or change may be more grounded in the Platonic philosophy of sense perception that is encrusted in Western education and culture.

94. Clarke, *African Christology*, pp. 1-2: "The approach to theology taken in the council of Nicea, AD 325, which declared that Jesus was *homoousios* (one in being or one in substance) with the Father, and the council of Chalcedon 451 statement that the two natures of Christ (the divine and the human) are without division or separation, is not an African approach to theology."

they thought, represented revealed truth and therefore did not recognize how their own cultural, social, and political influence would determine the shape of their Christological construction.[95]

What Clarke does not also mention is that in the fourth century (306-337), Christianity had been transformed from a minority religion in the Roman Empire to *the* imperial religion, following the conversion of Emperor Constantine. So, while prior to 313 Christianity could be characterized as having been a voice of justice and dissent against empire, afterward it had been co-opted as the state religion and partner in power, unfortunately with the very devastating results of persecuting "pagans" and heretics.[96]

Yet, creeds themselves were prompted by the encounter of Christianity with Greco-Roman culture and religion. So, if Christologies were from the very beginning the products of the encounter of the gospel message with different cultures, then one wonders whether there is need to revisit the creeds themselves, given the more recent Christian encounters within African, Asian, and Latin American cultures.

For Further Reading

Achtemeier, Paul. "Christology in 1 Peter: Some Reflections." In *Who Do You Say That I Am? Essays on Christology,* edited by Mark Allan Powell, Jack Dean Kingsbury, and David R. Bauer, pp. 140-53. Nashville: Westminster John Knox, 1999.

Bediako, Kwame. *Theology and Identity: The Impact of Culture upon Christian Thought in the Second Century and Modern Africa.* Oxford: Regnum, 1992.

Elliott, John H. *1 Peter: A New Translation with Introduction and Commentary.* Anchor Bible 37B. New York: Doubleday, 2000.

Katongole, Emmanuel, ed. *African Theology Today.* Vol. 1. Scranton: University of Scranton Press, 2002.

Mbiti, John S. *African Religions and Philosophy.* London: Heinemann, 1969.

Mugambi, J. N. K. *Christianity and African Culture.* Nairobi: Acton, 1989.

Schreiter, Robert, ed. *Faces of Jesus in Africa.* Maryknoll: Orbis, 1991.

95. Clarke, *African Christology,* p. 6.
96. Samuel Lieu and Dominic Montserrat, eds., *From Constantine to Julian: A Source History* (London: Routledge, 1996), pp. 213-14.

CHAPTER 8

Biblical Christologies of the Global Church: Beyond Chalcedon? Toward a Fully Christian and Fully Cultural Theology

K. K. YEO

Introduction

Understanding who Jesus Christ was in Scripture has been a vexing problem ever since Jesus asked of his disciples: "Who do you say that I am?" (Matt. 16:15; Mark 8:29; Luke 9:20). The world has changed, but the theological challenge remains the same: understanding who Jesus was and who Christ is to readers in 50-100 (New Testament times), 325 (Council of Nicaea: the unity of nature between Christ and God), 451 (Council of Chalcedon: two natures in one person of Christ), and 2014 (these essays from the Western and Majority Worlds). With the rise of historical methods, new hermeneutics, and voices from the Majority World,[1] it is evident from the assortment of Christologies in the biblical witnesses that while Jesus is singular, Christology is plural, as the essays in this volume also reveal.

All contributors to this collection face two issues: first, the unity and diversity of biblical Christologies — that is, the question of the center (organizing principle) and the unity (underlying aspect in the diversity) of the Bible — and second, the meaning and task of theology

1. All Christologies (understandings of Christ) have "soteriological biases" regarding how Christ will fulfill various human needs or predicaments. Philipp Melanchthon says, "To know Christ is to know his benefits" (cited in Wilhelm Pauck, ed., *Melanchthon and Bucer*, Library of Christian Classics 19 [Philadelphia: Westminster, 1969], p. 21). It is important, however, that we know the person of Christ through his work in our lives (i.e., Christological anthropology), not through our experience (i.e., anthropological Christology).

– that is, the method and content of Christology as well as Scripture-reading. I begin with a hermeneutical question regarding the unity-diversity issue of (i.e., the differences and similarities between) biblical Christologies and that of Chalcedon. Next, I proceed with a theological discussion of the ontology of Christology (implied from the ontology of Christ): what it *means* to be "fully God and fully human," as the global church partners among ourselves in the *logos-dao* Christology, and as contextual Christologies from the Majority World move forward to a global Christology. Finally, I attempt to begin an ecumenical discourse through a distinctly Chinese Christology of *renren* (a person who loves) that helps us to understand Christ(ians) as the image(s) of God. It will be clear that my attempt here is to write and embody, as much as possible, a fully Christian-biblical and fully Chinese-cultural Christology.

Chinese Christian Christologies

When we survey the landscape of biblical Chinese Christologies, it is apparent how adolescent Chinese Christian scholars are in becoming "fully biblical and fully Chinese." The majority of Chinese biblical scholarship still betrays the assumption that biblical interpretation can be a-cultural (naïvely or deliberately), and some of these readings have become tacitly Western to the point of replacing whatever is Chinese.[2] Among those Chinese writings that attempt to be aware of their dual-nature-in-one person identity, it is noteworthy that particular biblical texts and topics are favored in Christological studies. The Chinese Christological palate favors John's Gospel over the Synoptics, particularly the philosophical word *logos* and *dao*.[3] If Synoptic Christologies are discussed, they are linked to the kingdom-of-God discourse pertaining

2. On historical survey of Christian Chinese theologies and biblical interpretation, see my article "Chinese Interpretation," in *The Oxford Encyclopedia of Biblical Interpretation*, ed. Steven L. McKenzie, 2 vols. (Oxford: Oxford University Press, 2013), 1:103-12; also my "Paul's Ethic of Holiness and Chinese Morality of *Renren*," in Charles H. Cosgrove, Herold Weiss, and K. K. Yeo, *Cross-Cultural Paul: Journeys to Others, Journeys to Ourselves* (Grand Rapids: Eerdmans, 2005), pp. 104-40.

3. See multiple essays addressing this hermeneutics in He Guanghu and Daniel H. N. Yeung, eds., *Sino-Christian Theology Reader*, 2 vols. (Hong Kong: Institute of Sino-Christian Studies, 2009). See also the works of Liu Xiaofeng (in China), and *The Biblical Library* series (K. K. Yeo and Liang Hui, eds. [Shanghai: Shanghai VI Horae Publishers, Inc.]).

to the socialist sociopolitical reality of modern China.[4] Paul's writings to the Gentile readers are preferred over Jewish documents (Hebrews, James) in the New Testament, as Chinese scholars are preoccupied with Pauline Christology that speaks to a moral self or Confucian morality.[5] A more in-depth investigation may reveal that the books of Hebrews and James are actually rich resources for Christian Chinese Christologies since they reflect themes pertinent to the Chinese such as the revelation of God in historical past (tradition) and fulfillment of Christ (for Jewish and Chinese cultures); Sabbath rest, Christological-redemptive rest, and *tai-ji* (Great Ultimate) as well as Confucian musical delight *(yue)* and ecstasy-elevation *(xing)*; Christ in space and time and the cyclical and linear worldviews in Hebrews and China (*yin-yang* space and time);[6] the wisdom Christ in James and the *Daoist* sages in Chinese cultures; and wisdom Christology and metaphoric language of Chinese.[7] Christological texts in the Apocalypse are used often in a dualistic sense to address the Chinese cyclical worldview and the moral vacuum of present-day China. A more engaging cross-cultural reading awaits future Chinese scholars as the Apocalypse and Chinese texts are read through lenses such as the sacramental Lamb of God and various Chinese rituals of cosmological anthropology; poetic justice in worship in the Apocalypse and aesthetic transformation of selfhood and nationhood in Chinese culture; and the process and goal of history and a Chinese worldview.[8]

There is fresh air around the table when Chinese scholars continue to read their cultures biblically, and read the biblical texts in their own languages. Taking seriously the composite contexts of Scripture and the complex horizons of the Chinese world (whether in China or overseas) with its multiple nationalities, regional groups and dialects,

4. See the works of Wu Leichuan, T. C. Chao, Y. T. Wu, Jia Yuming, and Bishop Ting Guang-hsun.

5. See the works of scholars in the previous footnote, and also Watchman Lee and Wan Sze-kar.

6. K. K. Yeo, "The Meaning and Usage of 'REST' (*katapausis* and *sabbatismos*) in Hebrews 3:7–4:13." *Asia Journal of Theology* 5 (1991): 2-33.

7. K. K. Yeo, *Zhuangzi and James* [in Chinese] (Shanghai: Huadong Shifan Daxue VI Horae, 2012).

8. K. K. Yeo, "Hope for the Persecuted, Cooperation with the State, and Meaning for the Dissatisfied: Three Readings of *Revelation* from a Chinese Context," in *The Book of Revelation in Intercultural Perspective,* ed. David Rhoads (Minneapolis: Fortress, 2005), pp. 200-221.

diverse cultures, pluralistic religions, and sociopolitical realities, Chinese Christologies like those in the *Sino-Christian Theology Reader* have begun to address the following topics: (1) the reinterpretation of the biblical understanding of revelation (Chia Yuming) and reason (Chow Lien-hwa) and the incarnation of Christ (Chao Tzuchen) in the present cultures of China; (2) Christian ethics of resurrection hope in the Bible (You Xilin) in light of the consanguineous Marxist ideology of the New China; (3) faith in Christ and the interaction with other faiths (Chow Lien-hwa); (4) Christ and Chinese Marxism (Zhang Xian) and secular humanism (Wang Xiaochao); and (5) Chinese feminist theology (Gao Shining, Kwok Pui-lan, and K. K. Yeo).

Biblical Christologies and Chalcedon: Diversity (Contexts) and Unity (Ontology)

Like the pluralistic milieus of the New Testament and the Chalcedonian Council, the authors of the essays in this book gather in our diversity two millennia later still naming Christologies (plural) from our particular contexts (United States and Europe, Palestine, sub-Saharan Africa, Kenya, Latin America, Mexico, the Philippines, and China) and yet befriend one another as we seek the unity and fullness of Christ. Neither biblical writings nor Chalcedon's creedal formulations represent an abstract (see Martínez-Olivieri's caution that abstraction that "leads to historical apathy") and comprehensive (possibly leading to an authoritarian voice) theology of Christ. Rather, they are historical documents, embedded in particular space and specific time, though their impact has endured beyond their contexts.

The Proclaimer (Jesus) became the Proclaimed (Christ); that is, only Jesus is normative, and no Christology is absolute. For example, Chalcedon was correcting the error of the Nestorian division of Christ's two natures and the Eutychean error that Christ had only one nature. Based on biblical witnesses and employing Greco-Roman philosophical acumen, the creed defines Christological orthodoxy by holding to the full deity of Christ, the full humanity of Christ, the distinction of the two natures of Christ, and the unity of Christ's person.[9] Follow-

---

9. The creed holds "the two natures existed before the union but became one at the Incarnation, . . . Christ is declared to be one Person in two Natures, the Divine of

ing what Mbuvi calls a "culturally constructed" creed, many Western Christologies hold to the two natures of Jesus as neither a mixing, a union, nor a compound of divine-human substance, but the personal and functional unity with God (although Christ has an independent will). This view does not contradict New Testament Christologies. In the New Testament, Jesus' divinity and humanity are non-conflicting, as revealed in Jesus' relationship of self-surrender and self-dedication (humanity) to the personal community of the Triune God (divinity) in order to exhibit God's reign.

The subtitle of my essay "Beyond Chalcedon?" does not bring into doubt the validity of the creed to address the controversies at that time. Rather, the question is a hermeneutical one: is orthodoxy as formulated in the creed comprehensive enough, given its contextual response to the Nestorian and Eutychean heresies? It is notable that it was not accepted by the Oriental (Armenian, Coptic, Ethiopian, and Syrian) Orthodox churches.[10] The question "Beyond Chalcedon?" can best be answered if we compare and contrast Chalcedonian Christology with that of the New Testament and note the limited *catholicity* of its explicitly stated Christology and the subsequent problem of violence against the Copts (as highlighted by Ezigbo).

Vanhoozer writes in his essay that "What is normative in Chalcedon is not the particular concepts but the underlying judgments, not a particular metaphysical scheme but the underlying biblical ontology." I agree with Vanhoozer that "a particular metaphysical scheme" is not normative, but Vanhoozer's proposal needs further discussion. For whatever these "underlying judgments" and the "underlying biblical ontology" are, they are still related to the "particular concepts" about the ontology of Christ (fully God and fully human). After all, Christ's reality (two natures in one person) is the reality out of which the Triune God has created the world. I would argue, it is this ontology of Christ that Western Christology struggles with when discussing "high Christology" or "low Christology," Christology "from above" or Christology "from below." It is the same Christological issue that liber-

---

the same substance as the Father, the human of the same substance as us, which are united unconfusedly, unchangeably, indivisibly, inseparably" (cited in F. L. Cross and E. A. Livingstone, eds., *The Oxford Dictionary of the Christian Church*, 3rd rev. ed. [Oxford: Oxford University Press, 2005], p. 318).

10. E. Fahlbusch and G. W. Bromiley, eds., *The Encyclopedia of Christianity* (Grand Rapids: Eerdmans, 1999-2003), vol. 1, p. 464.

ation theology affirms by holding to "both heavenly savior and earthly liberator" (Martínez-Olivieri), and the same issue raised when African Christology believes in indigenous spirituality and Christian faith. My reservation is not with the concepts, but the *scope* of the concepts, with the single lens of Chalcedon. That is why I still prefer using the compound lenses of the biblical Christologies.

Indeed, the biblical ontology of Chalcedon is *selective*. The "beyond" I refer to in the subtitle of the essay is not intended to invalidate Chalcedon. My proposal to the global church is to return to the richness and variety, thus the *true catholicity*, of New Testament Christologies, and the expansive nature of biblical hermeneutics evident in the fourfold Gospels and the Pauline Christologies. The fact that we are given four Christologies of the Gospels based on the evangelists' variegated and nuanced portrayals of the historical Jesus reveals the cross-cultural hermeneutical task of theology in the lived experience of the first readers:

1. Responding to a Jewish Christian community in the midst of a Gentile world, the Gospel of Matthew constructs a Christology of Jesus as the new Israel, new presence of God (Emmanuel), new Moses and new Law, new David and new kingdom, new covenant and new faithfulness. Matthew's *biblios geneseos* (book of genesis-genealogy, 1:1) is a new scriptural reading of the Old Testament in light of Jesus Christ, thus fulfilling rather than abolishing the Old Testament.

2. Aiming to encourage the persecuted Roman Christians in the 60s, the Christology of the Gospel of Mark is about the crucified Messiah (Mark 8:29; 12:35; 13:21; 14:61; 15:32), who is the Son of God (i.e., the fully human One; 1:1, 11, 24; 3:11; 5:7; 9:7; 15:39). This good news (1:1) of Mark is about a Christology of the cross and service.

3. Luke's ordered narrative has a Christology of the universal Savior (1:47, 69; 2:11), as he defends the legitimacy and goodness of Christian faith to the Roman Empire, and as he narrates the reign of God expanding in the empire.

4. Addressing issues in Pharisaic Judaism, John's Gospel writes the Book of Signs (1:19–12:50) about a Christology of the transcendent Wisdom-Jesus tabernacled in human history, the Great "I AM" who created and worked miraculously in the chaotic world.

It was not the purpose of the Chalcedon Council to read the Christologies of the fourfold canonical Gospels in light of their historical meaning. We can see how the council was reading the New Testament faithfully, but contextually, with a cross-cultural hermeneutic that addressed their philosophical and contextual issues, those being the challenges of the Nestorians and the Eutycheans. The focus on the two natures of Christ and the discussion regarding the technical usage of Greek and Latin (at times using slippery terms such as *homoousios* [same substance] in Ezigbo; "white mythology" in Vanhoozer) certainly is true to the spirit of New Testament Christologies *selectively,* thus it was not their intention to embody the richness of the Gospels' and Paul's Christologies. Chalcedonian Christology, being a contextual Christology, does not attempt to provide a comprehensive Christology of the global (catholic) church.

Global Christologies seek creative dialogues toward: (1) a *catholic* faith based on biblical Christologies that honor multiple and interacting worldviews; (2) a global theology that respects cross-cultural and shifting contexts in which faithful communities embody real-life issues; (3) a translatability of the Scripture that upholds various dynamic vernaculars and hermeneutics; and (4) a round-table symposium of proclaiming and worshiping a biblical Christ portrayed in varied Christologies.

One of the best examples of diversity in unity regarding Christologies can be found in the biblical witnesses in the epistles of Paul. Gadamerian hermeneutics of pre-understanding and horizon-fusing is evident in Paul's understandings of Christ.[11] To the Thessalonian Christians, he speaks of Christ the Coming One who is the Judge and their hope. To the Galatians, he speaks of Christ the Crucified One, lifting the curse of the Law, thus bringing in the nations (Gentiles) as the people of God (together with the Jews) to be the new creation in Christ. To the Roman Christians, he speaks of Christ as God's Righteousness to judge, save, and welcome all regardless of race (Jews or Gentiles) and culture (Greeks or barbarians) so that they may become God's beloved community. In speaking to the Corinthian Christians, Paul seeks to bring them to a higher spiritual awareness via the "crucified Christ"

---

11. For more, see K. K. Yeo, *Rhetorical Interaction in 1 Corinthians 8 and 10: A Formal Analysis with Implications for a Cross-Cultural, Chinese Hermeneutic* (Leiden: Brill, 1995), pp. 15-43.

(1 Cor. 1:23; 2:2), in order to deconstruct the civilization ideals of power (Romans), religion (Jews), and wisdom-philosophy (Greeks). Through such self-deconstruction, they are then able to reconstruct a holistic life found only in the "weakness" of God, a "miracle-less" faith, and "foolish" understanding. To the Corinthian Christians in 2 Corinthians, when contesting the theology of the super-apostles (11:5; 12:11), Paul speaks of Christ as the Reconciler of humanity to God (5:11-21), of the congregation with its church leader (Paul, chapter 2), as well as of the Macedonian believers with the Jerusalem church (chapters 8–9). For Paul, the unity of his Christologies in all his epistles is Christ "who has died, is risen, and will come again," yet we see in individual epistles that his Christologies translate dynamically into different foci, shed light on various themes, and always speak forth in a prophetic and priestly way to the needs of the congregations. The compound lenses of Paul's Christologies are certainly much more powerful and expansive than those of Chalcedon. In keeping with previous chapters in this volume, the following section is my Christian Chinese attempt to listen to the voices around the table. It is also an opportunity for me to project my voice, so that together we can embrace global Christologies and go "beyond" the scope of Chalcedon, reaching back to the fountainhead of Christologies, the Bible.

Global Christologies and (Beyond) Chalcedon: Biblical Mandate and Eschatological Truth

Our task is not to construct only *one* abiding and unifying principle from the four corners of the earth in order to arrive at a coherent, systematic Christology of the Bible. Rather, we wish to encourage faithful interpretations of biblical witnesses in their polyphonic, yet harmonized, proclamation and theologizing of Jesus Christ from diverse cultures. There are two ways we can do this: (1) discern and celebrate (a mutual learning process) the commonalities and the differences of biblical Christologies of the global church; or (2) covenant with each other to work together toward a Christian ritual of confession and loving Christian friendship when contentious points of our biblical Christologies emerge.

The way the global church is diversified in unity demonstrates its priestly and prophetic calling in the world, thus transforming it (Gener calls this "missiological Christology"). The church will live out the biblical mandate of preaching, translating, and exegeting Jesus Christ as it acknowledges the eschatological nature of Truth.[12] The ontology of Christ is ultimately not simply significant in and of itself, but rather in the ontology of Christological theology. That is, Christ's ontology enables "every tribe and language and people and nation" (Rev. 5:9; 7:9; 13:7; 14:6; cf. Acts 2:1-13) to be "fully Christian and fully Chinese-Palestinian" in their *theologizing,* which constitutes part of Christian worship. Jesus Christ is the Reality that makes all realities, cultures, and meaning-systems true, beautiful, and good. Because Jesus Christ does not speak heavenly tongues in his revelation of God, Christianity does not have a sacred language. The gospel of the church is neither culture- nor language-specific.[13] Jesus is the Eternal Word enfleshed (John 1:14), as the gospel of Christ and Christian doctrines are always proclaimed and understood "incarnationally" within their own cultures "in-linguistically."

All the essays in this volume are akin to eight sides of a prism that allow us to view Jesus Christ from, and in interaction with, their various vantage points. An individual on his or her own is limited in the ability to reflect Christ's glory and meaning. But all facets, when held together and in tension, reflect Christ's fuller glory in eschatological openness and richness of meaning. As a Christian Chinese, I find a lot of overlapping concerns and conclusions in our biblical interpretations, and my views on many theological and interpretive issues are greatly clarified and expanded by these. Many essays contribute to the discussion of the symbiotic relationship between the spirit and human worlds (Ezigbo, Mbuvi, Spencer, Gener) and the fluidity between past and present worlds (Katanacho, Yeo). All essays see the hermeneutic act of theology as something salvific, whether to the individual, the community of women (Latin American feminist discussion in Martínez-Olivieri) or the poor (Gener), the system of oppression (Katanacho and Martínez-Olivieri), or even the culture (Gener and Yeo).

All eight essays follow the path of the biblical paradigm that war-

---

12. K. K. Yeo, "Response: Multicultural Readings: A Biblical Warrant and an Eschatological Vision," in *Global Voices. Reading the Bible in the Majority World,* ed. Craig Keener and M. Daniel Carroll (Peabody: Hendrickson, 2013), pp. 27-37.

13. As Lamin Sanneh writes, Christianity from its beginning until now has been "a translated religion without a revealed language" (Lamin Sanneh, *Whose Religion Is Christianity?* [Grand Rapids: Eerdmans, 2003], p. 69).

rants us to take "local language, context, and culture" seriously for a good cause. When theology is translated into local tongues, and the Bible is used to address contextual issues, the culture is transformed (or fulfilled or converted and turned to Christ, rather than substituted; see Ezigbo), and the Scripture demonstrates its sacredness. It is sacred in the sense that the Bible has the power to speak life across space and time. Moreover, these essays highlight another aspect of global theology, that is, how global Christologies are understood and lived out in their contexts around the roundtable, for the purpose of edifying others. Let me use the example of the Chinese translation of John's Gospel, and show how it has helped me to appreciate a Chinese Christology of *dao* that enabled me to see Christ more fully than simply reading the word *Word* in the English version or *logos* in the Greek Bible.

A Chinese Christology of Dao

The Greek word *logos* is translated as *dao,* a Chinese word having three meanings: (1) the cosmic or creative principle; (2) the personal truth or embodied wisdom; and (3) the verbal word (speech) or communal dialogue.

(1) Jesus is portrayed in John's Gospel as the Creator of the cosmos, evident in the parallel motif of the first chapters of John and Genesis. God-Jesus is the Creator of order from chaos, light from darkness, and meaning from void.

The word *logos* in Stoicism and the word *dao* in Chinese thought have similar ideas: the foundation of truth and the principle that holds all things together. John probably used the word *logos* because it held a cross-cultural meaning for both Jewish and Gentile readers that the universe has coherent structures sustaining itself. The notion of *dao* speaks of wholeness and integrity in the Chinese understanding of the universe. Indeed, Jesus, as the creative *dao,* takes human form and keeps on working and performing miracles. These works and miracles are called "works" (*erga* in Greek) and "signs" (*semeia* in Greek) in John's Gospel and reflect the glory of the Father.[14]

---

14. For example, the so-called first miracle Jesus performed at Cana, turning water into wine, is for the sake of "revealing God's glory" (2:11). The resurrection of

(2) The *logos* Christology speaks of Jesus as personified wisdom, as the word *dao* would be understood by Chinese readers. *Dao* means wisdom, truth, and knowledge that has the character and vitality of life. In the same light, Jesus as the wisdom-*logos*-*dao* comes to us through the Hebrew tradition of wisdom (*hokmah* in Hebrew) as we have known it in Proverbs 8 – the personal wisdom and the personal Creator, presented in female imagery. Understood in a patriarchal setting, the use of female imagery is certainly a creative and cross-cultural endeavor (see also Martínez-Olivieri's and Spencer's discussions on Christ and women in different cultural contexts). The wisdom-*dao* Christ has personhood; he is not just an abstract principle. Thus, Jesus Christ the personal *dao* has to be an *incarnated logos*. The personal *dao* takes the form of flesh and blood, wear and tear. "In the *dao* was *life*, and the *life* was the light of humanity" (1:4). Two favorite words John uses in the Gospel are *ginoskō* (know) and *alētheia* (truth). Truth is equivalent to wisdom in John's Gospel, personified wisdom with which one can interrelate. To know is to embrace and be embraced by the embodied truth as one enters into that I-thou relationship. So the *dao* was "full of grace and truth" (1:14), "grace and truth came through Jesus Christ" (1:17).

(3) If the creative-*dao* Christ speaks of theological creativity, the wisdom-*dao* speaks of incarnated personhood, then the rhetorical-*dao* speaks of communal dialogue, since the universe is a communicative life-world, not an isolated island. Jesus is the rhetorical-*dao*, as the Chinese Catholic Bible translates: "In the beginning was the speech [Protestant Bible in Chinese uses *dao*]." The creation is more than *ex nihilo* (out of nothing), it is also a creation of meaning from meaninglessness via God's saying, "let there be . . ." God created the orderly universe (cosmos) by means of word-speech.

Jesus is the Word of God that makes sense of human language. Jesus is the rhetoric of God that allows the Holy One and human beings to communicate with him. Jesus manifests God by means of what he says. The direct speech of Jesus in John's Gospel is imperative because the revelation of this *dao*-Christology of God is happening on Jesus' own lips. So the self-claim of Jesus ("I am the . . .") is unique to the Johannine Gospel.[15]

Lazarus from the dead is also for the sake of "God's glory" (11:40). The greatest sign is, of course, the cross (12:23), where Jesus reveals the glory of God.

15. I am the bread of life (6:35-40); I am the light of the world (8:12; 9:15); I am the

John is aware that while words have their creativity, they also have limitations. When the limitation of words is evidenced, silence is used in John (e.g., 8:24: "If you (pl.) do not believe 'I am,' you will die in sin"). The question is: "I am" what? The Greek text is silent.[16] Words cannot really express and reveal who "I AM" is.[17] That words cannot really express who God is does not mean that speech is useless. It is all the more necessary to use words. John, the master of language, uses irony, metaphor, and dialogue as ways to transcend the limitations of language. That richness of *dao*-speech is reflected in *Daode Jing* (the scripture of Daoism by Laozi).[18]

Although language has its limitations, it still is the best medium by which to express the mystery of the unknown and to be in constant conversation with truth within a community. The Johannine Jesus is in constant conversation with God and people: Jesus' conversation with Nicodemus on being "born again," with the unnamed Samaritan woman concerning the living water, and with the Jews concerning the "Wonder Bread." Jesus talks to God the Father in chapter 17, which is truly "the Lord's Prayer." The rhetorical *dao* reveals the truth by telling, praying, and listening to truth. He is the truth (14:6), but few seem to know the truth.[19] When the Spirit of truth (14:17; 15:26) comes, "he will guide us into all the truth" (16:14).

---

good shepherd (10:11); I am the gate (10:7); I am the resurrection (11:20-27); I am the way, the truth, and the life (14:6); I am the true vine (15:1).

16. Erroneously, some of the English and Chinese translations say, "If you do not believe I am the Christ" or "If you do not believe I am he"; that addition of "the Christ" or "he" is unwarranted. Silence is a better expression here.

17. Also, the twofold ending of John, 20:30 and 21:25, hints at the same meaning. John 20:30, "Jesus did many signs . . . that are written in this book," and John 21:25, "so many other things that Jesus did if recorded in the books, the world could not contain them," are not stating the obvious; they are the acknowledgment that Jesus the Word of God cannot fully be expressed by our words. Thus, Jesus is the Great "I AM" mentioned in Exodus 3:14 ("I am who I am").

18. "The *dao* that can be told of is not the eternal *dao;*
The name that can be named is not the eternal Name.
The Nameless is the origin of Heaven and Earth;
The Named is the mother of all things." (*Daode Jing,* chapter 1).

19. As Pilate asks, "What is truth?" (18:38). Truth is to be located in theological discourse. Jesus tells Pilate that the rhetorical *dao* came into the world "to bear witness to the truth" and that "every one who is of the truth" hears his voice (18:37). Jesus prays that the Father may sanctify his followers in the truth, for his "word is truth" (17:17, 19).

K. K. Yeo

The *logos-dao* Christology of John 1:1-5 reminds us of the passion and boldness of John to communicate the gospel of Jesus Christ cross-culturally. He dares to work with the biblical text (Hebrew Scripture) together with the Greek philosophical tradition of his time. And those who follow in John's footsteps, as the ones who translate the Bible into other local languages, will discover unique Christologies in the vernaculars of people all over the world.

Chinese Christology *(Renren)* and Contextual-Global *Imago Dei* Christologies: Christ(ologies) *as* the Image(s) of God

The most challenging issue in Christological discussion across cultures is the contesting soteriologies (work of Christ), and thus the competing Christologies, especially in the heated milieus of religious claims.[20] Many essays in this volume wrestle with this aspect of Christology (Ezigbo's discussion on African theology; Mbuvi's discussion on the missionary denigration of African religion; Gener on Asian plurality of religions), differing only in degree.

We believe that Jesus comes not to abolish the old, but to fulfill and to renew it. This is true of the Jewish Law and of cultural ideals as well. My task is to offer a Christian Chinese Christology (and soteriology)[21] that explains Jesus as the fulfillment of the Confucian ideal of "being human" *(ren)*.

Confucius's "soteriological concern" is that people do not know how to coexist together, and that the government-politic has used force to alienate citizens, that rituals *(li)* make us fallen, and music *(yue)* that beautifies our souls is corrupted. According to Confucius, the greatest cultural danger is that people thought they could love God without loving people. So Confucius teaches people to actualize the mandate of heaven *(Tianming)* by committing themselves to love *(ren* = human-relatedness), for what makes human beings *(ren)* is love

20. For various views on the relationship between Christianity and other religions, see John Hick and Brian Hebblethwaite, eds., *Christianity and Other Religions, Selected Readings* (Philadelphia: Fortress, 1981).

21. See K. K. Yeo, "Christian Chinese Theology: Theological Ethics of Becoming Human and Holy," in *Global Theology in Evangelical Perspective: Exploring the Contextual Nature of Theology and Mission*, ed. Jeffrey P. Greenman and Gene L. Green (Downers Grove: InterVarsity Academic, 2012), pp. 102-15.

(*ren,* see *Analects* 12:22), thus the term *renren* (who love). The similar biblical concept is love *(agapē).* *Ren* (love) is not simply a psychological term related to the ontological aspect of human beings; rather it is inclusive of virtue or spiritual condition.[22] *Ren* (love) connotes all the moral qualities that govern relationships among people, thus human-relatedness has love as the cardinal principle.[23] In other words, to be a *renren* is to express and to participate in the holy as a dimension of all truly human existence. "Virtue does not exist in isolation; there must be neighbors," says Confucius (*Analects* 4:25). "In order to establish oneself, one helps others to establish themselves; in order to enlarge oneself, one helps others to enlarge themselves" (*Analects* 6:28). Therefore, the "lostness" of humanity is primarily brokenness, isolation, and de-humanization. Thus (here I am going beyond the Confucian anthropology and soteriology toward that of a Christian, or better still, a Christian Chinese anthropology), the salvation Jesus offers and epitomizes is that of wholeness and worthiness of humanity — human beings are created *as* the image of God (1 Cor. 11:7; James 3:9). Humans represent God in managing the earth and reflecting God's glory in the world (they are the light of the world).[24] Jesus has revealed for us what it means to be fully human, in his being both with God and with people. Jesus' openness and empathy toward sinners, outcasts, the separated, the disowned, and the rejected reveal the extent of his full divinity encountering his full humanity. Christ is fully human, and together in one person he *is* also the *imago Dei* (Col. 1:15; Heb. 1:3) who lives and gives his life

22. Herbert Fingarette, *Confucius — The Secular as Sacred* (New York: Harper & Row, 1972), pp. 37-38. Mencius says, "Human-heartedness *(ren)* is the mind of human beings; righteousness is the path of human conducts" (Mencius, 6a, 11).

23. Fung Yulan, *A Short History of Chinese Philosophy,* ed. and trans. Derk Bodde (New York: Macmillan, 1948), pp. 69-73.

24. The image (Hebrew *tselem,* Greek *eikon,* Latin *imago*) and likeness (Hebrew *demuth,* Greek *homoiosis,* Latin *similitudo*) of God is the ideal-fully human mentioned in the Bible (Gen. 1:26; 5:2; 9:6) having similar denotations of royal lordship (Ps. 8:5; cf. Heb. 2:6-8), esteem (rather than as slaves to gods, as some ancient Near Eastern creation myths propose), and physico-spiritual uniqueness (immanence representative of the transcendent Creator God on earth) as that of Confucian understanding of ideal man *(junzi).* On the Genesis text, see Claus Westermann, *Genesis 1–11: A Commentary,* trans. John J. Scullion (London: SPCK, 1984), p. 146; on human beings as "God's vice-regent on earth," see Gordon J. Wenham, *Genesis 1–15* (Waco: Word, 1987), p. 31.

totally for others and for God, not himself. In doing so, he has not lost but has fully encountered himself and the Triune God.[25]

New Testament Christology has no problem understanding Jesus *as* the *imago Dei*, but speaking of human beings, the Hebrew preposition *beth* in the Old Testament texts (Gen. 1:26-27; 5:1-3; 9:6) is often translated as "in" (God has an image and we are created *in* his image, or *has* his image) rather than as "as" or "in the capacity of" (God has no image of his own other than we, being created *as* his image).[26] I take David Cline's view (*as* rather than *in*), but I explain the content of image as relationship with God (thus dwelling in God's Spirit-presence) and among people (thus communion-friendship with others in order to be fully human). The function of such relationships is to represent God.[27] The first dimension of *imago Dei* is reflected in humanity's corporeal-animated creatureliness that encounters God, his word, and his presence. It is that gifted ability to enter into relationship with God (with all we are — mind, heart, soul, will, body) that allows humans creatures *to be* God's image in the world.[28] Second, the image of God as seen in the creation account, with the clause "male and female he created them," not only emphasizes that both male and female are created "as our image" and "as our likeness," but also explains "image" and "likeness" as the social self (or *co*-humanity of male and female in the first *pair* of humanity) relating and encountering each other toward psychosomatic wholeness, intimacy-fulfillment, and glory-dignity.[29]

The human predicament is that one tends to live apart from God's presence (not for God's glory) and subsequently lives a narcissistic life that leads to losing one's self (Matt. 10:39; Luke 9:24; John 12:25). The alienation between I and self, between self and other, between other

25. "In Christ there is no male or female" (Gal. 3:28). This does not speak of uni-sexuality in Christ but of the equality of male and female. See also Martínez-Olivieri's and Spencer's essays.

26. The latter view is that of David Cline; see his "The Image of God in Man," *Tyndale Bulletin* 19 (1968): 53-103.

27. See also Karl Barth, *Church Dogmatics*, III/1 (Edinburgh: T&T Clark, 1958), pp. 197-98.

28. See Claus Westermann, *Genesis 1–11: A Commentary*, trans. John J. Scullion (Minneapolis: Augsburg, 1984), p. 156.

29. See Hans Walter Wolff, *Anthropology of the Old Testament*, trans. Margaret Kohl (London: SCM, 1974), p. 159. As Cline writes, "It is the *homo* [human], not the *animus* or the *anima*, that is the *imago Dei*" (Cline, "Image of God," p. 86).

and the world, between humanity and God is called the distortion or corruption of the *imago Dei.* That constitutes sin, falling short of the glory of God (Rom. 3:23). Jesus is the Christ precisely because in his incarnation, life, death, and resurrection, he lives fully *as* the *imago Dei* (2 Cor. 4:4; Col. 1:15) and thus reconciles and restores the broken *imago Dei* to be the new humanity-creation (Rom. 8:29; Eph. 2:15; 4:22-24; Col. 3:9-11) for us. Human beings as created as the *imago Dei* does not mean that they are divine beings. Rather, humans are always *creatures* of God because the inbreathing of God's breath-Spirit, thus making the human "a living *nephesh*," does not make the human a divine being. For humans do not possess a divine part (spirit); Cline writes: "breath is not a 'part' of man, but the principle of vitality itself, which remains in God's possession and may be withdrawn by Him as He pleases."[30] But Christians living as the new humanity are being changed into the likeness of Christ from one degree of glory to another (2 Cor. 3:18). Ezigbo is correct when he says, "Theologians need the vision of other theologians . . . to successfully imagine, understand, and appreciate the breadth, width, and length of the person and significance of Jesus Christ (Eph. 4:12-13)."

The "fully human" language in both Confucian ethics and biblical Christology emphasizes complete love for others (Rom. 13:8). Jesus can complete salvation because he is fully God *and* fully human. Only the fully divine, who is infinitely righteous and glorious, can forgive infinite sin against God and cover the infinite shame and curse against human beings themselves: namely, that we have fallen short of God's glory. Through the power of righteousness, justice, and glory, only the fully human Jesus can restore and save "less than human" humanity from the power of sin. Thus the unity of Jesus' divinity and humanity is God's work of reconciliation based on Jesus' faithfulness and love. The divine can enter the sphere of humanity and become "fully human," *yet* Jesus is *still fully divine,* and eschatologically, the "all in all" (1 Cor. 15:28; Gal. 3:28; Eph. 1:23; Col. 3:10). No human being can be fully divine and "all in all," but the unity-communion we (the fully human) can have with God (the fully divine) is a divine gift and invitation to us all.

Christ manifests the I-Thou relationship with God and with people most perfectly. This line of thought is close to Confucius's understand-

---

30. Cline, "Image of God," p. 89.

ing of the transcendence of heaven, best known in its representation of immanence in ethical life. It is the virtue of human beings that reveals the beauty, order, and sacredness of heaven. The mandate of heaven has endowed us and is calling us to be moral-spiritual selves, to thankfully receive God's indwelling Spirit in us. As God's image, we are summoned "to live as God's representative within creation, that is, to be that image through whom God's presence and self-manifestation in creation may be found."[31]

Conclusion

As God's image, we are called to be free expressions and diverse representations of our oneness with God, with one another, and harmony with God's world, just as the global church should be. Indeed, as God's image, we the new humanity in Christ are moving to the eschatological reality of the glorified church by virtue of the Lamb of God, the Alpha and the Omega. Christ makes sense of all our theologies, including our Christologies. The God of the Bible is Christlike; creation has Christ as the firstborn, and humanity created as God's image is re-created as *imago Christi*. God's world, after all, is not anthropocentric but Christocentric — in creation, redemption, and consummation.

For Further Reading

Brown, Raymond E. *An Introduction to New Testament Christology.* Mahwah, N.J.: Paulist, 1994.
Cosgrove, Charles, Herold Weiss, and K. K. Yeo. *Cross-Cultural Paul: Journeys to Others, Journeys to Ourselves.* Grand Rapids: Eerdmans, 2005.
England, John C., and Archie C. C. Lee, eds. *Doing Theology with Asian Resources, Ten Years in the Formation of Living Theology in Asia.* The Programme for Theology and Culture in Asia 1983-1993. Auckland, New Zealand: Pace, 1993.

31. Stanley J. Grenz, "Jesus as the *Imago Dei:* Image-of-God Christology and the Non-linear Linearity of Theology," *Journal of the Evangelical Theological Society* 47 (2004): 623.

He Guanghu and Daniel H. N. Yeung, eds. *Sino-Christian Theology Reader,* 2 vols. Hong Kong: Institute of Sino-Christian Studies, 2009.

Kärkkäinen, Veli-Matti. *Christology: A Global Introduction.* Grand Rapids: Baker Academic, 2003.

Patte, Daniel, et al., eds. *Global Biblical Commentary.* Nashville: Abingdon, 2004.

Pelikan, Jaroslav. *Jesus Through the Centuries: His Place in the History of Culture.* New Haven, Conn.: Yale University Press, 1999.

Yeo, K. K. *Musing with Confucius and Paul: Toward a Chinese Christian Theology.* Eugene, Ore.: Cascade Books, Wipf & Stock, 2008.

Contributors

VICTOR I. EZIGBO (Ph.D., University of Edinburgh) is Assistant Professor of Systematic and Contextual Theology at Bethel University in St. Paul, Minnesota. His areas of research are African Christian theologies and Christologies, African indigenous religions, and postcolonial theological discourses. He has written a book and several articles in the areas of African theologies, Christologies, and spirituality. He is also the founder of the Centre for Research in Global Christianity (CRGC).

TIMOTEO D. GENER (Ph.D., Fuller Theological Seminary) is President of the Asian Theological Seminary, Manila, Philippines (www.ats.ph). A practitioner of local theology and a distinguished member of the World Evangelical Alliance Task Force on Ecumenical Affairs, he has coedited *The Earth is the Lord's: Reflections on Stewardship in the Asian Setting* (2011), published jointly by OMF Lit and Asian Theological Seminary.

GENE L. GREEN (Ph.D., University of Aberdeen) is Professor of New Testament at Wheaton College in Illinois. Previously he taught New Testament and served as Academic Dean and Rector of the Seminario ESEPA in San José, Costa Rica. He is the author of four biblical commentaries written in Spanish and English, coauthor of *The New Testament in Antiquity* (Zondervan, 2009), and coeditor of *Global Theology in Evangelical Perspective* (InterVarsity Academic, 2012). His current research focuses on the intersection of the Christian faith and cultures, both ancient and contemporary, and the theology of Peter.

YOHANNA KATANACHO (Ph.D., Trinity Evangelical Divinity School) is a Palestinian Evangelical who studied at Bethlehem University (B.Sc.), Wheaton College (M.A.), and Trinity Evangelical Divinity School (M. Div.; Ph.D.). He serves as the Academic Dean for Bethlehem Bible College. He has authored several books in English and Arabic, including *The Land of Christ: A Palestinian Cry; A Commentary on Proverbs; The Seven 'I AM' Sayings in the Gospel of John,* and *The King of Peace and His Young Followers.* He is also one of the authors of the Palestinian Kairos Document.

JULES A. MARTÍNEZ-OLIVIERI (Ph.D. candidate, Trinity Evangelical Divinity School) is Assistant Professor of Theology at Seminario Teológico de Puerto Rico. His blog is available at www.theodrama.com. He is completing his doctoral dissertation in Systematic Theology at Trinity Evangelical Divinity School. A Puerto Rican, he serves as an academic and minister with the Christian and Missionary Alliance.

ANDREW M. MBUVI (Ph.D., Westminster Theological Seminary) is Associate Professor of Biblical Studies and Hermeneutics, Shaw University Divinity School, North Carolina. He has published a book on 1 Peter entitled *Temple Exile and Identity in 1 Peter* (T&T Clark, 2007) and is currently working on a commentary on 2 Peter-Jude in the New Covenant Commentary Series for Cascade Books.

STEPHEN T. PARDUE (Ph.D., Wheaton College) is Assistant Professor of Theology at the Asia Graduate School of Theology in Manila. He is the author of *The Mind of Christ: Humility and the Intellect in Early Christian Theology* (T&T Clark, 2012). He grew up in the Philippines and moved back there after finishing his doctoral work. His areas of research include virtue theory, contextual theology, and the doctrine of providence.

AÍDA BESANÇON SPENCER (Ph.D., Southern Baptist Theological Seminary) is Professor of New Testament at Gordon-Conwell Theological Seminary, South Hamilton, Massachusetts, and Extraordinary Researcher at North-West University, Potchefstroom, South Africa. Born and reared in Santo Domingo, Dominican Republic, she earned her Ph.D. in New Testament at Southern Baptist Theological Seminary and the Master's of Theology and Divinity at Princeton Theological Seminary. She has served as a social worker, college minister, and Founding Pastor of Organization of Pilgrim Church in Beverly, Massachusetts.

Listed in *Who's Who in the World*, *Contemporary Authors*, and *Who's Who of American Women*, she has authored numerous books and articles, including *Pastoral Epistles* (New Covenant Commentary), *Beyond the Curse: Women Called to Ministry*, *Paul's Literary Style*, *2 Corinthians* (Daily Bible Commentary), and cowritten or coedited *Reaching for the New Jerusalem: A Biblical and Theological Framework for the City*, *The Global God*, *Global Voices on Biblical Equality*, *The Prayer Life of Jesus*, *Joy through the Night: Biblical Resources on Suffering*, *The Goddess Revival*, and *Marriage at the Crossroads*. She has been a visiting scholar at Harvard Divinity School and El Seminario Evangélico de Puerto Rico.

KEVIN J. VANHOOZER (Ph.D., Cambridge University) is currently Research Professor of Systematic Theology at Trinity Evangelical Divinity School. Previously he served as Blanchard Professor of Theology at Wheaton College Graduate School (2009-12) and, before that, as Senior Lecturer in Theology and Religious Studies at the University of Edinburgh, Scotland (1990-98). He is the author or editor of sixteen books, including *The Drama of Doctrine: A Canonical-Linguistic Approach to Christian Theology* (Westminster John Knox, 2005) and *Remythologizing Theology: Divine Action, Passion, and Authorship* (Cambridge University Press, 2010). He is married to Sylvie and has two daughters (and fifteen doctoral students). He is an amateur classical pianist and serious reader, and finds that music and literature help him integrate academic theology and spiritual formation.

K. K. YEO (Ph.D., Northwestern University) is currently Harry R. Kendall Professor of New Testament at Garrett-Evangelical Theological Seminary (Evanston, Illinois) and Academic Director of the Christian Studies program at Peking University (Beijing, China). He has authored and edited more than twenty-five Chinese books and eight English books on cross-cultural biblical interpretation and Christian spirituality, including *What Has Jerusalem to Do with Beijing?* (Trinity Press International, 1995) and *Zhuangzi and James* (in Chinese, 2012). He was born and raised on the Borneo island of East Malaysia. He and his wife, Kungsiu, and their three children reside near Chicago, but he commutes to China frequently to serve the global church there.

Index of Authors

Abesamis, Carlos H., 69n, 70
Achebe, Chinua, 144n
Achtemeier, Paul, 151, 157n
Acosta, Raul, Jr., 125n
Adeyemo, Tokunboh, 45, 57n
Akiva (Rabbi), 114
Al-salam, Faruq Abed, 104n
Al-Saqa, Ahmed Hijazi, 104n
Ali, Michael Nazir, 73
Alves, Rubem, 85
Ames, William, 11
Anderson, Allan, 75n
Appiah-Kubi, Kofi, 147
Aquino, María Pilar, 139
Arevalo, C. G., 61n
Aritonang, Effendy, 73n
Assman, Hugo, 81, 84
Assmoah-Gyadu, J. Kwabena, 55n
Ateek, Naim, 104n
Awad, Alex, 106n
Awolalu, J. Omosade, 152n
Aye-Addo, Charles Sarpong, 146n
Azariah (Bishop), 60

Bach, Johann Sebastian, 34n
Baille, D. M., 14n
Baker, William, 105n
Barth, Karl, 23, 27-28, 176n

Bauckham, Richard, 24
Beasley-Murray, George, 106n, 119n
Bedford, Nancy, 87-88, 94, 95n, 98, 99
Bediako, Kwame, 39n, 46, 48, 50-52, 143, 146, 147, 149, 150n, 158n
Belding, J., 62n
Bernasconi, Robert, 46n
Bertram, G., 47n
Beti, Mongo, 144n
Bettenson, Henry, 128n
Bevans, Stephen B., 59n, 60n, 63
Bird, Michael F., 64, 66n
Blau, Joshua, 109n
Blomberg, Craig, 106n, 110n
Boff, Clodovis, 84, 138, 139n
Boff, Leonardo, 84, 87, 89, 90n, 127n
Bonhoeffer, Dietrich, 13-14
Bretall, Robert W., 31n
Brodie, Thomas, 119n
Bromiley, G. W., 166n
Brown, Jeannine, 118
Brown, Raymond, 116n, 137n
Bujo, Bénézet, 50n, 51n, 148n
Burridge, Richard A., 64
Butler, Alfred Joshua, 40n

Capaque, George, 76n

Carson, D. A., 107n, 119n
Castro, Emilio, 85
Chan, Simon, 72n
Chao, T. C., 164n
Cikala, Mulago gwa, 146, 147n
Cimok, Fatih, 127n
Clark, Clifton, 160-61
Clark, Francis X., 62n
Claver, Francisco F., 62n
Clement, 155
Cline, David, 176-77
Confucius, 174-75
Coote, Robert T., 59n, 62n
Cosgrove, Charles H., 163n
Crisp, Oliver, 23n, 25n, 26n
Cross, F. L., 166n
Culpepper, R. Alan, 106n

Daldianus, Artemidorus, 130, 131n
Dalton, William J., 156, 158n
Daniel-Rops, Henri, 127n, 137
Danquah, J. B., 146, 147n
Darragh, Neil, 65n
Dawson, Gerrit, 26n
de Mesa, José, 60n, 61n, 66n, 68n, 69
de Mesa, Karl, 77n
de Pantoja, Diego, 74
de Santa Ana, Julio, 85
Derrida, Jacques, 15
Dodd, C. H., 108n
Donfried, Karl P., 137n
Dube, Musa W., 145
Dy, Ary C., 74n, 75
Dyrness, William, 59, 60n, 150n,
    151n, 153n

Ekem, David, 150n
Elliott, John H., 156n, 157n, 159n
Enz, Jacob, 113
Escobar, Samuel, 67n, 68n, 85, 88
Euripides, 131n
Eusebius, 125n
Evans, C. Stephen, 18n
Ezeh, Uchenna A., 49n

Ezigbo, Victor I., 43, 44n, 46n, 49n,
    53n, 56n, 57n, 166, 168, 170, 171,
    174

Fahlbusch, E., 166n
Farrar, F. W., 125n, 127n
Farrow, Douglas, 26n
Fasholé-Luke, Edward, 50n, 150
Feinberg, J. S., 156
Fingarette, Herbert, 175n
Fitzmyer, Joseph A, 137n
Forsyth, P. T., 18
Fowl, Stephen, 31n
Frei, Hans, 23-24
Fung Yulan, 175n

Galvin, John P., 17n
Gandhi, Mohandas K., 71
García, Alberto, 88
García, Sixto J., 126n
Gaventa, Beverly Roberts, 137n
Gavrilyuk, Paul, 13n
Gener, Timoteo D., 65n, 68n, 170,
    174
Gibellini, Rosino, 83, 84n, 90n
Gil, Rosa Maria, 139n
González, Antonio, 83n, 88, 97, 99,
    134n
González, Justo, 123, 127n
Goppelt, Leonard, 151n, 159n
Greeley, Andrew M., 130
Greene, Colin J. D., 20n
Grenz, Stanley J., 17n, 178n
Guang-hsun, Ting (Bishop), 164n
Guthrie, Shirley C., 66n
Gutiérrez, Gustavo, 81, 82n, 83n
Gutmann, Joseph, 152n

Habets, Myk, 14n
Hallencreutz, C. F., 146n
Hammond, Dorothy, 46n
Handy, Robert T., 126n
Hansen, Guillermo, 93, 94n
Harper, Susan Billington, 60n

Harvey, Richard, 104n
He Guanghu, 163n
Healey, Joseph, 55n
Hebblethwaite, Brian, 19n, 174n
Hector, Kevin, 33
Herzog, Frederick, 115n
Hick, John, 19-20, 174n
Holmes, Christopher R. J., 28
Holter, Knut, 152n
Hoskins, Paul, 111n, 114n
Hwa Yung, 76n

Idowu, E. Bolaji, 41n, 42, 45n, 145n,
  146, 147n, 150n
Irarrazabal, Diego, 136, 137n, 138n,
  139n, 140n
Irenaeus, 80n

Jablow, Atla, 46n
Jayakumar, Samuel, 63
Jenkins, Philip, 14, 62
Jenson, Robert, 28, 66n
Jobes, Karen, 155, 156n
Johnson, Elizabeth, 22, 134
Johnson, Luke Timothy, 66n
Jones, Paul Dafydd, 27n
Justin Martyr, 38, 39n

Kabasélé, François, 148n, 154
Kähler, Martin, 25
Kapic, Kelly M., 23n, 30n
Kärkkäinen, Veli-Matti, 64, 65n
Kasomo, Daniel, 158n
Kasper, Walter, 19n
Katanacho, Yohanna, 105n, 115n,
  117n, 118, 170
Kato, Byang, 44, 45-46, 48, 148, 149n
Katongole, Emmanuel, 145
Kegley, Charles W., 31n
Kelly, J. N. D., 123n
Kho, Triawan Wicaksono, 73n
Khoury, Rafiq, 119n
Kim, Stephen, 107n
King, Fergus J., 159n

Kolié, Cécé, 148n
Kombo, James H., 149n
Köstenberger, Andreas, 119n
Kroeger, James H., 60n
Küng, Hans, 19n
Küster, Volker, 64
Kysar, Robert, 103n
Kyung, Chung Hyun, 61n

Lee, Watchman, 164n
Leith, John H., 160n
Levenson, Jon, 153n
Libânio, J. Batista, 81n
Lieu, Samuel, 161n
Lincoln, Andrew, 119n
Lindblom, Gerhard, 141n, 152n,
  154n, 155n, 158n
Liu Xiaofeng, 163n
Loden, Lisa, 106n
Lonergan, Bernard, 32n
Lott, Timothy L., 46n
Lotz, David W., 126n
Lozano-Díaz, Nora O., 137n, 139n
Lua, T., 62n
Luther, Martin, 155

Ma, Wonsuk, 76n
Macaulay, Herbert, 52
Macleod, Donald, 16n
Maggay, Melba, 76n, 78n
Manus, C. U., 146n, 148n
Martínez-Olivieri, Jules, 167, 172,
  176n
Mbiti, John, 42, 46, 50n, 145n, 146,
  147, 150, 157n
Mbuvi, A. M., 145, 149n, 166, 170, 174
McCormack, Bruce, 30, 31n
McGrath, Alister, 16n
McGuckin, John, 126n
McIntyre, John, 15n
McKim, Donald K., 65n
McKnight, Scot, 4n
Melanchthon, Philipp, 162n
Mencius, 175n

Mendoza, Celina A. Lértora, 86n
Miettinen, Kari, 41n
Migliore, Daniel L., 29n
Míguez Bonino, José, 85, 87n, 99
Miranda, Dionisio, 63n
Mitchell, Stephen, 128, 129n
Mngadi, Christopher Simon, 152n
Moloney, Francis, 116n
Moltmann, Jürgen, 25
Montserrat, Dominic, 161n
Morimoto, Anri, 61n
Morris, Thomas V., 27
Morrison, Craig, 109n
Motyer, Stephen, 114n
Moulder, James, 105n
Moule, Handley, 20n
Mugambi, J. N. K., 142n, 143n, 157n
Mulago, Vincent, 54n
Munayer, Salim, 106n
Murphy-O'Connor, Jerome, 131n
Muwayesango, D., 145

Nestlehutt, Mark, 105n
Netland, Harold, 34n
Newbigin, Lesslie, 65n, 69n, 72
Ng, Wai-Yee, 108n
Nicholls, B., 62n
Niebuhr, Reinhold, 31n
Nilsson, Martin P., 131n
Norris, Richard A., 126n
Núñez, Emilio Antonio, 85-86
Nyamiti, Charles, 49n, 148n
Nyende, Peter, 150n

Oakes, Edward T., 19n
Obusan, Teresita, 77
Oden, Thomas C., 146n
Oduyoye, Mercy Amba, 48, 143n, 148n, 149
Origen, 155
Ositelu, Gabriel, II, 145n, 147n
Ott, Craig, 34n

Pack, Frank, 103n

Padilla, C. René, 85, 96n, 97, 98n
Pannenberg, Wolfhart, 19n, 25-26, 89n
Pantoja, Isabel, 126
Pauck, Wilhelm, 162n
Pausanias, 130n
Pazdan, Mary, 110n
Phan, Peter C., 61n
Pieris, Aloysius, 61, 72
Pittenger, Norman, 21n
Pius IX (Pope), 127
Pobee, John S., 145n, 147n, 148n
Price, Richard M., 137n

Raheb, Mitri, 104n
Rahner, Karl, 62n
Ramsay, W. M., 131n
Rausch, Thomas P., 66n
Rea, Michael C., 26n
Reinhartz, Adele, 104n, 112
Reumann, John, 137n
Ricci, Matteo, 74
Ricoeur, Paul, 23
Rieger, Joerg, 40n
Rinaldi, Bonaventura, 138n
Ritschl, Albert, 17
Rodriguez, Jeannette, 136n, 139n, 140n
Rodriguez, José D., 87n
Rosales, D. D. Gaudencio, 61n
Ruckstuhl, E., 106n
Rufus, 155-56

Salinas, Daniel, 86n
Samuel, Vinay, 67n, 70, 71n
Sanneh, Lamin, 143n, 170
Sanon, A., 147n
Sawyerr, Harry, 146, 147n
Schaff, Philip, 137n
Scherrer, Peter, 131n
Schillebeeckx, Edward, 19
Schleiermacher, Friedrich, 16
Schreiter, Robert, 142n, 147
Schweitzer, Albert, 143n

Schweitzer, Don, 22
Sen, Keshab C., 71
Setiloane, G. M., 146, 147n
Singgih, Emmanuel Gerrit, 62n, 63,
    65n
Singh, David Emmanuel, 73n, 74n
Sobrino, Jon, 87, 90, 92n
Song, C. S., 61n
Song, Minho, 60n
Songer, Harold, 103n
Spencer, Aída Besançon, 130n, 131n,
    132n, 133n, 135n, 136n, 170, 172
Stendahl, Krister, 59
Stephens, Sunil, 71n
Stibbe, Mark, 103n
Stinton, Diane B., 50n, 51n, 52n, 148
Stoll, David, 86
Stott, John R. W., 59n, 62n
Strange, James, 107n
Strauss, Mark, 132n
Sugden, Chris, 67n, 70, 71n
Sugirtharajah, R. S., 67n, 71, 72n
Svendsen, Eric D., 136n
Sybertz, Donald, 55n

Tacitus, 129
Tahaafe-Williams, Katalina, 59n
Tamayo-Acosta, Juan-José, 95n
Tanner, Kathryn, 25
Tatlock, Jason, 153n
Taylor, John, 42
Tennent, Timothy C., 69
Thaumaturgus, Gregory, 126
Thayer, Joseph Henry, 132n
Thiongo, Ngugi wa, 144n
Thomasius, Gottfried, 18
Tillich, Paul, 20
Torrance, T. F., 22, 24, 35

Ukaegbu, Faith, 54n
Ukpong, Justin S., 152n

Vähäkangas, Mika, 149n
Vanhoozer, Kevin, 166, 168
Vazquez, Carmen Inoa, 139n
Velasco, Carmiña Navia, 140n
Villa-Lobos, Heitor, 34n
Von Allmen, Daniel, 64, 65n

Wace, Henry, 137n
Wachege, P. N., 148n
Walker, Williston, 126, 127n, 129n
Walls, Andrew, 5, 11, 12, 29, 33, 38n,
    39n, 40n, 47
Wan Sze-kar, 164n
Weiss, Herold, 163n
Wenham, Gordon J., 175n
Westermann, Claus, 175n, 176n
Whitehead, Alfred North, 20
Wiles, Maurice, 20n
Wilken, Robert, 13n
Wilson, Everett, 75
Witherington, Ben, III, 78n
Wolff, Hans Walter, 176n
Wostyn, Lode, 69
Wright, N. T., 4n, 66n, 67n
Wu Leichuan, 164n

Yango, Emo, 74n
Yeago, David, 31
Yeo, K. K., 75, 163n, 164n, 168n, 170,
    174n
Yeung, Daniel H. N., 163n
Young, Frances, 105n
Young, Jung Lee, 61n
Yuming, Jia, 164n

Zorilla, C. Hugo, 139n

Index of Subjects

African Initiated Churches (AICs),
144 45, 147

Buddhism, 72

Chalcedon, 32, 94
    Council of, 14-15, 39, 160, 162, 165,
        167
    definition, 34, 40, 95-96, 105, 119,
        123, 141, 142, 160, 168
Christology
    ancestor, 49-52, 158-59
    Chinese, 74, 163, 174-75
    feminist, 22, 94, 124
    from above, 14, 88, 166-67
    from below, 14, 18-19, 88-89, 91-92,
        166-67
    global, 29, 168-71
    liberation, 89-92, 114-16, 147
    missiological, 60, 67-78, 170
    neo-missionary, 43-48
    Pauline, 31, 39, 164, 167-69
    Petrine, 151
    revealer, 52-58
Churches, African Initiated. *See*
    African Initiated Churches
Contextualization, 39-40, 58, 64

Globalization, 1, 62

Hinduism, 71-72

Incarnation, 24-25, 107, 109, 165, 177
Islam, 73-74, 104, 111

Jesus
    as Creator, 171-72
    as Good Shepherd, 117-18, 151
    as Healer, 147
    as High Priest, 134
    of history, 16, 18-19, 66, 91, 99-100
    humanity of, 21-22, 69-71, 93, 109,
        129, 133-34
    as Lamb, 133, 154
    as Liberator, 89, 140, 147, 158, 167
    as Logos, 171-74
    as Mediator, 49-50, 129, 132, 134,
        140, 147
    as perfect sacrifice, 133-34, 151,
        153-55
    as Servant, 70, 105, 132
    suffering of, 75, 123, 140
Judaism, 106, 108, 119-20, 129, 149,
    164, 167, 174

Liberation, 83, 87, 114-15, 135, 138-39, 147

Mary, 123-40
  Theotokos, 123, 137
  Mother goddess, 126, 128, 130
Metaphysics, 15-17, 19-21, 28, 30
Missionary, Western, 41-43, 74-75, 144-45

Nicene Creed, 31, 34, 39-40, 95-96, 123, 160, 162

Pentecostal, 53-54, 75-76, 78, 85, 145
Poor, 83, 91, 135, 139
Praxis, 81, 83, 91, 94

Religion, African, 44, 49, 142-44, 149, 152, 160
Resurrection, 25-26, 66, 90-92, 154, 156-57, 165, 177
Roman Catholic, 126, 136-39, 160

Sacrifice (animal, human), 141-42, 150-53, 155, 158

Index of Scripture References

OLD TESTAMENT

Genesis   106
1–2   118
1   112
1:26   175
1:26-27   176
1:26-28   131, 132
2:7   118
2:24   131
5:1-3   176
5:2   175
9:6   175, 176
11:1   131
11:6   131
22   153
28:13-14   107
28:17   107

Exodus
2:11   113
3:14   173
4:4   113
4:22-23   114
12   151
12:12-13   113
13:3   114

13:12   153
13:14   114
13:21-22   113
14:8   113
14:20   113
16:4   113
16:15   113
19:1-16   138
20:2   114
24   151
29:3   32
32–33   113

Leviticus
16:11-19   152

Numbers
19   151
27:16-17   117

Deuteronomy
5:6   114
6:4   24, 129, 131
6:12   114
7:8   114
8:14   114
13:6   114

Joshua
24:17   114

Judges
6:8   114

1 Kings
2:10   157
11:43   157

2 Chronicles
32:33   157

Nehemiah
13:15-23   112

Job
9:30-33   132

Psalms
2:9   138
8:5   195
118:26   115

Proverbs
8   172

Isaiah
26:17–27:1   138
66:7-13   138

Jeremiah
17:21-22   112
34:13   114

Ezekiel
33:21–37:28   118
34   118
34:23-25   118

Micah
6:4   114

Zechariah   116

NEW TESTAMENT

Matthew   167
1:1   167
1:18-25   124
1:23   135
2:13-15   124
2:19-23   124
6:25-34   57
10:39   176
12:46-50   136
13:55-56   124, 125
16:15   162
20:25-27   132
20:28   132
28:19   131

Mark   25
1:1   167
1:11   167
1:24   167
3:11   167
3:20-22   136
3:31-35   125, 136
4:41   24

5:7   167
8:29   39, 58, 162,
                  167
8:31   47
8:33   47
9:7   167
10:45   132
12:35   167
13:21   167
14:61   167
15:32   167
15:39   167

Luke
1:29   135
1:31-32   135
1:34   135
1:35   135
1:38   135
1:42   135
1:45   135
1:46-55   124, 135, 137
1:47   167
1:48   138
1:48-49   135
1:51-55   137
1:52-53   139
1:69   167
2:4   124
2:11   135, 167
2:16   124
2:33   124
2:35   135
2:43   124
2:49-50   136
2:51   135
4:18-19   140
4:22   124
5:29-32   140
5:36-39   140
6:20-26   140
6:36–8:1   140
8:19-21   136
9:20   162

9:24   176
11:27-28   125
17:4   47
17:21   16
24:25   26

John   6, 103-22, 167
1–9   108
1–2   107
1   107, 118
1:1   107
1:4   172
1:11   113
1:12   115, 116
1:14   12, 25, 107,
                 111, 170
1:17   172
1:18   107
1:19–12:50   167
1:32-34   107
1:45   124
1:47   107
1:51   107, 111
2   113, 116
2:1-4   135
2:1–4:54   110
2:11   107-8, 171
2:19-21   109
2:21   110
3   111
3:2   111
3:6   115
3:8   111
3:14   113
4   110
4:20-25   111
4:23   57
4:34   21
5   113, 116
5:9   112
5:16   112
5:17   112
6–8   109, 113
6:4   113

6:31	113	17	113, 173	11:7	175
6:33	114	17:1	109	15:28	177
6:35	113	17:17	173		
6:42	124	17:19	173	**2 Corinthians**	
6:53-58	113	18:1	119	2	169
7:22-24	112	18:26	119	3:18	177
7:23	112	18:37	173	5:11-21	169
7:30	109	18:38	173	5:17	28
7:37	114	19:25	135	5:18	132
7:50	111	19:25-27	124	8–9	169
8	114	19:27	125	11:5	169
8:12	113, 114, 172	19:39	111	12:11	169
8:44	104	19:41	119	13:13	131
8:56	115	20:15	119		
9	111, 116	20:22	118	**Galatians**	
9:14	112	20:30	173	1:11-12	131
9:15	172	21:25	173	3:20	132
9:34	115			3:28	176, 177
10	116, 118	**Acts**			
10:7	173	1:9-11	26	**Ephesians**	
10:11	173	1:14	135	1:23	177
10:22	117	2:1-13	170	2:15	177
10:33	133	4:12	35	4:12-13	38, 177
11:20-27	173	6:7	12	4:22-24	177
11:40	172	8:26-40	146		
11:50	133	9:4-5	131	**Philippians**	
11:55	108	10:2	149	2:6	31
12	115	10:22	149	2:7	18
12:23	109, 172	12:24	12	2:8	133
12:25	176	13:36	149	2:11	35
12:27	109	17:4	149		
12:37-40	113	17:17	149	**Colossians**	
13	108	19:20	12	1:15	175
13:1	109	19:27	131	1:19	28, 39
13:1–20:31	116			2:15	76
13:33	116	**Romans**		3:9-11	177
14:2	26	3:23	177	3:10	177
14:6	118, 173	13:8	177		
14:17	173			**1 Thessalonians**	
15:1	173	**1 Corinthians**		2:13	131
15:1-5	116	1:23	169		
15:26	173	2:2	169	**1 Timothy**	130
16:13	116	5:7	133	2	132
16:14	173	5:21	133	2:4-5	131

2:5	132, 133	9:12-18	134	3:18-20	154
2:5-6	140	9:27	134	3:18-22	155, 160
2:5-7	129	10:14	134	3:19	159
2:6	132	10:21-22	134	3:22	158
3:2	130	11:6	22	3:25	151
3:12	130	12:24	132	4:4	151
5:7	124	13:8	11, 32	4:5	155
5:9	130			4:5-6	159
		James	164	4:6	155
2 Timothy		3:9	175		
3:15	48			**2 Peter**	
3:16-17	48	**1 Peter**	6, 141-61	1:20-21	48
		1:2	141, 149, 151,		
Hebrews	134, 164		155	**Revelation**	
1:2-14	134	1:2-3	151	2:26-28	138
1:3	175	1:3	154	5:9	170
2:6-8	175	1:15-16	149	7:9	170
2:11-18	134	1:18	154, 155	12:1	137-38
3:1	134	2:4-10	151	12:10	138
4:9	112	2:5	149	12:17	138
7:17	134	2:8-12	141, 142	13:7	170
7:21	134	2:9	149	14:6	170
7:24	134	2:18-22	151	14:12	138
7:25	134	2:20-22	153	19:15	138
8:1	134	3:5-7	149	21:5	28
8:6–9:15	132	3:18-19	151, 156-57